SONGLINE OF THE HEART

A Navigator's Guide to Resurrecting
Your Heart, Home & Habitat

Shelley Darling

Manor House

Songline of the Heart / Shelley Darling

Cataloguing in Publication Information:

Title: Songline of the Heart / Shelley Darling
Names: Darling, Shelley, author.
Description: Contents/subtitle: A navigator's guide to resurrecting your heart, home and habitat

ISBN 978-1-988058-76-4 (softcover)
ISBN 978-1-988058-77-1 (hardcover)
Also available in digital form via Kindle ebook
Identifier: LCSH: sh85038609
Subjects: LCSH: Divining (Dowsing); Divining rod;

BISAC: OCC005000: (Body, Mind & Spirit, Divination, General, Dowsing); OCC033000: OCC011020: OCC010000: OCC019000: SEL016000: BIO026000:

Front cover photo of the Author playing didgeridoo by Cliff Oliver, Creative Surf photography La Jolla.
Back cover author photo: Nikki Incandela photography

Interior art:
Part 1: Lyre Bird: Whitemay / iStock
Part 2: Bald Eagle: benoitb / iStock
Part 3: Tuatara Reptile: ivan-96 / iStock

First Edition
Cover Design-layout / Interior- layout: Michael Davie
Edited by Susan Crossman, Crossman Communications
298 pages / 78,168 words.   All rights reserved.

Published Nov. 15, 2021   / Copyright 2021
Manor House Publishing Inc.
452 Cottingham Crescent, Ancaster, ON, L9G 3V6
www.manor-house-publishing.com   (905) 648-4797

Songline of the Heart / Shelley Darling

This book is dedicated to my father and my mother whose courageous choice to live their dreams was, for me, an endless source of inspiration.

My father, who initiated the greatest challenge as I sailed through my life, was my hero. As a child, I viewed him as a skilled navigator, and in later years I watched as my parents sailed around the world for more than 10 years, with my dad at the helm of their custom-built 48-foot boat.

My mother's career involved reaching out to children in need, and yet she had the courage to let go of her prestigious life—one most people would consider a dream-come-true—and chose instead to sail into unknown waters with my father. Together, they ecstatically embraced—with joyful fervor—the vast ocean. They met people from many indigenous cultures on their travels, and they loved engaging with their families in their everyday life. Together they lived in simple harmony with the elements and the Earth.

I watched in awe as my parents sold everything they owned and took the risk to live a dream that had started as an idea, a potential, a possibility held deep within my father's heart. My parents have inspired me to live courageously, to treat others as I would want to be treated, and they have instilled in me the value of always responding with an exuberant "yes" to the inner urgency of manifesting my dreams.

Endorsements/Reviews:

Mamoudou Conde'- Les Ballets Africains Founder, Nimbaya, formerly known as Amazones Women Master Drummers of Guinea: *"The essence of this reading is phenomenal, as it transcends the normality of how sound and music is used to cleanse, heal and join all forces together for the betterment of our present collective circumstances."*

Sharon Joy Kleitsch, Connection Partners:
"I congratulate Shelley for hosting the spirited inquiry and encouraging important ponderings about what Dowsing may mean to our lives. it is time to reclaim this important art, science and evolution."

Trudy Johnston, Director and Founder, Vim + Zest Personal Branding: *"The raw power of Songline of the Heart lies in Shelley Darling's tenacious courage in navigating 'the unseen' to journey into the tenderest reaches of the heart and the spaces we live in."*

Barry Brailsford, Author, *Song of the Old Tides:*
"The realms of consciousness, the power of the human mind to connect with our earth's forces in ways that seem to defy reason, is the amazing new frontier we are beginning to explore. Yet, our ancestors recognized this power, knew it was a vital part of who we are...Shelley has opened fascinating pathways into that ancient realm of mystery."

Claire Kanter, World Navigator, Special Ed. Music Teacher:
"So much is encompassed in this book, that my heart is full. Shelley has experienced life to its fullest and thankfully has taken us all along on her inspirational journey. Read, enjoy, and fill yourself with her life! Shelley is a true emissary of love and light. I am proud to have her as my daughter."

Foreword

It takes great courage to step into the unknown and unseen, to follow the pull of dowsing rods that say *things are not as they seem*. And to follow through to see where forces that defy the known and accepted may lead.

The realms of consciousness, the power of the human mind to connect with our earth's forces in ways that seem to defy reason, is the amazing new frontier we are beginning to explore. Yet, our ancestors recognized this power, knew it was a vital part of who we are and used it to find water sources for their village wells, to locate iron ore, copper and tin, and more. They accepted that forces we cannot see, but run true, is a good space to learn within.

Shelley has opened fascinating pathways into that ancient realm of mystery. Now it is open to you to explore too.

- **Barry Brailsford**, MBE, MA (Hons), archeologist, historian, former Principal Lecturer at Christchurch College of Education, and author of ***Song of the Old Tides*** and many other titles.

My soul is the writer...

She had been hidden in the dungeon of my subconscious, a little girl sitting on the cold stone staircase, silent, as I rebelled, reacting stridently to the circumstances in my life.

She sat motionless, waiting for my attention.

In the beginning I had no clue, she, was the key to accessing my inner humanity that would ultimately give rise to the unearthing of the Songline of my heart...

-Shelley Darling

Songline of the Heart / Shelley Darling

Note to the Reader:

January 2015: I had a dream...

On the surface of a still lake in a small wooden waka,[1] I stood tall beside Barry Brailsford, a New Zealand author, archeologist, historian, and former Principal Lecturer at the Christchurch College of Education.

Barry was teaching me a formal sacred prayer called a Karakia, his evocative words eliciting from within me a deep state of resonance, reverence, and respect.

We stood together above the crystalline, calm blue waters that reflected the soft muted light of a few slow-moving cumulus clouds hovering high above the lofty wavering reeds.

Tuti Hinekahukura, elder of the Maniopoto tribe of New Zealand, once respectfully asserted that, "Barry's work is a journey into the strength, power, and spiritual wisdom of indigenous people. It honors the precious knowledge placed in his hands by our elders."

Those were honoring words indeed.

In April of that same year, Barry travelled from New Zealand to Montecito, California, to stay with my dear friend Cheryl. Auspiciously, I had arrived a few days earlier. We gathered one evening under a pastel-painted sky, as the Earth completed another turning, just as in my dream.

In front of a still Koi Pond, Barry offered a Karakia in the Maori language of Aotearoa, New Zealand, thus opening the way for the Sacred Evolutionary Dowsing Consortium's first public event, "Hearts Across the World."

---

[1] A "waka" is the Maori word for "boat."

Songline of the Heart / Shelley Darling

Standing in front of a bed of sunlit-softened flowers, with the Santa Barbara mountains behind him, Barry tightly gripped and emphatically gestured with his *Tokotoko*—a ceremonial carved Māori walking stick —in accordance with the movement of the chant. I, with his permission, was filming, for the very first time in public, this ancient Karakia.

Like me, many people have understood the Maori to be the native indigenous people of New Zealand, yet a mysterious turn of events was to teach me of the legendary Polynesian people who had traveled the long tides, landing in New Zealand more than 2000 years ago. It was told they traveled in a waka, like the one in my dream.

They were people of peace, and their message was one of loving kindness.

Karakia

Na te maramatanga ki te nakau o te Atua
Kia Koha te maramatanga ki te nakau o te Tangata
Kia koha te maramatanga ki te Ao
Ma te maramatanga
Ma te Aroha
Ma te kaha, e whakau te whakara nui te Ao
Tihei mauri ora

I ask that the light of creation itself,
Come into our hearts and minds,
That we might walk in the light,
That we might walk with compassion in our hearts,
That we might have the courage to carry our dreams into tomorrow.

May we choose the breath of life.

Table of Contents

Foreword – 5
Introduction – 11
Prologue – 22

Part I: A Significant Time – 27
Chapter 1: Cathar Oracle – 29
Chapter 2: Road to Truth – 41
Chapter 3: The Quickening – 55
Chapter 4: Charmed Convergence – 69
Chapter 5: Voice of the Land – 83

Part II: A Moment of Awakening – 91
Chapter 6: Return to Wholeness – 93
Chapter 7: The Mountain – 107
Chapter 8: Global Contact – 125
Chapter 9: White Buffalo Calf Woman - 135
Chapter 10: Sacred Buddhas – 155
Chapter 11: Divine Spark – 169

Part III: A Shift in Perspective – 173
Chapter 12: Call to Presence – 175
Chapter 13: Compass of Joy – 189
Chapter 14: Living Resonance – 197
Chapter 15: Tracking the Southern Serpent – 211
Chapter 16: Tale of the Peace Trail – 219
Chapter 17: Wisdom of the Ancestors – 233
Chapter 18: Navigator of the Heart – 253

Epilogue: Return to the Birthplace of the Gods – 263
Acknowledgements - 269
Appendix A: Evolutionary Dowsing – 272
Appendix B: Ancestral Bridge Journey – 275
Appendix C: SED Consortium – 277

Praise for the Author – 285
About the Author – 295
References and Resources – 296

Through Dowsing...

I began to experience a more powerful connection with the voice of the land. Each dowsing seemed to support an empowered awareness of the land with a conscious recognition of one's personal power and appropriated guardianship of the land by the Ancestors.

The personal transmissions that occur through each dowsing deliver messages to the individual and their families, awakening and renewing their relationships with each other, while simultaneously restoring and harmonizing the energy of the land.

My experience has since continued to support these findings, with the strength and conviction of a power and unfolding wisdom, which opens the "Heart Field" through Dowsing. This connection with the Quantum or Unified Field, transforms and uplifts children, families and their communities, as shared in their personal stories.

*—**Shelley Darling***

Introduction

In November 2009, I left for Australia on a personal walkabout. This pilgrimage was a profound journey that held in its grasp the keys for self-transmutation, empowered self-expression, and profound magic. The surge of joy that arose as dowsing came into my life catalyzed a momentous change that even the Tower Tarot card couldn't have possibly revealed.

— **Shelley Darling**

For many of us, a moment arrives in life, when we become a conscious traveler in our journey. No longer able to turn away from the incessant call of our soul's design and purpose, the challenge, if consciously chosen, awakens us to a veritable magic, an interconnected web of universal intelligence. When we perceive this magic, it gives us cause for celebration in any moment and, potentially, in every moment.

In April 2008, a profound shift took place in my life, one that ultimately led, in short order, to the dissolution of my marriage and business, and the loss of my home. I had been at a turning point where I felt called to more consciously address any old residual patterns of control. I contacted all my clients and students, clearing any energy that might be in the way of our connection and my personal evolution as an authentic mentor and guide.

Although I grew up in a caring family, from my perspective, kindness had not been a virtue celebrated in my family. Even today, although my parents love each other, and have been together for over 60 years, the way they communicate sometimes is harsh and, to my perception, not always kind.

The challenge I took on in this life was to figure out how to bootstrap the experience of loving kindness.

Songline of the Heart / Shelley Darling

With sincerity as my companion, I called up the courage to trust, and acknowledged this lack in my own life. I modeled transparency for my clients, which miraculously resulted in them feeling safe and mutually respected. This allowed our relationships to flourish, and it meant we could continue on with their personal integrative work.

Dowsing came into my life serendipitously, seemingly out of left field. As I dowsed my clients' homes, I found myself in complete awe of how quickly my clients themselves evolved. They became enthusiastic and developed profound confidence and trust in their personal internal guidance systems, often in ways that had previously seemed unimaginable to them.

But by the fall of 2008, I was beginning to experience an unusual illness in my "nether regions."

Despite countless medical appointments, no one, not even the doctors, could come up with either a diagnosis or a cure.

Convinced my problems had come from a new alkaline water machine a friend had given to my husband and me to try during the nine-day "Love and Relationship" training we had held at our new house, I immediately called in haste to return it! It was the only variable I could think of at the time that had changed in my life. Apparently, I was reaching for any answer that would soothe my mind.

Like many others who live with unresolved illnesses, there seemed to be no end to the fiery pain and angst I was experiencing. I became desperate.

I went to every doctor I could find, to no avail. I remembered back to 1990 when it was discovered that I had a tumor in my spinal column. To my parents' dismay, I was as ornery as they come, determined to buck Western Medicine, and find my way to an alternative healing solution.

Songline of the Heart / Shelley Darling

Though I seemed to be getting better, and had undertaken a heroic healing journey, I finally agreed to the eight-hour operation conventional medicine had recommended and, with my health returning, I found my equilibrium and realized the importance of both Eastern and Western Medicine.

Eighteen years later, having exhausted my search for allopathic medical solutions, I called on my higher guidance for help, and somewhat humorously, I found myself closing my eyes and trusting, finally placing my finger on a name in the yellow pages.

Wild as it might sound, I found a competent, older Chinese-certified doctor who had studied in both China and the United States. He had me boiling artful concoctions of herbs and roots, which I then poured in the sink as I sat perched, butt naked in the sink, doing my best to cool down the raging fire between my legs.

Ultimately, the illness receded with the help of Chinese herbs. My dream marriage collapsed and, at my daughter, Heather's, urging, I agreed to make a pilgrimage to Australia, where she was living at the time. Through a magical onset of synchronicity, I discovered and learned about the Cathar people of medieval France, and their absolute faith in the "Way of Love." This knowledge set in motion the resurrection and restoration of my soul.

Following the Divine Breadcrumbs

After an initial four-month visit to Australia, I returned elatedly a few months later, following the divine breadcrumbs that began with my dowsing client and new friend, Cheryl. While I had been visiting her, she had been giving me incessant nudges to also visit New Zealand. She put in my hands the book *In Search of the Southern Serpent,* which had been written by Barry Brailsford, and a well-known British dowser, Hamish Miller.

As life was going to have its way, the journey I emphatically said "yes" to inspire a profound awakening. It enhanced my education around dowsing sacred sites and introduced me to the history and lore of a confederation of ancient people called Waitaha, who, like the Cathars, lived the "Way of Peace."

Today, the resurfacing of dowsing as more than simply a farmer's tool for looking for water offers a unique, practical, holistic bridge back to a world that is natural and revelatory.

The sacred science of dowsing allows us to open our eyes and hearts to an embodied experience of living inherently bonded to our surrounding habitat, one we can actually *feel*. This allows for a great transmutation, one that invites us to rise up from our experiences of separation, and judgment, inviting us to live attuned with our heart, as we joyfully experience and express our wholeness.

Evolutionary Dowsing became the style of dowsing I developed over the years, and now teach internationally. It's a whole-system, transformational experience with far-reaching effects for the health of our families, neighbors, and communities. This dynamic process uplifts individuals, simultaneously bringing to balance and harmony the non-beneficial energies held in our homes and in the land.

We are in constant lively interaction with the natural world and unseen forces around us, even if we are not consciously aware of these energies. My purpose unfurled with stunning clarity as I deepened into the mystery of the "Way of Love" that revealed itself through my exposure to the Cathars of France and the Waitaha people of New Zealand, separated by continents and centuries, yet united by their steadfast devotion to love and peace.

I traveled, spoke, and taught Evolutionary Dowsing while I stepped ever more in tune with these two exemplary influences. Through my experience of dowsing, as a conduit for clearing harmful frequencies from my clients' environments, I was noticing a shift, "a quickening," as I now like to say, for each person to easily access their higher consciousness and remember their sacred relationship with the land. This in turn activated a personal evolution, as well, and gave the people I worked with greater clarity of purpose, and an embodied return to wholeness.

Raising our Consciousness

There are many types of dowsing, as well as many tools used for dowsing. Dowsing has been and still is being used for seeking water, minerals, and treasures. My personal passion, experience, and understanding as a professional dowser is that dowsing is an ancient science. It has the power to directly affect the raising of our Consciousness and affect the healing of separation on the planet. Dowsing elevates the frequency of a space, creating "harmonic coherence" or, as I say, a "quickening." It not only clears dense and stressful energy from the environment, but it also opens our inner circuitry to a powerful relationship with our higher consciousness. Dowsing bypasses the mind, accessing a deep state of awareness that is attuned to a much broader range of energetic signals. Today we recognize the increased scope of dowsing to include the mystery of human Consciousness interacting with that of the Earth.

Through my epic dowsing experiences, I've learned that our homes and land want to support us in ways we cannot imagine. Similar to brain waves in our body, our homes have "brain waves," too, which are made up of light frequency and vibrations which are very much like what we have in our bodies. We now know these waves can be scientifically measured. We know we can raise our own consciousness through meditation, prayer, and positive thinking, so consider that our houses too, can be assisted to holding a higher vibration which supports our greater health and wellbeing, and an illuminated path to our soul's purpose.

Songline of the Heart / Shelley Darling

I can't tell you how many times I have heard from my clients prior to a dowsing session that they, "feel stuck," only to find, upon initiating a dowsing assessment of their house, that, to their amazement, the dowsing rods will either be at a standstill, or barely sway back and forth. It's as if the rods are telling a story. My client, watching the rods, will feel into their communication and, aghast, shout out "that's me, that's exactly how I feel in my life!"

Dowsing harmonizes the energy in the environment, allowing a full light spectrum activation of the land, our homes and our businesses. One might say that dowsing a house assists it to allow all manner of "subterranean infections" to rise to the surface to be healed. I feel moved to say that this ancient art is a very practical, and applicable alchemical practice.

As the dissonant energies shift and become vibrant positive frequencies, the overall energy resonant in the client, their home, and the land on which they live spontaneously recalibrates, activating a greater positive flow in their life.

Over the years I have explored this at length, and I've been awed by how dowsing eliminates environmental dissonance, triggering in us an enlightened, more evolved state of Consciousness.

In fact, I revel in how this work offers a pathway for sacred communion with ourselves, with others, and with Nature. In the past in Europe—where dowsing has had a long and respected history—it was said that only a certain type of person was ever given the capacity to dowse.

With years of experience behind me, I can now confidently say that anyone can dowse; we're all innately connected to Spirit Consciousness, which is the intelligent force behind the movement of the dowsing rods.

Inevitably, each individual will find their own particular use for dowsing, one that will either enhance their chosen profession, or one that will, as in my experience, allow a person to find that dowsing is their destined vocation.

It's humbling and gratifying to see dowsing creating dynamic momentum in people's personal transformations. It opens a sacred pathway to a revitalization of their relationship with their heart, home, and habitat.

Working with Groups

Over time, I began to shift from working one-on-one with people, to working with groups as well.

I had already been facilitating groups in the practice of "Heart Resonance" and as I embraced my role as a navigational guide, a bolt of inspiration struck, and I created the "Ancestral Bridge Wisdom Journey,"[2] and the "Sacred Evolutionary Dowsing Consortium."[3] You will learn more of these programs toward the end of this book.

Today, my business, Evolutionary Dowsing, is the aggregation of more than 35 years of engaging in practices of ancient and evolutionary healing modalities, drawing on the powerful synergies of Ancient Wisdom, Evolutionary Dowsing, Feng Shui and Heart Resonance in a process that engages the energies of the body, mind, spirit, and soul, as a living, whole-system experience.

---

[2] Shelley Darling, "The Ancestral Bridge Journey," shelleydarling.com
[3] Shelley Darling, "Sacred Evolutionary Dowsing Consortium," www.evolutionarydowsing.com.

The dowsing protocols I use represent an extraordinary tool for cultivating individual inner peace and sustained joy. What's more, when a few houses in an area are dowsed, a field is generated that begins to positively shift the energy in the larger community. This process sets the conditions for people to more proficiently trust their own experience and guidance, while expanding their understanding, skill set, and capacities for greater presence and participation in an ever-evolving, unified field of Consciousness.

My journey has been, and continues to be, a conscious unfurling of my ability to stand tall in the power of my knowing, living in service to the whole. This story is a metaphor for how you can personally presence your love, your power, and, with courage, trust your voice.

The subject of leadership was first brought to my attention by my former husband's, best friend, Richard, who had dedicated his life to understanding the Art of Palm Reading. Just before the collapse of my marriage he had read my palms, and turning my hands over and over, said I had the leadership line, yet at the moment it was not developed. He categorized me as a "Spiritual Psychologist" whose destiny was to work with mass consciousness. He stated more than once that if I wasn't living my fullest expression, the result would be a lack of intimacy...and, lastly, *I wasn't meant to live my life as a "Senator's wife!"*

I had fallen into the core habit, fueled by my beliefs, of giving away my power, all of which was supported by the belief that my personal power was either "too much" or "not enough." My underlying fear generated by the experience of having been subject to another's domination and disregard gave me cause to resist my own inner sacred authority. My journey opened me to the reclamation of myself as a navigator, revealing we're all born to be extraordinary, unique leaders.

Understanding the magnificent movement of migrating birds, or dolphins moving in pods, we see the beauty and brilliance of leadership in resonance. When we honor and uplift each other's unique gifts, we easily fly together as one coherent whole. As evolutionary leaders, choosing to compassionately embrace our differences, we find ourselves reveling in the joyful diversity of all life. When we tap into the "Songline of our heart" we consciously align with the energy, mystery, and intelligence of Nature itself. We we naturally foster loving kindness, empowered peace, and greater prosperity for all.

An Experiential Odyssey

My hope for you, dear reader, is that the experiential odyssey offered in this book will kindle your own soul's remembering and will inspire a renewed relationship with the spirit of the land, inviting you to awaken to your ancestral lineage. Awakening and bridging your personal lineage with ancestral Spirit—and the ancient ways—allow for a deeper respect for the indigenous cultures that hold communion of Spirit and matter as a natural pathway to our inherent wholeness. May you experience an opening to the magic beyond your five senses, feel the reciprocity of life's gifts, and trust you have precisely what you need to meet the current challenges.

    This book is designed to increase your understanding and practice of dowsing while empowering you as the navigator of your own personal waka. As a beacon of love, the relational transformation of your heart, home, and habitat will amplify your light. I know that in following this story, you'll be inspired, gain practical information—about the sacred science of Evolutionary Dowsing and more—and, if you wish, discover how to become an Evolutionary Dowsing Specialist, healing and restoring balance to property, home, business, or school.[4]

---

[4] To receive the invitation to become an Evolutionary Dowsing Specialist contact: connect@evolutionarydowsing.com.

If you feel motivated to expand your horizon and work with others as a planetary healer, alchemist, or dowser, you will be given resources to assist with that goal at the end of this book.

What many people experience as they align with the emergent energy or impulse of the Unified Field—or some say Creator, God, Source, or Creative Consciousness—is a strengthened connection to their internal guidance system. Following your "Compass of Joy," as Barbara Marx Hubbard called it, by its very nature, leads us to the realization and manifestation of our fullest expression.

Whether you are new to dowsing, or have dowsed for years, this book confirms dowsing is a golden bridge between the awareness we live in every day and a world of new visions and possibilities, wonder, awe, and joy. If you choose to learn more about Evolutionary Dowsing, begin with the knowledge that you can directly affect your environment in a way that supports, you, your family, your business, and even your community, simultaneously.

You will begin to see, ever more clearly, the importance of shifting the energy in your home environment, and by strengthening your dowsing skills your relationships will be enhanced, affording you greater health, while opening the way for greater success and alignment with your evolutionary purpose. Your home will become a happier place to live and work, your children will have more focus, and everyone will sleep easier!

The only warning, I feel necessary to share is that in activating the energy in your home, business, and land, your life WILL recalibrate itself to your highest potential. It WILL move you in the direction of consciously living what is innately true for you; anything other than that will transmute or dissolve. In other words, be prepared for changes.

Your Life Will Change

If you are a person who is merely surviving, if you are afraid of your own power and if you are not in true alignment with your heart, your energy and your life WILL change. This unified "Heart" Field will recalibrate itself so you can embody what you love and more precisely live your dreams.

This story and the dowsing experiences I share in this book, are my gift to you, which will open the field for the "magic" to happen in your life. The question I ask every individual before dowsing is: ARE YOU READY?

A past history of struggle and painful experiences will be replaced with more consistent and delightful days, and the challenges of life will transmute. You will feel a greater sense of harmony, presence and peace.

Experience my journey as yours. Take this information and run with it. Add it to your deepest knowing, share and co-create with others in service to the greater whole. BE the fullest expression of your greatest dream and know the return will be much greater than you ever have imagined.

Are you willing to trust the inner call that is trying to capture your attention and stand in your power? Are you ready to say "YES" and take an evolutionary leap into living in alignment with your soul's destiny? Remember, *"There is no circumstance in which love is not the answer."*

Welcome to the world of Evolutionary Dowsing! May this book be a navigational guide that expedites the experience of LOVE on all levels.

- **Shelley Darling**, Topsham, Maine

shelley@evolutionarydowsing.com.

www.evolutionarydowsing.com.

Songline of the Heart / Shelley Darling

Prologue: Chartres July 7, 2019

Standing in the sacred garden in the shadow of Chartres Cathedral, I could hardly believe the miracle that had brought me here. A small and humble outdoor labyrinth lay a stone's throw from my feet, while the ancient lime tree in the center seemed to expand its branches in a joyous welcome, playing host to the international group of people with who were gathering around its trunk. A hot July sun beat down on our reverent heads and an air of awe permeated the environment.

We had all been called to attend Ubiquity University Wisdom School's[5] week-long course on *The Cosmic Dance of Astronomica* in the ancient city of Chartres, France. Astronomica is the highest of the classical Seven Liberal Arts and it had been reintroduced to the "modern" world by the Chartrean Masters of the 11th and 12th Centuries. Ubiquity University had again resurrected the model through course work offered to people seeking enlightened wisdom. We were to spend the next week in intimate study of the cosmos and the interconnectedness of all things in the Universe.

The calling to Chartres had been seeded in January 2009 when I read Kathleen McGowan's just-released *Book of Love*. Its message penetrated deeply in my subconscious, and spoke to an unfulfilled promise within, while sparking a sense of mystical remembrance of the Cathar people of 13th Century France. Little did I realize this book would come to have a profound impact years later when my own book, *Songline of the Heart,* literally came to life in real-time—a descendant, it would seem, of the Cathars' devotion to pure love.

---

[5] Mayteck, "Three Courses You Don't Want to Miss This Summer in France," *Ubiquity University*

A thread of Divine grace seemed to be moving within my life, when literally 10 years after I read that profoundly touching book, I was able to find last-minute accommodation at the hotel where the course in *The Cosmic Dance of Astronomica* was to take place.

A room opened up for me at the Hotellerie St. Yves,[6] which had been built on the site of a very old priory founded a thousand years earlier; it was situated less than 50 meters from the famous cathedral of Chartres. The hotel had been built in tribute to St. Yves, the notable bishop of Chartres who oversaw church affairs from the year 1090 to 1115. At the time, Chartres Cathedral was famed as a destination for pilgrims devoted to Mary, Mother of Jesus, and it was a Christian center that served as the site of the "School of Chartres."

In reading the history of Chartres, I learned that St. Yves had been known as one of the greatest scholars of the medieval era because of his knowledge of canon law. He was both a lawyer and a cleric, two distinctions that most probably earned him the appointment as Bishop. Apparently, St. Yves was also a prolific writer.

I couldn't help smiling when hearing of St. Yves' work *Prologus*, which evokes St. Paul's message and quote of loving one's fellow man, as one would love oneself. I was touched by these words, *"He was called to teach. His lesson was love. It was all that mattered."*

I had been undecided about whether to take this trip to Chartres, but an unusual and complex dream had spurred me to undertake some esoteric research that eventually led me to listen to a recording made by Anne Baring, an author and Jungian Analyst who had written articles on the Sacred Feminine and the Sacred Masculine.

---

[6] "Hotel," *Hotellerie St. Yves,* http://maison-st-yves.com/en/history.

In the recording, Anne spoke about the Black Madonna, whom I felt had appeared in my dream as a woman with a golden necklace. Known as the Queen of Heaven, she usually is pictured with a golden halo around her head.

The Black Madonna, as Anne explains,[7] represents Mary Magdalene and the lineage of those whose path and practice was the Way of Love.

Not fully understanding, I was intrigued by a dream in which all the objects were black, and only the Black Madonna's necklace radiated like the sun. She stood at the crossroads of the past, present and an unknown future, which spoke to my heart. It led me, ultimately, to decide to heed the call to go to Chartres.

Prior to arriving, I read Baring's work, *Mary Magdalene: Consort of Jesus and Apostle to the Apostles*. In it, she described a newly found document:

> "*An astonishing document has recently come to light which confirms the very close relationship between Jesus and Mary Magdalene.*
>
> *In 2010* The Gospel of the Beloved Companion: The Complete Gospel of Mary Magdalene, *has been translated with a commentary by Jehanne de Quillan and published by Editions Athara, Foix.*
>
> *It is believed to have been brought from Alexandria to the Languedoc in the early to middle part of the first century and to have been translated into Occitan, the language of the Languedoc, in the early part of the twelfth century.*

---

[7] Anne Baring, "The Two Mary's of Chartres," *Return to Mago E-Magazine*, January 12, 2021.

> *Since then, it has been closely guarded and passed from hand to hand, generation to generation until the present time. It gives the passages that are missing from the Gospel of Mary that is already known and that is one of the texts in the Nag Hammadi Library.*
>
> *It makes it clear that Mary Magdalene was the "Beloved Companion" and also, when this Gospel is compared word for word with the Gospel of John, that this Gospel was also written by her."*[8]

Anne was clearly drawing a parallel between the Cathars of the olden days and the sacred feminine for which Chartres Cathedral was so powerfully known.

Tears came to my eyes as the opening ceremony of *The Cosmic Dance of Astronomica* began.

Our group filtered silently through the old stone corridors of the priory and down a set of ancient stone steps worn smooth by the passage of a thousand years of footsteps.

As we entered the garden, we were each gently blessed and showered by sacred water shaken from a fern leaf held by Timote, a Maori ceremonialist. He also sung us a Karakia, a sacred prayer for which the Waitaha people—a peace-loving branch of the Maori family—are known.

As fate would have it, the Waitaha featured prominently in the book I was writing at the time—this book—and I was dumbfounded at the coincidental appearance of this man at this place, in this time.

---

[8] Anne Baring "Mary Magdalene, Consort of Jesus and Apostle to the Apostles," *Anne Baring*, www.anne-baring.com.

Songline of the Heart / Shelley Darling

We formed a circle around the lime tree and turned to face the steps. As if in slow motion, Timote lifted his eyes toward Anne Baring herself, and reached for her hand.

Gracefully they walked hand-in-hand together, joining the energies of the Waitaha with the Cathars in a union of Peace and Love.

Here and there their eyes met in gentle acknowledgement of the grace of the moment as they walked clockwise around the sacred Lime tree in the garden. In the silence of the moment, and in a state of timeless presence, I became aware of my book; all the diverse threads of my life—which hadn't previously come together—coalesced perfectly in that moment.

How was it that these two peaceful people—a gentle indigenous man from New Zealand with an abiding love of the sacred, and a scholarly elder woman whose life's work spoke to the Divine Feminine and the Way of Love—came together to open the way for the week's studies?!

The process of writing this book has been intense and surprising. What began as an idea to reconfigure the dowsing manual I'd used as a teaching tool into a simple informational book turned into an unfurling odyssey that eventually led me to exploring a question that had stirred deep within my soul.

The question that had been nudging my heart and mind to respond was this: is it possible that the Cathar and the Waitaha people, who lived generations apart in time, were somehow of the same lineage?

I could never have predicted the majestic richness that came my way as I delved into the mysteries of dowsing, the Cathars, and the Waitaha. And I am deeply grateful for the magical journey this continues to be.

Part I
A Significant Time

The Call is Heard

"...and what about the promise?" she cried out loud.

Her inner waters flowed as she veiled herself in a moment of deep remembering.

"...and what about the promise?"

Chapter 1:   Cathar Oracle

One day you will tell your story of how you've overcome what you're going through now, and it will become part of someone else's survival guide.
— **Brené Brown**

Slumped deep in my seat, I gripped the cover of the book I was reading, oblivious to the patter of conversation around me or parade of people passing by as they made their way to the tiny washrooms at the back of the airplane. The woman beside me was nervously rustling a copy of a newspaper dated January 9, 2009.

I was riveted to the book's story unfolding in front of me, and my 14-hour flight from Los Angeles to Sydney, Australia, gave me ample time to devour this book that was unlike anything I had ever read before.

Though the whisps of meandering thoughts of leaving San Diego, my husband, and the community, continued to arise, I was enchanted and alert. The *Book of Love* was the second book in the "Magdalene Line Trilogy" penned by author Kathleen McGowan. It was a non-fiction spiritual thriller about the legacy of the Cathar people who had lived in southern France during the Middle Ages.

Kathleen had spent years traveling and researching the history and practices of the Cathars, and I would later learn that the controversy the book had generated required her to take action to honor and protect her sources of information.

Previously, I had been living in a rustic, high-beamed apartment in a restored barn that had been generously offered as a sanctuary to me during what I now refer to as my three-day "homeopathic dose of homelessness." The book—a gift from a friend—had arrived only hours before my flight to Australia.

I was in a time of devastating pain. Grabbing the book and barely able to see through my tears I drove wildly to a rendezvous with my youngest daughter, Nina, who was to take the car keys after dropping me off at the Los Angeles airport and leave them hidden on the driver's front wheel for my now-former husband.

Clumsily climbing into her black Lincoln SUV, a quiet hush took hold of the moment. Soothed by my daughter's encouraging words, I let go, consciously choosing to leave my old life behind, and in the next breath, willingly, I took a quantum leap into the unknown.

I would be staying with Nina's sister, my middle daughter, Heather, who had pleaded and lovingly demanded I leave my home in San Diego and stay with her for a while in Australia. She lived on her boyfriend's remodeled houseboat that was anchored in a small cove beneath a forested park where immense slabs of sandstone held ancient Aboriginal carvings of the Ku-ring-gai people.

Little did I know I was at the beginning of what was to be an epic journey.

I had planned to dip into the book to calm my agitation and shift my focus to the long flight to Australia. But I soon became entranced by the story Kathleen McGowan told of the highly devout Cathar people.

As I turned the pages, I seemed to be returning to a time that resonated deep within me. I learned the Catholic Church had deemed the Cathars a threat to the established hierarchy. The Cathars were subjected to religious inquisition and a military crusade that ultimately stranded them in the hilltop castle of Montségur, France. A nine-month siege in 1243-44 saw holy crusaders attempt to starve them out. When the Cathars finally admitted defeat, these valiant people chose to walk down the mountain at Montségur—singing—to their deaths by fire in the field at the base of the mountain.

What particularly captured my attention in the *Book of Love* were the lengthy references to something called the "Hieros Gamos," a twin-soul partnership based on honesty, truth, and Divine love. I had been devastated by the tumultuous ending of my marriage, one that had been prophesized when my husband had drawn the Tower tarot card—twice in one expanded reading—just scant months earlier. The Tower card foretells impending collapse. I had not seen it coming.

So now, soaring to a change of scenery in Australia, I was in the process of letting go of my marriage, and the dreamer's dream of love that dwelled still in my heart. I felt the inexplicable synchronicity of this book's appearance in my life.

Turning my head toward the window, hiding my face while sobbing silently, my thoughts drifted to the experience of the Cathars, as well as the impending mysterious promise that seemed to be igniting within me the flame, once again, regarding my search for love and truth.

Some years later I discovered the work of writer Lisa Renée who also spoke of the Cathars and the Hieros Gamos:

The term hieros gamos is used generally to refer to the sacred marriage between two divinities, or between a human being and Mother/Father God, or between two human beings, under certain special conditions; the ultimate alchemy of forces which harmonize polar opposites.[9]

Was this a possibility for me, someday, as well?

---

[9] Lisa Renée, "Hieros Gamos," *Ascension Avatar*, https://ascensionavatar.wordpress.com.

Rubbing together my now damp, slightly sticky hands, I feverishly continued: The *Book of Love* opened with journalist Maureen Pascal receiving a mysterious package that appears to be an ancient document written in Latin and signed in code.

Maureen realizes the significance of the document inside and, remembering a previous message from Jesus, she dedicates herself to fulfilling her "promise" and continues her search for the *Book of Love*, the gospel supposedly written in Jesus' own hand. Along the way, she encounters the extraordinary story of the Cathars.

The origins of the Cathars are something of a mystery, although there is reason to believe their ideas came from Persia or the Byzantine Empire.[10]

Much of their faith seems to have rested upon a form of Manichaeism (duality) brought to Gaul in the 8th Century by missionaries from Bulgaria and Yugoslavia.

The Cathar doctrine, encapsulated largely in the *Gospel According to John*, provided a highly desirable antidote to the religious confusion and misery that existed at the time.[11]

> "They knew another time would begin again sometime in the future as it was prophesized by the seers within the group and that many who had once been Cathar would meet again, and they would hold the knowing that they are Light and Love and hold the space for others to come to know the true nature of all that is… "That future time has arrived…"[12]

---

[10] Despite my many resources on the origins of Catharism, there are varied opinions as to the exact origins of the Cathar people.

[11] Judith Mann, *The Legend of the Cathars*, (Pacific Rim Press, November 27, 2012, Kindle Edition)

[12] Robert C. M. MacGregor, "The Immortals," *The Modern Alchemist*, https://didanawisgi.tumblr.com.

The Purified Ones

Between the 11th and 14th Centuries the Cathars lived mainly in Southern France—in the Midi-Pyrénées, the Haute-Pyrenees and the Languedoc. Due to the way they lived their lives, they were called "the pure ones," "the purified ones," or "the Cathars," Katharos being a Greek word meaning "purity."

The Cathars didn't identify themselves through labels or churches. They established themselves in small private spiritualist groups that had no particular name, no particular religious symbols, no cross or church, no incense, elitism, or hierarchy. They followed a simple path of spiritual consciousness, living in alignment with Spirit.

Extraordinary kindness was natural among the Cathars and devotees chose a path of joy acknowledging the connection to Light, Love, and Universal Consciousness. Later I learned the Cathars were also respected for their wisdom in the healing arts, toning, and singing, and were well versed in using herbs, geomancy, sacred geometry and, it is said by some, even tarot.

Women had a voice in the community, as noted by Jungian analyst and philosopher Anne Baring in her story of a notable female Cathar, Esclarmonde de Foix. Baring notes Esclarmonde's life demonstrated "the Cathars evidently succeeded in giving women a respected and active social role as teacher, priestess and healer. There were even women surgeons, for the Cathar Ancients were trained in the arts of healing."[13]

Apparently, Esclarmonde was an expert herbalist as well as an Archdeaconess and, as a *Parfait* she was allowed to administer the supreme Cathar rite of the *Consolumentum*. This was usually given at the point of death, but it was also the ritual used when an initiate became a *Parfait*.

---

[13] Anne Baring, "Awakening in the Holy Spirit," *Anne Baring*, https://www.anne-baring.com.

The training to become a *Parfait* was long and challenging and made more difficult by threats of persecution.

First, there was a two-year training period during which the student would receive intense education on the cultivation, preparation, and uses of herbs. They were taught about the stars and the ways of Nature. They learned how to weave, sow and harvest crops, and they were taught how to build simple houses. The *Parfaits* avoided eating meat and dairy products, although they could eat fish.

After their two-year apprenticeship, Cathars who were in training to become *Parfaits* had to endure a 40-day fast on bread and water before entering the next phase of their training, which exposed them to the secret lore of plants, metals, and stones, and the study of mathematics, astronomy, and music.

They also had to learn sacred texts, known to include a text called *The Secret Book of John,* as well as the *Gospel of John.* Also, "*The Book of Love,*" said to have been written by Jesus or Mary Magdalene and given to John.

The book's existence was revealed to Inquisitors of the Catholic Church during the campaign against the Cathars and led to their torture. There was also said to have been another equally treasured book called *The Secret Supper* or *La Cêne Secrete.*

The final part of a Cathar's parfait-related training prepared them to be priests. They became celibate once they started training for priesthood but before this they married and had children. The Cathars were carefully taught to administer the *Consolumentum.*"[14]

---

[14] Anne Baring, "Awakening in the Holy Spirit," *Anne Baring,* https://www.anne-baring.com.

This conferred upon them acknowledgement that they were pursuing the activity of a fully Awakened Spirit, committed to being present to who they "BE."[15]/[16]

> **Man and Purity**
>
> *Man, according to the Cathar creed, has three natures: the body, which is the abode of the soul; the soul, which is the abode of the spirit; and the spirit, the divine spark. Through a life dedicated to ever increasing purity, the composite nature of man can undergo a double death and transfiguration, so that the formed spirit, born of the spark and nourished in the soul, will eventually separate, returning to the Light.*
>
> —**Judith Mann**

Ani Williams, a world-renowned harpist, singer, troubadour and researcher of female disciples in the Gnostic texts states:

> "The 11th, 12th and 13th centuries in Europe were a time of revolutionary ideas and produced a renaissance of love and beauty in music and poetry. This was a time of new writings on the Grail, the true quest of the human spirit for perfection, fulfillment of the soul's perennial dream for truth, love and wisdom."[17]

Although they lived in a time resonant with ideas of truth, love, and wisdom, in the eyes of the Catholic Church, she notes that the Cathars were considered heretics, and were systematically destroyed after crusades were launched against them in Southern France during the early 13th Century.

---

[15] Margaret Starbird, "Woman with the Alabaster Jar," *Sacred Mystery Tours*, http://www.sacredmysterytours.com.
[16] Judith Mann, "The Legend of the Cathars," *Biblioteca Pleyades*, https://www.bibliotecapleyades.net.
[17] Ani Williams, "Songs of the Eternal Dream," *Ani Williams*, https://aniwilliams.com.

The crusaders were primarily French men paid by the Catholic Church to besiege the peace-loving Cathars in their villages. "All those who belong, belong; they belong to the church of love."[18]

In 1244 the Cathars who had found refuge in the castle of Montségur were surrounded, and defeated, and they walked to their deaths singing, before being burnt on a pyre simply for living the "Way of Love."

In her article, "A Troubadour's Journey," Ani Williams speaks of the Cathars' plight, at a time when male superiority, control, and avarice were at their height.

> *"Throughout history, the quest for beauty, love and truth has struggled to survive amidst the quest for dominance and greed. During the medieval era, the dominant powers of church and state burned the Templars, they burned countless thousands of Cathars, they burned Joan of Arc, who tried to liberate her people from foreign rule.*
>
> *They even tried to ban the poetry and songs of the Troubadours and silence the voices of women. But the spirit of truth would not be silenced and rose again and again, from the dust and ashes, rising from the half-remembered promise patterned in the blood, held in the heart.*
>
> *Always they return, with the flame of hope for a better world filled with compassion, beauty and a song of love returning to the land."*[19]

---

[18] Chief Visionary Officer and Founder, "The Cathar Prophecy of 1244 AD/The Fountain," *Waking Giant News Service*.
[19] Ani Williams, "A Troubadour's Journey in Cathar Country: Part 1," *Ani Williams*, https://aniwilliams.com.

Songline of the Heart / Shelley Darling

The Spirit of Truth

In the first book of "The Magdalene Trilogy," called *The Expected One*,[20] Kathleen McGowan speaks of the story of Mary Magdalene's life with Jesus, following a thread of belief, which has left many people in a stew of perturbation, speculating that Mary Magdalene was Jesus's lawful bride, and mother of a "holy bloodline." To support this idea, McGowan points to the *Gospel of Philip*, a Gnostic Gospel discovered in Nag Hammadi. It claims that Mary Magdalene was Jesus's *"koinonos,"* which can be translated as "wife" or, as French scholar Jean-Yves Leloup suggests, "special companion."

Dr. Joanna Kujawa an author and biblical scholar, who sees herself as a Spiritual Detective, spent years researching the Magdalene line. She was inspired by Margaret Starbird's book, *The Woman with the Alabaster Jar*. Instead of writing a book debunking theories she had initially contested, she ended up providing more support for the idea that Mary—the same Mary of Bethany, sister of Lazarus, who had anointed Jesus—was indeed married to him. Starbird spoke about the entire romance genre that began in Southern France when troubadours started singing songs soon after the Cathars were burned at the stake. They focused on a "pure lady" in need of protection.

Dr. Kujawa states "the fascinating thing about Starbird was that she wasn't looking for fame or scandal, in fact even Starbird herself says in the introduction to her book that, "as a devout Christian and Biblical Scholar, she set out to disprove the assumptions of Mary Magdalene, intending to use her knowledge of scripture to prove the theories wrong in the book *The Holy Blood and the Holy Grail*. Yet as she kept digging into stories she found in the Bible and in medieval tales, she kept finding more evidence in support of these theories."

---

[20] Kathleen McGowan, *The Expected One: A Novel - Magdalene Line Trilogy Book 1, page 37 (*Simon and Schuster, 2007)

> **Poem #10**
>
> *Each day I am a better man and purer*
> *For I serve the noblest lady in the world,*
> *And I worship her, I tell you this in the open*
> *There is no day on which I grow not*
> *Finer and more pure,*
> *For this world holds no nobler lady*
> *Than she whom I do serve and I adore.*
> *And these – the words I speak –*
> *Come singing from an open heart ...*
>
> —**Arnaut Daniel**, 1180-1200

The Church of Love is Proclaimed in 1986

British dowser Colin Bloy visited Montségur in the Cathar country of southwestern France in 1978 and dowsed in the meadow where the 300 Cathar Perfecti (*Parfaits*) had been burned alive in 1244. The dowsing led them to a Latin text, which referred to the rebuilding of a church in Andorra in 1986. In March 1985 Colin was prompted to write the proclamation of the Church of Love to fulfill the 14th Century prophecy that the Cathar Church would be restored in 1986.

Colin said the words were not his—and this Church was proclaimed in Andorra on Good Friday, 28th March 1986. He notes: "This was written by my hand, but I would not claim authorship, it was taken down in ten minutes - just like that... I don't want you to get confused over the word 'church', because it means 'communion', ecclesia in Greek, nothing more."[21]

---

[21] Chief Visionary Officer and Foundar, "The Cathar Prophecy of 1244 AD/The Fountain," *Waking Giant News Service*

The Cathar Creed

This church has no membership, save those who know they belong
It has no rivals as it is non-competitive.
It is not self-seeking—it seeks only to serve.
It knows no boundaries, for divisions are an illusion.
It acknowledges all great teachers of all the ages who have shown the truth of love.
Those who participate, practice the truth of love to the best of their ability.
It seeks not to teach but to be, and by being, enrich.
It recognizes that the way we are may be the way of those around us, because we are that way.
It recognizes the whole planet as a being of which we are a part.
It recognizes that the time has come to shift from separation into oneness.
It does not proclaim itself with a loud voice, but in the subtle realms of loving.
It salutes all those in the past who have blazoned the path.
It admits no hierarchy, for no one is greater than another.
Its members shall know each other by their deeds and being, and by their eyes and no other outward sign, save the fraternal embrace.
It has no reward to offer, save that of the ineffable joy of being and loving.
Each shall seek to advance the cause of understanding, doing good by stealth and teaching only by example.
They shall heal their neighbor, their community and our planet.
They shall know no fear and feel no shame and their witness shall prevail over all odds.
It has no secret, no initiation, save that of true understanding of the power of love and that, if we want it to be so, the world will change, but only if we want to change.

Songline of the Heart / Shelley Darling

With my eyes incessantly closing, and the red-covered book dropping from my hands, I glanced out the plane window, and drifted into a sunless sea of immense wind-driven clouds. Within minutes, in a trance-like dream, I was transported back to a time when I'd been staying in San Francisco...

Immersed in a sea of thoughts, and driving back from a graduation of sorts, I was absentmindedly watching the red steel girders of the Golden Gate Bridge obscuring a fleeting view of the Golden Gate Strait, like slow frames in a movie. This narrow nexus point, between the Pacific Ocean and the San Francisco Bay, had been named by explorer John C. Frémont in 1846, just a few years before the discovery of gold in California. I marveled at its beauty.

My eyes searched beyond the brilliant setting sun to a large vessel heading out into the open water. Just hours earlier, surprisingly, I had emitted a profound scream from inside the brick oceanfront building that was now miles behind me, while giant rollers crashed onto the shore echoing the powerful emotions welling up within me.

I had been in the second level of 60-hour empowerment training, consciously diving deep into my body using a variety of emotional integration techniques.

"...and what about the promise?" my up-surging voice had demanded.

What was this promise and why was it still so hidden from my understanding?

Stretched out on the floor during the training, I had had a vision of a little girl sitting despondently alone on a set of angularly placed stone stairs in a dungeon. I had felt the words streaming out of her like a vaporous mist, rippling loudly, moving up through the distant cold stone pathway and rising up through my awareness. Hardly reachable, this long-lost child could see the light, but sat hunched over on the stairwell, as if waiting for someone to find her...

Chapter 2: Road to Truth

The "light" is the capacity to reconcile your experience, your sorrow, with every day that dawns. It is that understanding, which is beyond significance that allows you to live a life and embrace the disasters and sorrows and joys that are our common lot. But it's only with the recognition that there is a crack in everything.
- Leonard Cohen[22]

Long before I knew of the Cathars, or even imagined I would one day find myself seeking solace in Australia, I led a life dedicated to empowering others, helping them bridge out of the morass of the past and into the joy of a brighter future. I led a life of love. Or thought I did.

An on and off again relationship with my first husband, Peter, gave me three beautiful blonde, bumptious children, Isaiah, Heather, and Nina. Peter, an avid meditator, introduced me to the notion of the precious inward journey of loving oneself. Although I had sincerely tried to make a relationship that had begun at the young age of 21 work, after three children I finally chose life as a single mom.

Years later, after my youngest child, Nina, was on her own, I continued my soul searching. Landing in California, I dove deeper into the inner landscape of self-worth, self-ownership, and emotional integration. This adventure led to an empowered sense of self; at the time, little did I know, I was at the horizon of a new love relationship with a man who matched my desire to support, teach and create a community based on the mastery of one's heart.

---

[22] Leonard Cohen interview, A. Showalter, www.allanshowalter.com

Our transitional year found my new love and I enjoying a few weeks of vacation at a home in Kauai, across the road from the YMCA beach just a mile from the end of the Na Pali coast. Poised to move to San Diego County, we were beginning a fresh chapter in our lives as transformational coaches and trainers. One morning I woke up from a dream that had given me a vision of what was eventually to be called the "Aloha Foundation."

I enthusiastically described the vision to my partner, who was sitting in a meditative pose in a large red flowery high-back padded chair under a huge window that framed cloud-covered pastel mountains. As usual, we had begun our day honoring our ritual time for silence and meditation. Though we were in a restful, lush retreat, my partner was leaving his former business, and he felt pressured to get on with creating the "higher octave" of the work.

About 10 minutes later, as if struck by lightning, he jumped out of his meditative state, his eyes on fire. "I've got it!" he ecstatically exclaimed. It was at that moment the "ALOHA" Practice was birthed. It seemed my dream vision of the "Aloha Foundation" had sparked just the right inner synapse for his enlightened response.

"ALOHA" was an acronym, and it became the foundation for our work over the next eight years together. It was a re-coding practice designed to bring a person into the tactile experience of their body. In taking a person through the embodied experience of ALOHA, they would be able to relax, and feel the sensation of being open and receptive, while tuning into the energetic resonance of their heart.

The ALOHA practice represented the five dynamics of embodied awareness (listed below), which released fear-based patterns and restored alignment with one's breath, emotions, heart, mind, and spirit.

A: Aha! Become aware of the life force through your breath.

Feel the breath as it interacts with your body. Surrender your exhale releasing resistance.

L: Liquid Body: Open and soften your body into a wave-like flow.

Track the current of sensations with loving kindness and fluidity.

O: Oh, it's not serious! – Choose to generate a warm, reassuring smile.

Smiles ignite your heart. Humor is your mind and body's reset button.

H: Heart: Choose love now! Focus your attention and breath through your heart.

Generate a feeling of gratitude and love. Feel the warmth. Turn up the volume!

A: Aligning Belief: Choose to align with the truth about you at this moment.

Energy follows attention. Choose an unconditional loving current of thought, feeling it in your body.

The experience of ALOHA brought on by consciously bringing your loving attention to the elements outlined by this acronym, even during your busiest of days, was a powerful practical tool that supported awakening into your true nature. The result of this was the integrative experience of being grounded in your body. At that time the "Law of Attraction," had become a catch phrase and it was the focus of many communities. I had learned over the years, however, through my clients arriving desperate at our door, that affirmations, by themselves—though mentally in resonance with their deepest desires—didn't work in the long run.

For example, if you tried to place an affirmation such as "I am a millionaire magnet of financial wealth," onto a body whose core belief was "I'm not enough," it would simply bounce off the body like a bungee cord, eventually slinging the person right back into their survival or fear zone. Using the ALOHA practice, which included breath, body, mind, and heart, the body could naturally integrate and transmute the core belief, so then the person's Aligning Belief—the million-dollar check for their body—would be received and fully integrated. "ALOHA" became the basis for all core integration work we brought forward until the day we parted. It was a dramatic development that continued to echo powerfully in my world.

Following our retreat in Hawaii, we excitedly jumped into the metallic green Honda Pilot and moved to La Jolla, a colorful, vibrant town only 30 minutes from the Mexican border. Thrilled to be living close to the ocean, on our first day, we intuitively came upon a grassy area surrounded by a few iconic pine trees with a gorgeous panoramic view of the Pacific Ocean. We stood high above the expansive sea, mesmerized by glistening waves and saw a circular, well-mowed green area below, surrounded by a half-moon stone circle. At that moment, we noticed a tall, well-dressed, somewhat stoic-looking man in a black cummerbund, and a fashionably dressed woman in a soft white, flowing gown. They were getting married. We later learned this place was called, the "Wedding Bowl," and we later returned to this spot, to commit to the bonding of our love.

Time went on. My partner—now my husband—and I were thrilled to be leaving the quaint laid-back ocean side hamlet of Birdrock, having found a larger home that gave us the space to breathe and grow our business locally. Our modern home was at San Diego's Mount Soledad where a huge pre-stressed concrete cross towered at its top. From the peak, you could see 360 degrees in every direction with a 180-degree view of the sunrise across the mountains, and a panoramic sunset view over the ocean. It was outrageously beautiful, and it only a five-minute bike ride from our place to the top!

Pathway to the House

October 2006. Moving day. Exhilarated, I took one last look down the long cement path to our enchanted little house located below Mount Soledad, in the quaint, laid-back neighborhood of Birdrock. Little did I know I was saying goodbye to an iconic chapter of my life. Driving our rented U-Haul slowly up the large winding road to the top of the hill where the new house awaited us, we were in awe of the extraordinary views of the city below and the vast sunlit blue sky above. San Diego weather was temperate year-round, and I always thrived in a warm tropical environment.

Arriving at our destination, we cautiously backed the moving truck into the driveway, opened the previously dented back doors, and slowly and carefully unloaded all of our belongings. The paved driveway was short, though steep, and the doorway inside the garage seemed the easiest way in. From a distance, the sun's rays led my momentary attention to the long pathway to the front door. As if noticing the walkway for the first time, I sighed as I contemplated the situation, although I quickly shifted my focus to unpacking. As a Feng Shui practitioner, I understood the pathway to a house is reflective of how the energy is flowing, not only into the home, but also into one's life.

I realized then and there we had attracted another house with a long, straight pathway, signifying what I called, in feng shui terms, a "birth canal." It foretold a possible challenge in the flow of energy and how easily one's dreams could be manifested. My heart sank a bit more when I viewed how the pathway created a sharp left turn just before the front door. As usual, being an optimist, I creatively considered its remedial possibilities and smiled. Coming back to my normal senses, and choosing to feel a renewed optimism, I acknowledged with gratitude that this pathway at least wasn't as long as the one we had just left!

Songline of the Heart / Shelley Darling

Clutching the last four rectangular, well-used and softened couch pillows, I stopped to take a peaceful breath. Finalizing our arrival, and stepping forward with gusto, I reached forward to push the garage door button, my body tingling with excitement at the thought of settling in. To my surprise, no matter how many times that button was pushed, the garage door wouldn't close. The door was totally stuck open. Frustrated, I stretched my body to look out beyond the garage door. Half laughing, I sought my husband's attention and pointed to a man across the street, jumping up and down on his garage door, trying to get it closed. It was a funny scene for a brief moment...until we discovered there had been a huge split that had opened in the pavement, exposing a large cavity deep in the earth, behind our neighbor's house on the next street.

In fact, a 50-foot sinkhole had opened an hour earlier and was now threatening to take a few houses with it! People were scrambling to get out of their homes, and officials with orange cones were hastily closing the street. The electric company had already shut the power off on both streets, and we learned our house was at a safe distance, so we decided to stay in our house. Had I known then what I now know about dowsing, I would have instantly packed everything all up again, and hauled me and my husband away with all our belongings, *never to return*.

The house was seductive, an exquisitely beautiful, spacious contemporary home that included a 33-foot training room. There were plenty of French glass doors and the house was brightly lit. A wall of glass windows opened out into a small, well-manicured backyard, which seemed to be the delight of every hummingbird in the neighborhood. There was an expansive modern kitchen in which we could entertain clients and students, and eventually hold monthly evening community salons.

In the beginning of our house-hunting adventure, I had been staunchly resistant to this upscale home. Years earlier, in

Songline of the Heart / Shelley Darling

1990, while I had been in the process of healing from a tumor in my spinal column, I learned by experience the importance of cooking on a gas stove. I eventually became a gourmet macrobiotic vegetarian cook and caterer, compassionately spending 12 years of my life helping others with their health and wellbeing. This house didn't–accommodate a gas stove. This had been my only prerequisite for our new home, and I had put my foot down on the issue.

At one point, my husband met with the landlord, intent on sweetly coaxing me into letting go of the idea of a gas stove. Together they decided to call me. The landlord got on the phone and said he would look into putting a gas stove in. But needless to say, here we were, moving in on what felt like an auspicious day, with no gas stove.

Incredibly alluring, this big house had enough room for both of us to have our own private offices. There was an expansive master bedroom with an ensuite bathroom containing two white porcelain sinks. To my delight, I found a rickety old metal ladder and climbed up to the red Mexican-tiled roof, happily discovering a far-reaching sunset spreading over the mountains. Turning to face the East, I was rewarded with a more-than-peek-a-boo ocean view. To add to the magic, knowing we needed a safe way to reach the roof, I placed my order into the Universe and miraculously, while driving in the neighborhood a few weeks later I spied a beautiful wide, hand-hewn white pine ladder lying on the side of a small side street. Holding my breath, while resting it up against the side of the house, I exhaled with joy, delighting in how it fit perfectly.

Working with Couples

After the sinkhole situation had been diligently managed, we were now gratefully living in this elegant contemporary home and we were keen to get back on track with our teaching. We each had individual 1:1 clients and eventually created a cozy separate counseling room across from my husband's office where we worked cooperatively with couples. Together, we expanded our "Mastery of the Heart" trainings, taught the practice of ALOHA, and held retreats at our home while growing an expansive community of people.

Did I mention our mutual love of tennis?

San Diego was, in my eyes, the closest place to Hawaii without living on an island far out to sea. It was the perfect environment for outdoor tennis games, with the sun shining almost every day. It was here on the courts that our love was most playfully expressed. My years of tennis lessons and playing on the high school tennis team paid off. Tennis provided the balance in our working lives and our greatest delight was to meet at center court for a kiss when one or the other was not playing their best game, or simply to revel in our loving connection. This was the cherry on the top of a cake, one that in my mind would never crumble.

Silence. I used to be able to drop into silence...

July 10, 2008.

Nothing felt right all the way up to the moment of my departure for Los Angeles. My heart had been torn between staying with my husband for his birthday and going to attend my daughter for the birth of my youngest grandchild. My attention was split, and my mind and heart were racing as I drove to my daughter's ranch. I took out the new Bluetooth headset I had purchased with my husband the evening before and settled it in on both ears while trying to focus on making my usual morning calls. After a few hours of driving, with the traffic completely congested, I felt unnerved by the closely passing cars and near-accidents I had experienced. I finally passed through Los Angeles, otherwise known as the City of Angels. I became aware of a humming sound in my ears. Was it the new Bluetooth I had just put in my ears that was bothering me? Or was it simply the upset and devastation of leaving my husband on the day before his birthday? I could also sense something

Songline of the Heart / Shelley Darling

deep down, gnawing at my awareness, which in the moment I chose to ignore.

I soon forgot about the ringing, however, as I drove north beyond where Route 14 splits from Route 5, passing close to where the devastating Northridge earthquake had hit in 1994. Making the turn in Acton, I drove up the dusty and rocky gravel road, past the slightly tilted iron and wood gate, and on to my daughter's ranch. It reminded me of an old movie set with a roundabout, its center now turned into a circular pond for ducks and geese. The horses whinnied from the barn, as the expectant family members cheerfully sauntered out from the house. In the welcoming commotion, I was told that everything was arranged for the birth of my new grandchild.

Shortly thereafter, standing in the aged Mexican tiled kitchen, just under the hole where the light fixture had not yet been replaced, my mood swung low for no apparent reason, and I became totally distracted by thoughts of my husband. I tried calling again and again, but there was no answer. Gathering in preparation, we all quietly entered the room set for the birth. My daughters seeing me distracted and aloof, took me aside, away from the birthing tub, and with great conviction told me to straighten myself out. They strongly reminded me that the birth of my new grandchild was the priority, not the whereabouts of my husband!

For the next week, amid vast ranch lands, and an exquisite pool surrounded by more than 30 full blooming rose bushes, we celebrated the birth of my new grandson with members of my daughter's husband's family, who had recently arrived from Israel. My thoughts and feelings regarding the two-week separation from my husband were subdued, but not forgotten —they were just waiting, like a perfect storm, to arise.

I'll never know why the tinnitus—the name for the ringing in my ears—really happened. At the time, there wasn't any news on the effects of Electromagnetic Frequencies (EMFs) from cell or Bluetooth technology on the human body, at least none I knew of. Now, there's strong evidence the high-pitched sound I was experiencing and still experience, yes, can be due to an emotional change, and the new research is leading to possible EMF exposure. All I know is that from the day I drove north from San Diego to Los Angeles, the ringing hasn't stopped, and I've never used Bluetooth technology, ever again.

Returning to San Diego, I ecstatically fell into my husband's arms for a magical night of wild orgasmic love making. With my nervous curiosity quelled, I happily returned to business as usual. But from that night my health steadily declined. It was exacerbated by the ringing sound in my ears, and then worsened as a result of what felt like a wildfire in my genital area that no medical doctor could explain.

My husband watched with a loving yet apathetic eye. The energy between us was becoming strained. My health circumstance was eating away at my normal sense of daily joy and delight, so we eventually decided to go to a hot spring spa retreat in the mountains a few hours away. The plan was to relax and enjoy a few days of calm and cherished time together. The spa was in a beautiful country setting with a hot spring pool just a few minutes' stroll from our cabin. In a heightened moment of anxiety, sauntering down to the spring-fed pool, I realized the predicament of my situation and decided I wasn't too keen on going into the sulfurous spring water.

I watched with envy as my husband lavishly swam, not being able to float on his back, as I, oddly nervous, chatted with him inches away from the water's edge. Later, coming from the hot pool, I cuddled up close to him on the bed as he reached out his long tan, muscular arms for his Thoth Tarot deck, which he had thoughtfully brought with him for our sacred weekend. I lovingly watched as he perfectly shuffled the deck and was oddly surprised when I saw his relaxed face cringe as he slowly turned over the revelatory Tower card. The air became stiff as he stared, not pulling his eyes away from the card, after which his energy shifted, and he was extremely quiet.

> ## The Tower
>
> *The Major Arcana Tower card is a symbol of endurance and destruction, an allusion to sudden, maybe shocking realizations that crush old views. The area of relative security starts wavering, and our tower then falls, taking with it the walls around us that have become too narrow. It is rarely evil, but rather does it represent the necessary development we meet when there is a change required in our situation, On the positive side, this somewhat violent trump card will mean that we proceed to learn that losing the old secure fortress of our beliefs will reward us with a major step forward. And a good step forward sometimes requires a kick in the ...*
>
> **—Thoth Crowley**

The following morning, not wanting to leave us in the dread of that reading, my husband had a short soak in the crystalline blue spring pool, and intently chose to pull a new card. I observed the process just as intently, and with no small amount of curiosity. He kept shuffling and shuffling, and then pragmatically pulled a new card. We were both dumbfounded as he pulled, once again, the Major Arcana Tower card. Now searching for a deeper meaning, I scanned the tarot book like a pointer who has expertly found the hunted fox hiding in the thickened brush. A highlighted line caught my eye: "There is a sudden realization of the truth, with the will to change one's old ways to recreate life and start something new."

Unbeknownst to me, my husband was taking this tarot message to heart. We left the next morning after I handed the man at the desk my last bit of cash. This trip had been on me.

Upon returning to San Diego, the next morning, back at home in the brilliance of our sunlit, cozy couple's session room, he finally rose out from under the radar.

A Gnawing in the Bones

At first, we nestled close together on the velvety, soft green couch we had found together on Craigslist when we had first moved into our new home. And hesitantly my husband finally began to speak.

As his lengthy story unfolded, I awkwardly inched back, then pulled away from him entirely, and sat against the farthest pillow as he informed me his of tryst: a seven-month affair with the certified practitioner who he had recently been wanting me to consider as a potential business partner.

I now knew why I'd been having those uncomfortable feelings as I had been driving through the City of Angels, away from our home to my grandson's birth! My body's response had been trying to alert me, and the gnawing in my bones, and pulling on my heart, was something I now knew I ought to have responded to more attentively!

In looking back, I realized I wouldn't have been able to change the circumstances that had arisen, nor was I in control of this shocking collapse of our marriage. The situation shook me from the ground up.

Looking back, I could see the places of contention we had overridden. Even as mentors, always focusing on other's needs, we didn't take the time to communicate and work out our own personal issues and frustrations around lack of kindness, honesty, and, for me, financial accountability.

I was suddenly overcome with how, over the previous months, I'd been continually blaming myself for not trusting my husband. There, in our comfortable couple's therapy room, I backed up even further on the couch and squeezed myself high up on the ledge of the couch pillows, as far away from him as I could get. Now I was seeing life flash before me, and was in full recognition of how many times I had berated myself, turning inward, and asking myself "What's wrong with me?"

I had asked him several times over the previous months if there was anything going on between him and this woman, even after we had discussed his choice to take her on as a personal client. Looking directly in my eyes, he had more than once hissed back at me and adamantly insisted there was nothing happening between the two of them. I, in turn, continually blamed myself for not trusting him.

I discovered this woman had pushed him to finally tell me the truth, and I was dumbfounded! How could they possibly have been together for more than seven months at this point?

Emotionally devastated, and broken, I couldn't even speak the word "ALOHA" out loud. "ALOHA" had not simply been a word for me; it was my essence and driving force of my life. More than a greeting, it was a living breathing experience and the core foundation of our work in the world. My greatest joy had been watching my clients and our students transforming their fear, and integrating their emotions, while growing their capacity to unconditionally love themselves amidst their pain. I was traumatized and could no longer utter the word, nor use the acronym or process to find my way out of my own suffering. In fact, it would be over a year-and-a-half, before I was able to say the acronym "ALOHA" again, even as a mere greeting.

If there was any humor at all in the situation, it lay in the fact that my husband wouldn't agree to any type of couples counseling. Reminding him of the couple's strategy we ourselves had developed and implemented over the years, I pleaded with him. Our protocol called for a couple to agree to undergo no less than 12 sessions together, as we understood it took this amount of time to clear one's projections and limbic imprinting[23] to truly discover what the underlying constellation of experience within the circumstance was, and to make a clear decision about a relationship.

---

[23] Limbic Imprinting https://pathwaystofamilywellness.org.

Songline of the Heart / Shelley Darling

"All relationships begin with yourself" had been my husband's declaration in all our training sessions, although apparently it did not apply on the home front. His answer was simply "No, our contract is over."

Many months later, about to leave on my trip to Australia, he finally agreed to one "safe" session with his best friend. The best friend agreed, ONLY on the condition that my husband—the head trainer for all the trainings—allowed him to command the session and not interrupt or attempt to take over the session. Well, to his best friend's dismay, five minutes into the session my now "wasband" jumped at the chance to take over the session. What ensued was a verbal argument between him and his best friend. Unbelievably, I had to break it up and remind them both that this time together was supposed to be for us. Ten minutes later, our one and only attempted session abruptly ended with the best friend leaving in disgust.

Regaining Our Authentic Power

We come into this world wide-open to receiving love. When we do receive it, as our first primal experience, our nervous system is imprinted—programmed...If our first impressions are anything less than loving (for example, painful or frightening) then those impressions will imprint as our valid experience of love. It will be immediately coded into our nervous system as a comfort zone.

When the consciousness of birth shifts from anxiety and fear to love and safety, we have a chance to reach our greatest potential. We regain our authentic power, clear the pain of our ancestors from our system, and set the stage for our children to step into their lives as peaceful, empowered guardians of Earth.

Chapter 3: The Quickening

"Dowsing raises the frequency of our surroundings which creates a "quickening" where individuals can, without resistance, easily access their authentic self. Our homes, business and communities become energetic uplifted environments for greater connection, joy, and heartfelt purpose."
—Shelley Darling

Six months before the full marital breakdown that played out in our couple's session room, dowsing had come into my life.

In the profundity of the moment, a towering Belgian woman, a Feng Shui master no less, arrived at our home to hold an informational introduction to "memon," a German product. " She brought with her a gentle small-framed man, Peter, also from Belgium, who was to present a new type of environmental technology for harmonizing homes and the environment by neutralizing the impact of electromagnetic frequencies (EMFs).

Upon discovering I was ill, and staunchly ignoring my requests to continue on with her evening, she stood up, announcing she had her "dowsing rods" with her. Excusing herself she hurried off to her car to get them.

Coming back into the house with her rods swirling, I was thunderstruck on seeing them move with no apparent input from anywhere. "What's dowsing?" I asked. At that moment, this statuesque woman was clearly in charge. She commanded me to take her to my bedroom, and said, to my puzzlement, that she wasn't going to dowse the whole house. What did that even mean?! On entering the bedroom, she began to work with her L-shaped brass dowsing rods and asked me to lie down on the bed so she could reveal what she had discovered.

Songline of the Heart / Shelley Darling

She pointed out three geopathic stress lines in the room, caused by the crossing of underground streams of water and, to my surprise, they intersected exactly at the point on my body where I was feeling sick. I was stunned, as I hadn't told her I had a raging bladder infection!

She immediately remedied these lines of negative energy with three copper sticks, which apparently revealed some underground water, and gave me instructions to buy a large copper tensor ring made by a man named Slim Spurling, a metaphysical cowboy who lived in Colorado. Slim was an alchemical wizard who always dressed in a cowboy hat, and he understood Sacred Geometry, Egyptian Cubits and more. He had learned how to make a positive energy vortex go in both directions, creating a portal effect with the copper rings. Used on horses or humans, the rings were a powerful tool that could shift non-beneficial energies in seconds.

I was to place this ring on the floor under the bed between the two pillows belonging to my husband and me. In the morning, I woke up with no trace of the sickness that had been wracking my body the night before. My curiosity took hold and I discovered that this woman's managing director had recently moved to the next town over from us and was offering a weekend dowsing workshop. Understanding the magic of synchronicity and universally ordered sequences, I signed up.

The following weekend, spurred on by my experience, I placed the dowsing rods into my hands for the first time, immediately experiencing joy surging through my body. I had the absolute feeling of knowing I had done this before. In my research from the previous week, I had learned that dowsing was a tool that allows us to gather information not directly available to the conscious mind. It involves a journey beyond our five senses, bringing visibility to that which is invisible. Dowsing bypasses the conscious mind, accessing a deeper state of awareness, one that is attuned to a much broader range of unseen energetic signals.

Songline of the Heart / Shelley Darling

Exploring more, I found that throughout history, there have always been people on our planet who have held this knowledge of dowsing. In fact, dowsing rods have appeared in many murals around the world, such as the one on the walls of the Tassili Caves in Northern Africa's Atlas Mountains. There, a mural depicts a man with dowsing rods surrounded by a group of tribesmen. This mural has been carbon dated to be 8,000 years old.

As I continued my investigation into the ancient art and science of dowsing, I found myself researching the historical connections of this ancestral knowledge back to Egypt, France, China, and even Tibet. I discovered that during medieval times some people understood this vibrational science and knew how to find where the lines of energy were located on the Earth. They built sacred structures directly on these Earth lines. Not only that, but they would also identify how the energy was flowing, and plan entire cities using this knowledge.

As we began the weekend training, I had another direct experience of energy. While sitting on the couch in the front of the room I became aware of a growing headache and found it very difficult to listen. It wasn't until after lunch when we were taught to cure our "Personal Interference Lines" that I found I had three energy lines hitting me from the back, and after remedying them, I noticed my headache immediately disappeared. With the closing of the weekend, I enthusiastically embraced this knowledge of dowsing and began to immediately apply it to my own home and to my clients' houses.

By the time I was introduced to the ancient science of dowsing, I had spent more than 10 years living in California, facilitating individuals and couples in what I call "Embodied Heart Awakening." Straight away, I excitedly began applying dowsing to the lives of our business manager and my clients. Totally awed at the "quickening" of transformation that took place within them after their houses were dowsed, I continued to explore this new tool for my toolbox.

Where clients might have been struggling with a relationship or career, I found that after I dowsed their home, they would feel the freedom to step with more courage and vision into their dreams.

Our Homes are Containers for Energy

My fascination grew as I saw my client's lives shifted in transcendent ways. It was as if the energy shift in their homes induced a higher state of consciousness which positively affected their capacity to see their old patterns with new clarity so they could step forward with confidence and ease their challenges. I reveled in learning about the relationship between how our homes as containers for stressful energies inevitably affect everyone living in the house, some more than others. The transformations taking place in people's lives following a dowsing were extraordinary.

One of my first experiences applying dowsing came the day when our loyal and organized business manager was feeling particularly upset. She had been coming to our office daily, emotionally distraught and suffering a severe migraine. Although she was a great office manager, most days she would arrive in a state of emotional upset. She often spoke of feeling physically challenged, so the day after I had learned how to dowse, I jumped into action, reached for my shiny new 18-inch brass dowsing rods, and set about assessing and remedying the negative energy coming in the office. Three interference lines converged at her chair. Over the weekend I had learned that interference lines are negative energy lines caused from power lines, cell phone towers, and satellite dishes. The radiation can be measured and it enters a building through windows or outlets. A few minutes later, to my surprise, this stalwart lady came running to find me, coming to a halt in the kitchen. Twice she asked me what I had done. Her face was relaxed and her migraine was gone!

Songline of the Heart / Shelley Darling

Ecstatically happy, she begged me to come dowse her new one-bedroom apartment. I wasn't surprised to find very strong negative energy coming from a fuse box in her closet, located less than six feet from her bed. Under her pillow, radiating up from the first-floor apartment, was also a negative vortex. Watching, she looked wide-eyed with amazement as the energy vacuum spun the rods counterclockwise. Although these types of energies, and others, are invisible to our normal sight, they can weaken our immune systems and cause illness. The office manager came to work the next day describing how she felt so much better and for the first time had slept through the night.

You can imagine my disbelief when I walked into the office a week later and heard our wonderful office manager happily telling me she was quitting! I was completely dumbfounded and retorted, *"Wait a minute I just dowsed your house!"* Her humble answer was that she had always dreamt of having her own business, and she finally felt the courage to take a leap of faith to substantiate her heart's desire. I found that this type of response kept happening with my other clients, as well. It was as if the experience of having their home or office dowsed opened each person to naturally access and actualize their fullest potential.

Things began to rapidly shift as I felt the strength of my own convictions, especially with my new understanding of how dowsing can help relieve the emotional stressors in our lives. What I found daunting was that once my home had been fully dowsed, and complimented with feng shui remedies, my husband became more agitated. We were in the process of trying to figure out how to separate and his refusal to leave the house was making the whole situation more difficult.

With my new knowledge in hand, I stood taller in my power and decided to move my office from the back of the house to the front; this action seemed to enrage him. I can still see us standing in the middle of the hallway, between our two offices, arguing. It was as though the fact we were both now in the front of the home equalized the energy, causing an increase in hostility. Prior to finally leaving the relationship I re-dowsed the house and was flabbergasted to discover that our hostile behavior towards one another had created a negative vortex in front of the bathroom, where one had never existed originally!

Given this circumstance, I felt compelled to learn more. I jumped on an opportunity to attend an Advanced Feng Shui course. Years before, while living with a boyfriend in Florida, I had learned the principles of Feng Shui, and discovered I had an inherent knack for Feng Shui, selling my first house within minutes after its completion! My love of Feng Shui had facilitated me to developing an aptitude for ensuring more houses sold, even ones that had been on the market for a long time. This new course was certain to hone my skills even further.

On the second day of the training, I had an epiphany as I looked at one of the Feng Shui charts handed out during the class. I realized as soon as I set my eyes on the chart that on the evening I had been introduced to dowsing, the Feng Shui master who had dowsed my bedroom—the one who was giving this very course—would have had clear knowledge about how things really stood between my husband and me as soon as she stepped across the threshold of our bedroom. In fact, I remembered her telling me a story about a celebrity she had worked with whose rocky relationship with his wife had been saved after she had dowsed their home. Was it possible? Had she known?

Feeling exuberant about the possibilities this astonishing insight offered, and practically leaping out of my chair, I wildly hailed my Feng Shui teacher to come over. She confirmed my thoughts exactly! As it turned out, that very night, while driving from my home after the presentation she had given, she had told the quiet, subdued man from Belgium who had been with her that night about what she had uncovered. Her companion had insisted she could not be right, given his experience of the evening and of my husband, yet she stayed true to her story. I realized I hadn't been ready to hear that my marriage was in trouble the night my bedroom had been dowsed, and not even the story she had told had sparked my awareness of the possibility that something was going on. Something inside me had simply not been ready to know.

After months of illness, sacrifice, and disempowerment, the tumultuous dismantling of my relationship finally reached its logical conclusion. I owned that I hadn't been listening to myself and, most importantly, I hadn't been trusting my inner knowing which, by the way, had been screaming for attention through the fiery infection I had been experiencing!

Sacred Remembering

Now, some might say the experience of my soul awakening was not worth the physically and mentally rough waters I encountered for the following months. Yet, as always, with the dawning of any spiritual emergence, the alluring possibility of some unseen aspect of oneself being revealed continued to captivate me.

When our life is looked at as a full-immersion film, we can appreciate the exhilarating moments as well as the passive, peaceful ones. I sometimes think our spiritual emergence is like a river: we see it has tributaries, and there are eddies and full-on rapids of experience. We are flowing along inescapably down the river of our lives, guided by the bounds of the riverbanks. For some of us, had we known (and some might say that we did know) about this roaring ever-changing river, we might have refused the journey with a generous, "no, thanks..."

At an early age I was consciously searching for the meaning of life. In one of my first attempts at writing poetry as a teenager, I scribbled down, "Who was I? A rock, a pebble a stone, all the same but different." My grandmother said that when I had been a baby, nobody could hold or console me. I was a rebel from early on, and I was the only person I knew at the time of leaving high school who didn't go to college. When I asked my friends why they were going, not one person could give me an answer that satisfied me. *It was just the thing everyone did*...so I chose to defer and headed to the mountains of New Hampshire, living in the woods, close to Nature.

Eventually, though, my best friend, Buffy, and I decided to hitchhike across the country with my long-bodied brindle dog, Anna. Our plan was to pick grapes in Northern California, though when we arrived, we discovered that harvesting would not begin for another three weeks. On a whim, we chose to head across the border to the Baja California area of Mexico. On our first night, we were picked up by a couple who invited us to travel and spend a few days camping with them at the ocean. Given the husband was from the state of Baja, and his wife was from California, we enthusiastically agreed. Hungry, we chose to stop at a restaurant for some yummy local food while listening to stories of the couple's travels. We had been warned not to travel in the Mexican state of Baja California at night, but after some coaxing from our new friends, we started our evening journey to the coast.

We drove along in our new friends' improvised camper van under the wondrously open starry sky. Buffy sat in between the two front seats, while Anna and I sat behind the driver's seat on the couples' hand-made bed. All was well, until suddenly we swept too quickly around a large turn. The vehicle, in trying to balance itself, kept rolling and threw us all out wildly onto a grassy embankment. In a daze, I tenaciously searched the dark spacious wilderness for my friend and my dog. Stunned and aching, I called for my dog, who was unhurt, and I eventually found Buffy, who was lying unconscious in the gully at the side of the road.

I looked around but didn't catch sight of our new friends in the tenebrous dark night. Compelled to stay present, I brought my focus to my friend. I lovingly held Buffy close to my heart for hours, while she struggled for her life. Anna stayed quietly beside us both. For the longest time there were no cars, and as I realized how faint Buffy's breathing had become, I was forced to lay her down gently and grapple with the situation. I made my way back to the road in time to wave down a couple in a car driving past. They agreed to stop in the next town and send for an ambulance. Returning to my friend's listless body, I sat communing with God, wishing I had listened to the warnings I'd heard about Baja.

Lost in thought about Jesus Christ and how he had healed people—and questioning my own actions—I felt a growing sense of guilt. In the cool stillness of the black night, I wondered whether I might have had the knowledge to heal Buffy if I had followed my past inner whisperings, rather than resisting them so much. I hurt inside and out. Buffy was alive, yet barely breathing. The ambulance finally arrived an hour later with no oxygen.

I didn't even turn around to find out what had become of our new friends, as the ambulance lifted Buffy and drove at high speed to a hospital in the next town. She continued to breathe ever so softly, and when the medical staff finally placed the oxygen mask meticulously over her mouth, I watched her take her last breath. Almost immediately the Mexican police arrived. They uncaringly shoved me aside and left me alone in a tiny dark room with Anna. I was paralyzed and in shock. The police officers didn't help matters at all, as their eyes stalked my body. They tried to find ways get me to pay them for their services. I begged them to let me call my dad in Boston, and a day later, my dad—my savior—arranged for a taxi driver in San Diego to drive across the border to get me.

Buffy's body was to be held and later transported to the US. I watched the moving lines of people as I crossed the border back into California, USA, with the taxi driver and gave a huge sigh of relief. Somehow the taxi driver had learned that our new friends were okay. I sobbed profusely, hands held close to my wounded heart, gathering the strength needed to return from this hellish nightmare.

Back in Bethlehem

Three weeks later, my father paid for my return to Bethlehem, New Hampshire, where my journey to California with Buffy had begun. I faced her family and the exaggerated story and belief that I had left their Buffy on the side of the road to die. I stood stunned at the open casket where she lay dressed in a yellow princess dress, nothing like the wild funky young woman I had traveled with. I found myself walking away that day on a deep inner search. Compelled to stay in Bethlehem, I was invited to live in a house located in an area where the very religious Hasidic Jews walked daily with their families.

Mysterious circumstances unfolded weeks later when I was invited on a snowy wintry evening to the Christian healing group the mother of a friend had joined. I had never experienced anything like this. One woman played the piano while the others in full concert joined her. Then, oddly, they turned to the person by the center table as the room become deathly silent, until she began to speak in an unidentifiable voice. I was determined only to go as an observer, but something finally tweaked open inside me. Listening to my inner guidance, I thereafter began following a guru whose foremost teaching was, "What you're looking for is inside." This turn on the spiral led me to years of growing a dedicated relationship with the Divine. I learned to meditate, focusing my attention on truth, love, and inner light.

Eventually, I did go to a small experimental liberal arts college on the other side of Mount Agassiz, just a few miles away. Franconia College was a wild place where LSD, magic mushrooms and all-night parties were the norm. During my first semester at Dow Academy, a Georgian Revival wood-framed building in town, I studied ceramics. I loved working with the earthiness of the wet clay. My second and last semesters, I spent most of my time on the top floor of the decaying old campus building in the weaving studio. On sunny days I would prop myself on the ledge outside the huge third-story windows of the studio and contemplate the expansive mountainous view out towards Easton Valley. I was still moved by the deeper urging of a soul unsatisfied.

Still engaged in my search for love and meaning, I engaged in a few disconcerting relationships and continued my spiritual course. Ultimately, after the end of my first marriage, I went on to marry my second "Aloha" husband feeling I had found a soulmate who could meet me fully, love me unconditionally, and partner with me as an equal. What I hadn't even considered at that point was, that what I was really looking for was a "whole-mate," and that whole-mate, was me! The misery that accompanied the dissolution of our marriage had me heartsick and discouraged, while at the same time, deep inside, a growing inner trust supported the understanding that the innate impulse of creation, though seemingly chaotic, is always recalibrating into the highest order.

A Homeopathic Dose of Homelessness

After agreeing to separate, the trauma in my life hadn't settled. As he declared he would, my husband took over our house and the business we had built together and for the first time in my life, I found myself homeless. A client whose house I had successfully dowsed, offered to let me stay in a studio above the barn on her organic hydroponic farm. It was festooned with silvery spider webs but luckily, as I had no money for food, I would wake up each morning and walk to an abundant fig tree on the property, relishing its soft, ripe, delicious fruit. From there I would stroll through the narrow lanes of plants over to the leafy kale and the blushing, crimson tomato plants to complete my morning feast.

Songline of the Heart / Shelley Darling

On my first night there I had a dream:

I dreamt I was sleeping with my husband in our king-sized bed in the house we had shared in La Jolla.

We were in the living room, and there were huge glass windows behind us that faced the street. In front of the bed was a large brick fireplace. I got up from the bed and walked through the wide wooden doors that were standing open at the front of the house. I saw before me, beyond the doors, an illumination of golden light, and I felt a calling to walk through the doorway.

Subconsciously I knew this was a portal through which I would never walk back. Instead of trusting the calling, I turned quickly to my sleeping husband. Simultaneously, the huge dark wooden mahogany doors closed, shutting me out forever. I cried and cried, pounding on the doors. The doors never opened, and neither did I walk through to that gateway of light.

It was a pattern I kept reliving over and over in my life. I always seemed to be caught between two waves of indecision. Finding myself without the capacity to move forward and unable to go back. Was it the power and fear of the unknown that kept me from adventuring forward, or a desire to make sure I didn't leave those I have loved behind? *Or something else?*

I remembered how, earlier in my youth, as an avid horsewoman I was sometimes thrown off while riding or jumping my horse. I was innately endowed with a sense of knowing how to fall. It was almost as though, in slow motion, I could feel my body naturally soften and become like jelly and inevitably, phenomenally, I would not be hurt when I landed. I would hop right back up, kindly stroke my horse and begin again.

Songline of the Heart / Shelley Darling

With the breakdown of my marriage, it appeared that for the first time I had fallen off, landed with a great thud, and found myself unable to get back up. Something had to give.

Packing up my dowsing rods, I said goodbye to my life in San Diego and prepared to travel to Australia to spend time with my daughter, Heather.

I knew I needed to use the time to better understand my recent experience of betrayal, and my part in its creation. The unfurling of this spiritual quest was to catapult me into a fervent awakening that resulted in a developing relationship with the Cathars, Jesus, and Mary Magdalene, all of whom lived the teachings of the "Way of Love."

Three Promises: *The Book of Love*

Attempting to stay focused, two days before leaving for Australia, I received a call from my dear long-time friend, Jenny.

Jenny and her husband, Mark, had completed many training sessions with my husband and I, and they were the first fully certified trainers of our proprietary technique. Prior to the altercation with my husband, they had been looking to create a training center in the Northeastern United States, in Maine.

At the moment Jenny called, I happened to be driving near the top of Soledad Mountain Road, just past an overlook of the Pacific, next to a home that had a large bronze sculpture of three moving dolphins facing the wide expansive ocean.

As spirit animals, the Dolphins represent harmony and balance. They are the messengers reminding us of our capacity to navigate the depths of the sea with joy and ease.

Jenny elatedly began reading me a passage from the newly published *Book of Love* by Kathleen McGowan... I listened as she continued.

There are three promises made at the dawn of time, each of them sacred:

The first Promise is to God, your Mother and Father in Heaven. It represents your most divine mission, what you have come to accomplish in the image of your creators. It is the reason for incarnation, the purest intention of your Soul.

The second Promise is to the family of Spirit within which you are created and will belong through eternity. It represents your relationship to each of the Souls in your family and how you have agreed to assist them in their mission, and they in yours.

The third Promise is to yourself. It represents how you desire to learn and grow and love within the context of your incarnation.

Align yourself with these promises you've made, for they're sacred above all else. Remember and cherish them, and you will know the greatest joy available to humankind. For those with ears to hear: Let them hear it.

The words triggered the memory of my husband and I at our wedding. He asked for kindness and promised honesty. I committed to always speaking my truth with love.

Jenny held space as I spoke of our shared experience and long-gone hopes regarding the time and effort put into the growing of our personal training business.

Given the timing of this dynamic synchronicity, I immediately ordered the Book of Love, receiving it just hours before my flight left for Australia.

Chapter 4: Charmed Convergence

In the rugged expanse of wilderness, wildness resonates as spiritual communication, the call of the Soul, the call of the sacred world of Nature - the unveiled face of the Source. The call of the wild says that the mystery is inside you, was inside you all the time, you just needed to be somewhere where the call could resonate, where the voice of your Soul could be heard. This happens when you enter into the deep silence within, either out in Nature or in the depths of your heart.

—Jack Angelo[24]

With my dowsing rods packed away and Kathleen McGowan's "Book of Love" tucked into my bag, I unknowingly opened the door to an experience that, through trust, gave way to a realm of everyday magic and mystery in Australia.

I left a world I believed was my dream come true and moved into a world that not even in my greatest imaginings could I have considered a possibility. Past and present became one, and time converged. I knew every experience of what I was calling, "magic" was, in truth, simply a series of natural, interconnected synchronicities. These synchronicities seemed to surface when I was paying attention to the movement of energy, and open to a deepening sense of Nature's intelligent design.

---

[24] Jack Angelo, *The Healing Wisdom of Mary Magdalene: Esoteric Secrets of the Fourth Gospel*, (Google Books), (Simon and Schuster, Feb 22, 2015)

Richard Rudd explains in his "Gene Keys" book how magic refers to events that do not follow logical, sequential laws. Magic, he states, "is spontaneous, highly mutated, unpredictable and uncontrollable. Its greatest quality is that it is beyond meaning or understanding." He goes on to say, "We know from modern quantum physics that all matter is made up of vibrating energy fields. Magic is causal. It cannot be learned, mastered or imitated. Magic comes pouring through and becomes a phenomenon, a symbol of the breaking of the laws of form." [25]

Randomly, over the years, Ellen, my former sister-in-law from my first marriage will call me to share what she considers to be my "charmed experiences." She particularly loves the story of the time when I was stuck on Alligator Alley in Florida. People living in Florida have long known they must fill their car with gas before going across this dreaded 100-mile stretch of I-75 that yawns from Fort Lauderdale to Naples. For most, it is far from a thrilling adventure, as the idea of running out of gas on a lonely highway with alligators can be quite panic inducing. Over the years there have been many accounts of close calls on Alligator Alley, and although some of them are quite humorous, they were still a bit scary.

My own story, which unfurled when I was in my 30s, happened to be full of near-death magic. My daughter, then a teen, and I were traveling from the East coast of Florida near Fort Lauderdale to the West coast, where we were living on Fort Myers Beach. Leaving early in the morning was a good choice, yet we only made it about 15 miles, before I realized that even though I was incessantly pressing my foot to the gas pedal, the car was refusing to go any further. It came to a dead stop.

---

[25] Richard Rudd, *Gene Keys: Embracing Your Higher Purpose* Penguin Random House, May 1, 2013), pp 482-484.

Songline of the Heart / Shelley Darling

My despondent daughter, not very happy about this ordeal, sat frozen in the front passenger seat, refusing to budge. Rather than conspiring with her fear, I simply took a breath, paused, and when guided by a divine spark of inspiration, ran out onto the empty highway. Turning my face to the East I searched through the mirages tat hovered over the paved road. Out of nowhere a truck appeared, heading straight towards me. Flagging him down, I immediately realized this was a tow truck with a large empty flatbed! I laughed hysterically at what seemed to be a cosmic joke.

As the magic would have it, although my American Automobile Association (AAA) membership would only allow him to drive us 10 more miles, he decided to drive us all the way, north of Naples to Fort Myers Beach, and straight to my place of work. Going way beyond the call of duty, he kindly offered to tow my white Subaru station wagon to his shop, and generously offered to bring it back to me the next day, all fixed. This experience, though seemingly miraculous, was a "normal" in my world. My past sister-in-law, though, will inevitably exclaim, *"How is it, that you do what you do?"* when hearing another one of my "magical" stories.

Born with boundless curiosity and an innate sense of optimism, I've consciously kept growing my trust and foundational wisdom in God and the Universe through practices of heartful daily prayers, ceremony, invocations, and resonance attunements, focusing on aligning with what scientists call, the Unified Field. Barbara Marx Hubbard, a futurist who worked with Buckminster Fuller, spoke to this as connecting with the evolutionary impulse of creation itself.

I've experienced countless times how this strange magnetic attractor, scientifically proven, seems to be available to us when we slow down, pause, and become fully present. Like ocean navigators, I learned we must move beyond our five senses, listen, and feel into the movement of the wind, the inner and outer tidal currents, and follow the inner light of our guidance, or as some simply say, our intuition. I discovered how asking Spirit with sincerity to "show me" inevitably opens us to the direct embodied experience of the Field of Creative Consciousness, as a felt/sensed knowing.

Heart-Based Explorations

Heading off to Australia alone, with the *Book of Love* in my arms and a torn heart throbbing under my skin, I was expecting to navigate an alley full of ferocious, metaphorical "alligators." I felt sorely wounded, and conflicted, and I asked myself once again, "What is love?" I also wondered if things would have changed sooner if I had paid attention to my whispering doubts and acted upon my own inner guidance. At the point at which my marriage fell apart, the journey of stepping into my personal power felt a fair way off.

My intention was now to consciously choose to understand my experience of betrayal, reclaim my power, and rediscover my soul's purpose. I was leaving behind years of building a conscious heart-based business that exemplified practices of unconditional love and embodied integration. What did all that mean now?

While reading the *Book of Love* on the long flight to Australia I found a new promise being kindled in my scorched and tender heart. I stopped reading for a bit and became mesmerized by an in-flight movie about the recent true story of a young woman who had left home to discover herself. She flew to meet an indigenous tribe on an island, who took her into their community and showered her with exceptional wisdom and love. A new sense of aliveness flourished within her. I trembled at this prophetic message and sat for a few minutes musing about my past journey and what might now be seeding itself in my heart. It had now been more than six months since I had begun fighting the illness that was still wracking my body.

Songline of the Heart / Shelley Darling

My marriage had ended, and I was still no closer to full health. Would this misery and grief ever end?

I arrived at Sydney International Airport in Australia still feeling deeply exhausted and extremely weak, but I felt elevated by my discovery of the mysterious Cathars. My middle daughter, Heather, who years before had been my companion on the trek across Alligator Alley, was waiting for me at the arrivals gate and noticed the difficulty I was having walking out of customs. She offered to help me acquire some vitamins from the holistic clinic where she was working in Mona Vale, a suburb about 45 minutes north of Sydney.

We drove along some of the most beautiful coastline I'd ever seen to the Northern Beaches where Heather worked as a massage therapist. The air was cool, and a waft of sweet-smelling Jasmine drifted in the air. Relieved, and feeling supported, I followed her down a natural stone path to her clinic, a renovated cottage. I stopped for a moment to listen to the birds and reveled in these new surroundings. I was surprised to hear sonorous laughter in the woods surrounding the cottage and learned it was a Kookaburra, a bird that sounds more like a monkey than a monkey! The bird's welcome tickled my senses. It was as if this Kookaburra knew magic was about to happen.

Just inside the clinic, I could see what looked like four healing rooms, though something caught my attention. Turning to the right, I was drawn to a white painted table that held 30 or 40 business cards from various holistic healers. One colorful card caught my attention, literally jumping out at me. Unfolding the uniquely crafted card, my lower jaw dropped:

> *"Sanna Purinton, clairvoyant, Spirit facilitator, whose mission is to bring the voice of the Cathars into the 21st Century."*[26]

---

[26] Sanna Purinton, https://www.sannapurinton.com

I stood there stunned as Heather watched with curiosity. Although I have always loved "the magic," of this type of synchronicity, in this moment took me by surprise.

How was it I had barely even heard of the Cathars just 14 hours earlier, and now suddenly found myself within calling distance of a spiritual facilitator who sought to bring the voice of the Cathars into the 21st Century?

I gazed at my daughter and stated quite hastily "I think I need to meet this woman." Heather's smile should have let me know something was up, but my exhaustion had taken over my senses.

Sanna

One hour after arriving in Australia I was gifted a session with Sanna Purinton. Her deep commitment as a conduit for the Way of Love, through the Cathars' message, guided me through the most painful transition in my life with absolute magic and joy. I began to experience a deep unification within my body, mind, heart and spirit. I am in gratitude to Sanna for her transmissions of deep wisdom and truth.

—Shelley Darling

Apparently, Heather had been planning a surprise experience for me as a welcome gift, and had considered many modalities, trying to choose between a massage, a chiropractor or a naturopath; after much consideration she had scheduled an appointment for me, for the very next day, at the clinic with Sanna.

Songline of the Heart / Shelley Darling

After climbing up into Heather's boyfriend's new white steed—a shiny Land Rover—we drove down a windy, tree laden road alongside the bay.

I was enthralled by the beauty of the land and saw beyond my window a small, distant forested island. Heather laughed and quietly mentioned that the island was where we were heading.

First, we stopped at Church Point landing, a charming local spot and ferry landing on the Northern Beaches, where we would carry my bulging luggage aboard Heather's little "tinny,"—the name used in Australia for a small aluminum boat.[27]

The walk up to the landing looked like something I had only seen in a movie. There were benches and picnic tables with many "mates" laughing it up, carousing, and drinking beer after work, and a group was socializing around an old gum tree. Family members were all chattering as they waited for their kids, who were happily coming home from school. I delightfully rejoiced in wonder at this untamed scene. One group of boys shouted to Heather, keen on finding out more about her "mum."

Scooting Across the Bay

A friend of Heather's owned an idyllic Mediterranean holiday house called "EngleSea" on Scotland Island and on hearing of my health issue, she'd invited me to stay there to heal. I reveled in the discovery the only means to get to this magnificent sanctuary was by ferry or by tinny.

---

[27] In Australia and New Zealand, the word "tinny or tinnie," is a commonly used as a slang word for a small open aluminum boat.

Songline of the Heart / Shelley Darling

As we climbed aboard the tinny, I could see the kids and their families lining up for the ferry, waiting to leave from the dock. I was overjoyed at being out on the water once again. I searched the bay with its exquisite rolling hills and bush walking tracks dropping into the water. Heather masterfully drove the tinny, scooting across the unclouded bay until we saw the landing dock jutting way out beyond a small island cabana closer to the shore. Getting gingerly out of the boat I walked unsteadily up the meandering sandstone path to the house. Dragging my suitcase was challenging, but I was determined.

Fatigued, I made my way up five steps at a time, in a slow-motion journey to the doorway of the single-story waterfront house. It was demanding of my admittedly worn-out petite body. Heather timidly shared later how she felt scared and concerned watching me struggling to walk. Arriving at the top of the walkway, though, I was rewarded by a breathtaking view. I was overtaken by the extraordinary beauty of the native and tropical flowers on the island. Beyond the immediate area I also scanned the West Head landscape, with its sparkling sunlit ocean vista. I was bedazzled by the light reflecting off other boats racing from Church Point around the island.

> **The Smaller Room**
>
> *I stayed at the house many times, and never would go in the smaller room. It felt really strange and, as well, I would never go to the back of the house, either. It felt dark and yucky, and the one night when I had to sleep in there I couldn't sleep, and the light kept coming on and off in the room.*
>
> **—Heather Meyer**

My first inclination was to dowse the house and create a true healing retreat space. Heather had been instructed to offer me the master suite, and with a slightly forlorn face she showed me the other bedroom, which she wasn't sure about staying in.

Songline of the Heart / Shelley Darling

She explained to me the energy of the smaller room was not good. Previously she had stayed at the house with her "mate" and hadn't slept well.

Extending my heartfelt gratitude and appreciation to the homeowner who had been generous enough to let me come—and who at the time was staying in Sydney Harbor—I delightedly skipped to the oversized master bedroom, which was filled with an overabundance of light.

Looking past the off-white lacey linens on the bed, I was captivated. Standing on the freshly cleaned hardwood floors, I rejoiced in the extensive, resplendent view of the bay.

Lazily unpacking and stopping to gaze at the panoramic views beyond the windows I was enraptured by the azure Australian sky. My body reveled at finding a luxurious bathroom with a contemporary curved glass shower and a free-standing bathtub. Not having the energy to dowse that night, I placed the larger tensor copper intertwined ring I had brought with me under the bed and headed into the dreamtime.

The Kookaburras awoke me the next morning, instilling in me a sense of place and sanctifying within me a love affair with these fascinating native birds. Outside on the stone patio, Heather and I finished our morning "brekkie" and I took right away to dowsing the house.

Heather repeated how she hadn't slept well and spoke of having heard weird noises in the small bedroom. She had also heard bottles crashing to the floor in the kitchen for no apparent reason.

I set sacred space, first acknowledging and honoring the Ancestors of the land, asking for permission and guidance to dowse. After Heather spoke to me about the owner's marital relationship and her impending divorce, I went into action assessing the home with the intention to clear away any non-beneficial energy.

> ## A Negative Vortex
>
> *A negative vortex is an energy vacuum that spins counterclockwise, creating density in the home or on the Earth. Negative vortexes are areas of high energy concentrations and occur where two energy lines intersect at a 90-degree angle.*
>
> *Unlike positive vortexes, which flow upward out of the Earth, the energy in negative vortexes flows inward, spiraling down toward the Earth. People experiencing their effects will feel like they're trapped in a state of critical despair, and experience a drained immune system.*

I discovered both a negative vortex in the main dining area, and many geopathic stress lines, causing a feeling of contraction in this exquisite home. A Geopathic Stress Zone (Geo=Earth, Pathic=Illness), is like a Negative Vortex in that it creates a chaotic energy in the earth's magnetic field. They are created by water running beneath the Earth's surface—which gives off noxious radiation—or by two different soils coming together, or also by mining. They produce high levels of stress and can create pathological conditions in plants, animals, and humans. Not surprisingly, I found an earthbound spirit, or otherwise called an entity, in Heather's bedroom.

Fields of Energy

Using 18" copper rods to clear away any interfering energy by placing them on the periphery of the house walls, I turned my attention to focus on where the non-beneficial electromagnetic energy was coming from. I then used a large Sacred Cubit Ring as a positive vortex to remove the entity. The Sacred Cubit energy rings were conceived by the late Slim Spurling, a world-famous geo-dowser with an interest in metaphysics and a vision of planetary healing.

Songline of the Heart / Shelley Darling

A Sacred Cubit Tensor Ring is a great superconductor, neutralizing the magnetic field, and creating a positive spinning energy; its energy output is beneficial and healing. Sometimes called a Tensor Ring, it's an infinite source of energy that is neither electric nor magnetic and is created with the understanding of sacred geometry. Tensor Rings, or "Resonance Rings", as I like to call them, come in varying gages and sizes. They can be used in different ways: for example, they can enhance the energy of specific places in a home, used around plants, and placed under furniture. Their positive spinning field of energy, when placed on the timber floorboards on top of the area of the negative vortex, begins to clear the negative energy immediately.

After I initially learned to dowse, one of my first large dowsing jobs was for a woman with breast cancer, the wife of a military Veteran who, together with her husband, were running a hydroponic farm. Investigating the matter, I learned that the woman who had lived there previously had died of breast cancer before her husband had been able to fulfill her request to finish building a fence around the property.

Following her passing, as sometimes occurs, the lady's husband died. Common between the two couples was the location of their bedroom, and the fact that both women struggled with breast cancer.

During the dowsing, I determined that the husband's spirit was hanging around and unable to move forward because of the uncompleted business represented by the unfinished fence. I began communicating with this man's spirit, letting him know I was sorry about his wife. I thanked him and let him know it was okay to return home to the light or Source. With the completion of the dowsing, the man's spirit moved on and the bottle crashing in the kitchen, *oh, didn't I tell you*, finally came to a halt. Once the house was cleared, the environment felt more spacious, peaceful and calm.

> ## Scotland Island
>
> Scotland Island is located towards the southern end of Pittwater, in the land of the Guringai, the original inhabitants of the area. In nearby Ku-ring-gai Chase National Park there are numerous rock engravings carved by the Guringai people. There are also middens containing remnants of shells and fish. The terrain is steep, rising in places, and it takes about an hour to walk the island's 2.5-kilometer circumference.
>
> The only access is by water, and the island is reached by the ferry from Church Point. There's a wonderful regular ferry service, which began in the 1950s, yet with the changing season and the ferry schedule ending early in the day, most residents use a small dinghy or "tinny" to travel to and from the island.
>
> **—Shelley Darling**

Although Heather had no personal experience with dowsing, and wasn't sure she even believed in it, she was surprised at how good she felt staying in the bedroom the following night. She said it felt like a totally different room and she exclaimed that the dowsing had created a huge difference. She expressed with delight how the change in her experience revealed to her the validity of dowsing.

At the time of my arrival in Australia I felt wounded, and I was suffering deeply, physically, and emotionally. Heather's boyfriend, Chris, seeing my despair, enthusiastically invited us to go out in his boat for a tour. Around Heather's neck hung the most exquisite teal stone necklace, which contained a large amulet. She caught me eyeing it and graciously offered to let me wear it for the day. The unique shaped stone amulet lay exactly over my heart.

Songline of the Heart / Shelley Darling

It was a gorgeous summer day, and we cheered as Chris's larger aluminum fishing boat raced over the water past Scotland Island and towards the far-off beaches at Avalon, a town located due West on a peninsula that held a lighthouse jutting out from the land. Cutting through the deep blue water, we passed West Head and kept following the river north of the point at Avalon. Putting my hand in the water as the boat slowed, I leaned against the edge of the boat, trying to reach out a bit further. Immediately, I heard and felt a loud "CRACK. CRACK!" To my utter disbelief, I realized I had cracked two ribs in front of my heart. Embracing the pain, I realized I was not at all complete with my grieving process.

Chris was an adept fisherman, and I was touched as his fishing buddies, knowing I was ill, brought fresh-caught fish daily. They surprised me with a party one night and concocted some of the most masterful cooked dishes atop the stainless gas cook top I'd ever seen. What's more, the tender, fresh octopus was unlike any I had ever eaten!

After a jovial night of feasting, Heather said goodbye, and I watched as she steered her tinny across the bay, leaving Scotland Island behind as she headed to her houseboat in the little cove nestled below the Ku-ring-gai Chase National Park. I flopped down and rested my head in deep gratitude for this peaceful, lush, bush landscape setting.

With a daily ritual that included gratitude for the ancestors of this place and a bush walk, my own personal healing continued. A growing benevolent relationship developed with Sanna who, after my first session, continued to be a remarkable guide. I would make my way by ferry from Scotland Island to the mainland and catch the local large-windowed bus to the cottage clinic in the town of Mona Vale.

From my arrival, the innate generosity and kindness bestowed on me, by all the Australians I met was astounding. Two close friends of Heathers' on meeting me for the first time, surprisingly, handed me the keys to their brand new Mazda!

The Sacred Sites

Many of the sacred sites and powerful places in nature offer an energy portal, and those who are sensitive can feel what is being offered.

The ancient ones were sensitive to these places and they usually built their temples and sacred altars near or upon the entrance or opening to these portals.

You can scan the history of Earth and see ... the main portals and power places by observing where the ancient churches, buildings, stone circles, pyramids, even villages and whole cities, were constructed over or near these gateways.

Even today people travel to hold ceremonies and experience the ancient portals. There are many who travel to these ancient sites unaware of this energy and force. The impact to their personal awakening can be very subtle or it can be extremely profound.

—**Peggy Black**

Chapter 5: Voice of the Land

"Kanyini is the connectedness. Everything living is our family. The trees are our family just like the kangaroos, emus and all the other animals. Growing up, our oldies used to tell us we were connected to everything else, every other living thing. You're never lost and you're never, ever alone. It is my responsibility to care for everything around me. Kanyini is caring with unconditional love."

—Uncle Bob Randall[28]

Ten days later I left Scotland Island, rejoined Heather, and went back to live aboard the houseboat. My health returning, and the integration of my journey now underway, I was being asked to introduce my personal empowerment sessions to people. Prior to the collapse of my health, I had been offering these to clients in the US only after I had dowsed their homes. I had come to realize that without dowsing, people are living in environments that are not necessarily supporting them, or their family members. A home often holds harmful negative frequencies that can affect health, relationships, and finances. Although these non-beneficial energies are invisible, they can be felt, and can represent patterns of energy that are creating a block in the manifestation of one's intentions.

Dowsing focuses on working with the subtle and not-so-subtle energies of the home and land and serves to awaken, and strengthen, the remembrance of one's soul's purpose. My work with the energy of house and land, combined with my knowledge of certain integration processes for our body, mind, and spirit, created an accelerated pathway for my clients. Repeatedly I discovered that once the negative vortexes and

---

[28] "Interview with Uncle Bob Randall," Medibank, https://www.medibank.com.au

geopathic stress were clear, my clients would automatically feel more relaxed, and they found they had greater clarity in discovering new ways to live in alignment with their inherent value, truth, and evolving purpose.

We, as a collective, have now learned we can raise our consciousness through meditation, prayer, and positive thinking. We know, too, of the need for creative solutions for our planet in dire need of us to shift so we can co-creatively foster peace, social order, and justice. Consider that everything is energy, and our houses, offices, schools, and community centers, too, need to hold and maintain a higher vibration to support our greater wellbeing, interconnectedness, and wholeness.[29]

In Australia, I became aware of the powerful ancestral voice and spirit of the land. I found it fascinating, how the winged ones, stone beings, and animals of the bush had such a profound effect on my psyche. Never having experienced anything quite like this, I knew I was being guided and directed.

I was becoming sensitive to the subtle changes in the land's energy, and I knew how powerfully this could affect my life. This experience was setting the tone for a more grounded relationship within myself and with Nature. Having the opportunity to listen more deeply to my internal compass, I was soon to discover a sense of home I had not yet understood.

Keen to share her mum's gifts, Heather introduced me to Anna. Anna was the owner of the Kookaburra Clinic in Mona Vale, and she was an enthusiastic, passionate, open-hearted, zesty woman. She loved people, and her massage skills and cheeriness were well known in the community.

---

[29] Peggy Black, "The Power of Portals," *Intuitive Mind*, https://intuitivemind.com/chakras

We immediately had a wonderful connection and before our meeting was over, she asked me to dowse her clinic. One of the things I am always aware of and share with students and individuals for whom I dowse, is that as soon as a person makes the commitment to dowse, the transformational process begins. The one question I always ask is, "Are you ready?"

Walking onto the clinic property prepared to dowse, I began with an opening attunement, a spiritual practice of connecting with the vibration of a building and the land while standing with the owner and observing it from the street. Looking down the pathway towards the clinic's front door, I was dismayed to realize I could not see the door at all. What this meant to me as a Feng Shui specialist was that the energy flow to the house was hidden. Consider that the flow of energy, or Chi, needs to easily meet the front door, the front door being the heart of the home or office. If we have a blockage to our heart caused by fear, then the blood flow will be obstructed. We want the pathway to the home to be gentle, winding and moving forward in an unhampered way to the front door.

Greater Wholeness and Wellbeing

We focused for a few minutes on opening the energy of the clinic. I could feel Anna's full engagement and was warmed by her wholehearted declaration in creating her intention for the dowsing. Devoted to her clients, she set her intention for their health, wealth, and happiness first, while I supported her to expanding her intention to include a personal vision for herself. I see this happening to people who are very spiritual and dedicated to different modalities of healing. My work supporting my clients in living their Soul design, at times includes helping reframe their intentions towards greater wholeness and wellbeing for themselves, as well as for their family and clients. All dowsing begins with an acknowledgement and honoring of the Ancestors of the land. We ask for permission and feel gratitude to our beneficent guides and feel into an attunement for the individual and the environment. This immediately sets the process that will create a resonant and harmonic relationship with their home, land, or office. My intention is always to offer a transmission that opens my client's awareness and enhances their connection to their home and property. Although I am focused mainly on dowsing, as a Feng Shui specialist there are often a few golden nuggets I feel need to be shared with my clients to help them understand the Chi, or life force energy, and how it's entering their home. Later, they might choose to go deeper and give their home and landscape a full feng shui treatment. I have always felt dowsing and Feng Shui together create a portal to Heaven!

    Taking a few steps past the thinning bushes, I was now standing on the little stone path looking at the front door to the clinic, I invited Anna to feel into how the subtle energy was moving toward it. This experience helps people slow down enough to see and feel how energy moves, and it is eye-opening. Many times, I have posed such questions as, "Is the front door blocked by some trees? Is the path twisted or turning, or creating what's called a birth canal? Is the energy stuck?"

    Walking slowly to the clinic, I described my experience of the energy pattern. Anna's path to the front door, though supported by native plants, was long, with a 90-degree turn to the left near the door. I wanted Anna to have direct experience of the flow of energy as it moved. Taking time with her helped her feel the way the energy was moving. She loved the analogy of the front door being equated to the heart's capacity to receive and when she "got it" she uttered a big "Yes!"

Animal Totems and Dowsing

To our delight, as we were walking together down the stone-lined path, we felt the sudden swooping of a Kookaburra as it flew past us and landed on a tree just above our heads. It cackled with raucous laughter. I bent over in glee, knowing the bird was curiously assessing what was happening. I have learned over the years to pay very close attention to the animal totems that show up during a dowsing. The Kookaburra's energy medicine was a great sign, and I knew—just as the Ancestors had known—that he had arrived to open the way forward for us. I always invite my students to pay great attention to what happens on the way to a dowsing, as it is prophetic. The Kookaburra totem revealed an end to fears and insecurities that caused a difficult journey, and it opened the way for a restorative and nourishing new experience.

We continued walking slowly as I shared my insights on how to shift the energy to create more of a flow to the front door. I knew that as I shared this information, Anna's intuitive senses were opening. She was becoming more sharply aware in the present moment of these subtle energies and after my experience of dowsing I knew this would serve her going forward in her life. Where our eyes rest as we open the front door powerfully connects us to the flow in and around the space. Whether your eye hits a clear glass door, or half-wall, or kitchen, will influence a person's body. In the case of a clinic, it will also greatly affect clients' dispositions upon entering for their sessions. The design of Anna's clinic was perfect. She had already moved the office desk into the command position, facing the door, and her clients were being greeted by the happy practitioners, one of which was my daughter.

In Feng Shui, the command position is the area where you would be able to best position yourself to see what's coming through the door, and it's a metaphor for the energy coming into your life. The primary places to consider would be your bedroom or office, and the main room of your house. Imagine being poised, ready to receive a loving hug or a check, allowing the reciprocity to be felt by both the giver and you, the receiver. This exudes a renewed sense of solidarity and joy.

The office walls were covered with dynamic, colorful, art prints. I invited Anna to sit down in the middle of the room as I proceeded to do an assessment of the clinic. She was in awe watching the brass-sleeved dowsing rods spun both positively clockwise and negatively counterclockwise as I checked the energy—not only for the clinic, but for the other body workers as well. As in "EngleSea," the home on Scotland Island, it was important to check here, too, for geopathic stress, interference lines, and other stress zones that might be affecting the space.

I took time to explain to Anna that geopathic stress is an illness created by harmful energies from the Earth. The home or building becomes a container for energies that can come from water running under the building, different soil and sand mediums, or any spots where the Earth has been mined. We are now learning how fracking, the process of injecting liquid at high pressure into subterranean rocks and boreholes, also causes geopathic stress. Geopathic stress produces sick building syndrome, depleting our immune system, and it can cause adrenal exhaustion. Signs of geopathic stress can be, sleep disorders, fatigue, noxious smells, and frequent accidents in a particular area of the home or property.

Interference zones, unlike geopathic stress, are caused by cell phone towers, power lines and satellite discs. These issues, along with geopathic stress-related issues, can be remedied using activated copper rods—which I now call "Earth Cures"[30]—programmed crystals, and other spirituality-enhancing modalities. Copper is known as a conductive element and when cut to a specific length resonates and remedies the geopathic stress.

To Anna's delight we also discovered a positive vortex in her office entryway. A positive vortex energy spirals upwards, causing an enhanced, uplifting feeling. We feel this energy when we're near energy landscapes such as waterfalls, or at sacred sites around the world, such as Stonehenge, Avebury, and, in Australia, places such as Mount Wolumbin, Mount Kosciusko, and Ayers Rock, better known to the Aboriginal people as Uluru. In our home or offices, positive

---

[30] Activate your own Earth Cures: www.evolutionarydowsing.com.

vortexes are great areas for meditation, healing, and open communication with our higher guidance. Placing a tensor ring above or on a doorway entryway can generate a feeling of spaciousness, and clear people's energy fields upon entry. Anna, being a body worker, was thrilled to learn how these energy lines affect the physicality of her clients. She learned how interference lines affect our capacity to think, and they create confusion and unclear communication. They can also cause issues in our family relationships.

A Heavy Weight in Her Heart

As we approached her private office, Anna was surprised to see me following the dowsing rods when they pointed to a wood-framed picture on the wall. It was a photograph of her sister. She said it had great meaning for her and marked a time when there had still been a heavy weight in her heart regarding tension in their relationship. As her head dropped and a slight tear dripped down her cheek, I knew this needed reconnection and so healing the rift with her sister was to be an important part of the dowsing.

This is an example of how the dynamic application of dowsing, woven with my previous training in emotional integration techniques, creates the conditions to powerfully support the people I work with in having a direct inner awakening. I facilitate this type of experience through the intuitive information I receive and as a dowsing mentor my work is to simply use my skillset, act as a catalyst, stay in a state of pure presence, and allow for the new information and a synergistic revelation to take place within the client. In other words, this type of alchemical process allows the creative potential of the person to attune with the natural resonance of the Unified Field of Consciousness.

Anna stood still in front of the picture and I felt the energy shift and support her in the release of old patterns that had inhibited the healing of her relationship with her sister. I waited patiently for her to make the connections inside herself. The rods had brought us to this particular photo for a reason.

Tears now streamed down her reddened cheeks as the unresolved story integrated miraculously in minutes.

The dowsing was completed through the setting of the copper Earth Cures, as I now like to call them, in specific locations where they were needed, in a parallel formation around the periphery of the office.

Anna left that day feeling ecstatic and joyful. She was curious about what would happen as a result of the dowsing, and keen to learn more about the resonant energy she was now feeling succinctly in her body.

The next day she happily called me and shared how her clients were coming in and asking her if she had done something different to the space. Some thought she had applied a fresh coat of paint, and others were saying how they loved the energy and noticed a calming effect they hadn't felt before. She was overjoyed, renewed, and thrilled I was coming to dowse her family home. Dowsing is an efficient evolutionary tool and catalyst for shifting the energy of one's heart, home, and habitat. Watching Anna's revolutionary transformation restored her love of self and awakened her sense of sacred relationship to the land. As a dowsing mentor I, too, receive benefits from every dowsing experience.

Here in Australia, I felt the strong energies of the Ancestors and Nature Spirits, and I felt the timely appearance of the animal relations showing up.

It brings joy and peace to my heart each time I witness a person's transmutation during a dowsing. Similar to the iconic butterfly metamorphosis, Evolutionary Dowsing creates a harmonized environment that directly affects and uplifts the individual's heart, creating a positive field of momentum for living in alignment with their personal soul destiny path.

Part II
A Moment of Awakening

Shelley

When Shelley arrived in Australia, though quite sick, she was walking in wonder and innocence.

Everyone needs to know God is a page turner, first you think you know where you are and then comes that moment of "oh" where the wonder equates to innocence, which is the key to transformation, as it allows for a deeper connection to Spirit.

—Sanna Purinton

Chapter 6:   Return to Wholeness

And then a memory from Avalon surfaced in her mind, something she had not thought of for a decade; one of the Druids, giving instruction in the secret wisdom to the young priestesses, had said, 'If you would have the message of the Gods to direct your life, look for that which repeats, again and again; for this is the message given you by the Gods, the karmic lesson you must learn for this incarnation. It comes again and again until you have made it part of your soul and your enduring spirit.
—**Marion Zimmer Bradley**[31]

Sanna and her close-knit family lived in Avalon, and at the time she, too, had an office in Anna's clinic. She called herself a Spirit Consciousness Facilitator[32] and she had been born in Honolulu, Hawaii. She is of Inca and shamanic Mapuche heritage on her mother's side, and her father was American. The conjoining of her indigenous South American heritage, and her Hawaiian and Kahuna upbringing, served to open her to the wisdom and light of the Cathars in her adult life.

Sanna's commitment in this lifetime was to be a conduit for the awakening in what she called at that time the "Divine Entitlement." After the initial session Heather gave me, Sanna agreed to continue counseling me on a personal basis supporting my healing and integrating the fragments of my earlier experience.

---

[31] Marion Zimmer Bradley, *The Mists of Avalon*, https://onlinereadfreenovel.com. pg. 89
[32] Sanna Purinton, "An Exploration of Spirit Consciousness," *Sanna Purinton*, https://www.sannapurinton.com

Songline of the Heart / Shelley Darling

In our therapeutic sessions she spoke of her love for the Cathars who were dedicated to helping others understand their lifelong commitment to the "Way of Love." She spoke of the Cathars' love for each other, embracing honesty, humility, and truth.

I watched Sanna live true to the Cathar way of life. She saw me as an equal and joyed in the honoring of our unified quest for truth, love, and light. I shared with her how dowsing opens the field for more light to come into a home, generating a "quickening" in a person's consciousness so they can more easily access the truth of their being. She, in turn, shared her wisdom, while holding space for me to grow into mine.

Sanna's Kookaburra clinic office was simply decorated —a sanctuary space softly lit by two small windows. Following our initial session, I began my journey with an exercise Sanna called "emptying." Sanna opened our session with a unique Cathar prayer given to her by her guides. My heart opened as she spoke her reverent words with strength and conviction. She listened compassionately with steadfast presence, holding safe space while lifetimes of tears found their way to the surface of my being, revealing the source of my experience of betrayal.

I was grappling with the backwash of blame I had overlaid on my bleeding heart. Who had I been betraying? In not listening to the wailing voice inside, I had indeed been betraying myself for years. What was I afraid of? What contracts had I made with myself that led me to refusing my own power and giving it away?

I found myself in an experience of unrelenting grief. A deep sadness was bonded to my soul as though I'd held it in my body thousands of years. Years of tears flooded forth as in a trance I envisioned and experienced Indigenous people being slaughtered until there was no more blood to be shed. Threads of my life unraveled wildly in a timeless moment, and seemed to act as a colorful, eye-catching, incoherent spinning tapestry merging in communion with the spirit of all time.

Songline of the Heart / Shelley Darling

Since I had been 15 years old, I had had an innate connection with Indigenous people not simply of this lifetime, and my connection intensified during this session with Sanna. I knew my tears were indicative of a time when I'd experienced the trauma of a nation that was misunderstood, disrespected, and disregarded.

Sanna continued to reassure me with her wisdom and guidance. I was afloat in the mysterious process of reclaiming the truth of my being. She spoke about the fecundity of trust, and of the importance of being willing to continue to empty myself first. She spoke of the emptying process as one in which we seek to neither hold yesterday's pain sacrosanct, nor say our yesterdays have merit. It is a process where we choose to stay present to our internal judgments, and to view those judgments innocently. For many of us the issue is resentment, and we hold on to yesterday's information. Illness, held close, keeps things in a state of stagnation.

Sanna offered an additional inspiration regarding my husband's pulling of the Tower card that included the sun: it was a reminder, she said, that although the Tower falls, thereafter, begins the exaltation.

The Fire of Experience

The story of the giant sequoia is instructive here. Its bark is unusually fire resistant, yet its seeds, or cones usually only open as a result of a forest fire. Then and only then, with the thinning of surrounding plants, will the sequoia be able to grow successfully, in full sun in the mineral-rich soil. Similarly, the burning fire of my unwished-for experience had all but cleared out my life. I now sensed an opening to the sacred seed of my heart and had a sense it was beginning to blossom.

Sanna continued clarifying for me the process of calling in and embodying the Divine Masculine. She did this through her unique combination of metaphor and descriptive storytelling: "We all need to truly understand what the Divine

Masculine frequency actually means," she shared. "Elucidated, it means the Noble Man. The Divine Masculine represents the Noble Man in all of us. The Noble Man is the giver. We, as a culture think, the Divine Feminine is the giver. We think, 'if I give, I am a better woman. I give and give, yet actually we're taking on the debilitated state of the masculine frequency, not the true frequency of the masculine."

She said that the masculine has the vibratory seed within it, and if we hammer that seed, it simply provides us with some white cheesy gunk. The man's seed is the sperm, and when it goes into the fecund space of the Divine Feminine, then we have a magnificent outcome. The energies combined—the masculine seed and the feminine Gaia—just like on Earth, need to be primed correctly; in order to make that real, we need the infusion of the Divine Essence to make form.

Sanna spoke of the territory of the Divine Masculine and how people often talk about raising their vibration to higher and higher frequencies. We continue wanting to be an ascended Spirit, yet we haven't built a strong enough foundational grounding for ourselves. I had studied, researched, and worked with hundreds of clients using this understanding of what I knew as "Limbic Imprinting,[33]" and Sanna knew she was speaking my language. How fascinating that the evolution of my work, called "Embodied Heart Awakening" spoke exactly to this need to ground this force of love in our body—in essence, to come home.

When we attempt to evolve, raise our consciousness, and "ascend," our past traumas tend to override our body and we ultimately end up back in our old survival patterns. I like to call this the "bungy cord effect." As we move out of our survival zone into our desired destiny we need to, in present

---

[33] Elena Tonetti, "Limbic Imprinting at Birth: Creating Our Comfort Zone for Life," *Kindred*, https://www.kindredmedia.org.

time, integrate our feelings, while grounding and embodying all parts of our selves. This call to come home fully in our body, IS, our return to wholeness. The conversation of Divine Masculine stirred up a deep questioning in my consciousness. Was that gnawing feeling that day driving to LA, was it the Divine Masculine within me prodding me to wake up, realize my victimhood and take back my power?

The day I picked up the dowsing rods and felt a surge of joy, was this, my Divine essence revealing itself? It was true that when I was dowsing there was a shift in my frequency, and it activated what felt like the most dynamic elated expression of my soul. In fact, it got to the point where if I wasn't dowsing, things simply didn't feel in alignment.

"That is what the Divine Masculine, the lower body, wants for us: to celebrate life, to be in our joy." Sanna gave quite a belly laugh and spurted out the comment that laughter is birthed and exists in the lower body. Light bulbs went on! For years, I realized I had been way too serious, and that seriousness was an obstacle in my path. I had confused presence with seriousness, and therefore unknowingly continually projected that seriousness out to the world. I was now called to genuinely embrace my Divine Masculine, and to emerge from my pattern of self-abuse and endless sadness.

Sanna continued speaking of the Divine Masculine in our next session. "Today, we say that if you work at a computer desk with head down and bottom up, eating unhealthy food as a man, that is supposedly a more noble profession, than if you're a builder or carpenter, or a laborer of any kind. Only the one making money working at a desk, is a REAL person.

"Contemplate the story of Jesus and look at his energy field as a balanced Divine Masculine, how he functioned on the planet with so much compassion and a tremendous balanced femininity in the understanding of the physical realm," Sanna explained further. "Consider him, too, as a builder, constructing from thought, using his emotional, mental, and physical body...

that is, the Divine Masculine. When we look at the Divine Masculine, we need to look at the energy of the Noble Knight that is exalted."

I welcomed the interrelation of the Divine Masculine, the Divine Feminine, and the Divine Essence, and felt something sacred stir within me. I was enveloped by the harmonic vibration of the pure silence of the moment.

I left my session with Sanna that day in a deep state of calm and gratitude and walked through Mona Vale on my way back to Church Point. Reaching for some freshly made Sushi from a local shop on the main street, I felt an incessant urge to cross the street and sit beneath the giant gum tree. I was immediately showered by an earth-shattering symphony of cicadas.

River of Remembrance

The following morning, I wakened from a dream, and remembered how, after years of staying in my first abusive relationship, I finally had the clarity one evening to leave, sparking an opportunity to be embraced by a vision of Jesus Christ at his crucifixion, and as a fully embodied human being.

In my late 30s, in urgency, I moved Nina, my 14-year-old daughter, away from a troublesome relationship with her boyfriend, a drug dealer. We moved from New England to Fort Myers Beach, Florida and two sun-filled years later, she blossomed into a new relationship with the Israeli manager of the bathing suit store where she worked.

I chose to move into the enchanting tropical home of my then-boyfriend, Bamboo Charlie, in Estero, Florida. Calling himself a Bamboo Hunter, he made and sold bamboo flutes and didgeridoos. I was transfixed by his magic flutes, and in deep denial of this wiry, misunderstood, and unkind man's inability to love... as well as my own incapacity to love and stand in love for myself.

Songline of the Heart / Shelley Darling

Late one evening, I tripped and fell over one of his Didgeridoos—one he had left on the floor with a number of other instruments. He literally went berserk and began yelling and accusing me of hurting his "Didge." There was not a word of care or concern about the possibility I might have been hurt. Never hearing voices of any kind, a loud voice inside me spoke. *"What are you waiting for?"* it said. I took a very long extended breath in and stepped slowly in time with my exhalation. In silence I walked out of the room. This had not been my first taste of his abuse. Many times before I had quietly thought to myself, "just simply meditate, he will calm down and things will return to some semblance of normal." This time, without hesitation, I noiselessly swept the house of all my belongings and shut the front door behind me for the last time.

I called my beloved friend Trautel, who listened to my story and recommended I go to the training offered at Harbin Hot Springs that she herself had literally just completed. She spoke with clarity in a strong voice *"I promise you; you will be able to manifest everything you want if you take this training."*

I had been a devotee of an Indian Master for more than 20 years and I'd been in a relentless search for meaning for most of my life. Trautel's infectious enthusiasm led me to meet Mark, who agreed immediately to send me an introductory cassette tape about the program. Listening for less than two minutes, the words; *"it's the knowledge you can't get in college,"* rang a bell. Transfixed, I knew without a doubt that my Indian Master had been the source of those words. The synchronicity was enough to clinch it for me. Although finances were tight, my father surprised me with a kind and generous financial gift, allowing me to head to Northern California the following week.

The first and second level trainings seemed to open places within my psyche not yet available to my everyday consciousness. A mighty gateway was opened and in a brave moment after the second weekend at the Headlands adjunct to

Songline of the Heart / Shelley Darling

San Francisco Bay, I eagerly leapt into the next level where the man who was to become my husband was the trainer. This third level of the training was held at Harbin Hot Springs, a clothing-optional hot spring retreat center in northern California owned by the Heart Consciousness Church. The second day of this immersion took place in a large open-spaced woodland dome.

Dropping into an extraordinary experience of my grandmother's death while in a guided visualization, as if in a highly lucid dream, though quite awake, I was aware that my grandmother, now 91, was choosing to leave this earthly plane.

An inner voice welled up as an incessant scream, rose to the surface of my awareness, now the bellowing sound capturing everyone's attention. Six assistants and eventually the main trainer surrounded me. Safely encircled and physically held, I let my grandmother know I was now choosing to fully invest in my present incarnation, from the deepest inner sanctum of my being. I was saying goodbye, not only from the perspective of this lifetime, but from all the other lifetimes where she'd loved and protected me. It was now my turn to take full responsibility and *choose to inhabit my whole self*, finding the words to, in that very moment, give her permission to leave.

I stumbled around and made my way to the women's bathroom, still somewhat in a trance. I decided during the lunch break to go for a cleansing in the hottest spring-fed pool at Harbin. Walking past the circular conference building, I crossed an enchanting bridge over a gentle running creek, past the hand-sculptured dragon gate, and up the white-stone path to the spring-fed hot pool. This was quite an experience. You couldn't help walking by pods of naked bodies lying on the earth, and I still found myself physically shy and sensitive about my body.

Approaching the largest warm pool and pausing to watch the facilitators giving Watsu[34] sessions in the pool I was

---

[34] "The Birthplace of Watsu," *Harbin Hot Springs,* https://harbin.org/massage/watsu.

struck how the instructor cradled each participant as he seamlessly moved them through the water. Sunlit slivers of light danced in elegantly animated spirals and circles. My knees softened as I watched, as I relaxed.

Continuing on, through a small dark cave-like opening, stepping into the torrid pool, I was lucky to find only a few others lined up against the steaming stonewall. Tenderly slipping into the scorching water, I slowly made my way to the far corner of the misty pool. The cavernous atmosphere had a sacred, timeless feeling. I looked up to the elongated front wall, and my heart leaped out of my body. Shocked and speechless, yet fully present, I saw an image of Jesus, crucified on the cross, hanging from the cave wall above the hot pool.

Ascending More Consciously

I grew up Jewish, not Catholic, and I had never prayed to Jesus; nor had I ever gone to church. Yet, there, half-submerged in that cave, I saw Jesus fully embodied, his blood dripping into the hot pool from just above my head.

Taking one more look around the hazy dark pool, I was surprised to see everyone else was now gone. What was especially uncanny about the experience was that in the process of feeling my grandmother transition, I now seemed to have been catapulted into my own, full-on resurrection as I ascended more consciously into my power and evolutionary life purpose.

Stunned, I lingered in the hot pool, barely believing my eyes. Moving to the left I slowly waded through the scorching hot water to the three short stone stairs. As the cool air gripped my body, I quickly ran up the narrow cement path to the small, natural cold-water pool. I attempted to clear my thoughts by dousing away the experience in the frigid spring water. With cool water dripping from my feet, I walked down the path past the hot pool cavern, and I felt called to experience one more round of the hot purging water.

Once inside, yet again, I could hardly believe what I saw. Speechless, I tried rubbing my eyes clear. But there above me was Jesus again, though this time, he was in fully resurrected form. Sobered by the sanctity of the moment, I placed my hands directly on my heart, savoring this illuminated vision. Enraptured and blessed, my knees buckled, as a heavenly reverence for all that was being revealed took over. *But what was I to do with this?*

Breathing a bit harder now, I quickly turned to the upper walkway deciding to double douse myself once again in the cold pool. Trautel had taught me to never go in the cool waters only once. She always said that in order to have the complete experience, you need to dive in at least twice. Making sure of any last threads of unmet emotion, I purged myself in the freezing cold spring. Getting out, I stumbled over to the cold white marble bench that faced a beautiful stone Kuan Yin statue situated to the left of the cold pool. According to legend, Kuan Yin, the Goddess of Mercy, paused, hearing the cries of the world as she entered heaven and vowed to remain in the earthly realms to help humanity.

The memory retuned of my experience with Jesus, a fully integrated Noble Man, as I processed insights Sanna was helping me unfold. At Sanna's invitation, I turned my attention inward, ever more present with each breath. Connected, cleansed and purified, I was now on the fast track to healing.

Desperate for Help

Word was spreading of my dynamic dowsing of Anna's clinic. In her excitement, Anna enthusiastically spoke to Elizabeth, a gentle woman in her late 60s who was desperate for help with her home and property, located on the higher elevation of Bay View, in between Mona Vale and Church Point. Her place overlooked Heather's houseboat far below in the cove.

Songline of the Heart / Shelley Darling

As I drove up the windy rise of the tree-laden hill to her house, I was immediately aware of a shift in the energy. Elizabeth had been quite unnerved about the experiences she was having with her home and land. She had bought the land many years earlier and the purchasing process had been a fight from start to finish. Her neighbors were agitated, continuing to create trouble related to land rights, and she felt hopeless and ready to move. She was exhausted and done, although she loved the property and the beautiful dark brown octagonal home she herself had designed and built.

To my delight, the land was filled with native flowers such as Acacia, Banksia, and Grevillea, and some magnificently tall gum trees stood sentinel over the property. As she opened the front door to the house, I was aware of the stained-glass window and a winding staircase beyond it, which bypassed what turned out to be a very dark and quite ominous first floor. Upstairs, you couldn't help being captivated by all the original Aboriginal dot paintings lining the walls, and Elizabeth shared her love for painting with me as we toured the house.

There was also a small table upstairs with brightly colored dotted pictures of native animals on it, which brought lightness to the dreamtime experience. Downstairs, there was a long rectangular wooden table upon which was laid a tablecloth and napkins that had been hand painted by the Aboriginal women Elizabeth had met on her journeys. She delighted in taking me outside to the back deck and proudly showed me the ancient gum trees. I was awed by this paradise, with its bright floral colors and the incessant sound of the large colorful parakeets and white cockatoos that had now surrounded the house. What was going on here to make her want to move?

Sitting down in the living room to have a "cuppa," Elizabeth spoke of the sadness she felt over the fact she had stopped painting after she moved in. She handed me the printout of the pre-dowsing form I had given her to fill out. Prior to beginning an assessment, I always ask people to jot down bullet points of what's not optimally working in all areas of their life. This creates the opportunity to contemplate, listen and pay attention to the thoughts and feelings that might arise just below the surface of one's everyday consciousness. Also, important to note: *are there any parts of the home or office that you might not like or avoiding going into?*

We spoke about the experience of standing near a positive vortex, and I used examples of being close to a waterfall or connecting with a sacred site. Elizabeth noted her body experienced a feeling of being uplifted in those places, and how it gave her a sense of belonging and connection to her "higher consciousness." These circumstances always evoked a surge or feeling of joy. A negative vortex on the other hand, is a spiral of downward energy that taxes our immune system.

Using my dowsing rods, I demonstrated how to follow the direction of the rods and to Elizabeth's dismay we found the first, strongest, negative vortex in her bedroom. She was in awe as we followed the energy down the stairs, on the dark lower floor. Walking in I instantly felt the strength of the negative vortex, making the energy in the room feel heavy and dense.

An Immediate Epiphany

Listening to the land, I had an immediate epiphany about the rocky ground under Elizabeth's bedroom. You could even see out the window, how the bedroom flooring lay against some very large, noticeable stones. I envisioned these stones as forming a plateau at the top of a ridge high above the water, where the Earth and sky met at the point closest to Heaven. These places were where the Aboriginal people would come to pray and bring their elders as they transitioned to the stars; it also faced the Ku-ring-gai Chase Nature Preserve. I felt the sacredness of this site and understood that Elizabeth, in her deep compassion for the Aboriginal people, was in fact the chosen guardian of this land. In the moment of that transmission, I watched as her love for the Aboriginals grew and the land blossomed.

I began clearing the negative vortex, first by laying a large copper Sacred Cubit energy ring down on the floor, which, within three seconds, shifted the counterclockwise energy to a clockwise, positive, energy field. It is a superconductor that seems to neutralize magnetic fields.

The sacred geometry of the Sacred Cubit Tensor Ring, creates a pillar of light, not seen with our everyday eyes. At this point any stuck energies, entities, or Earthbound spirits from the neighborhood, if ready, will move through the gateway back to the Source. None of this negatively affects the individual, their family members, or the house. The process simply allows any discordant energy to disperse and dissolve.

For the most part these energies do move on, yet once in a while, they need some extra attention, gratitude, and information to encourage them to leave. The vortex is finished by placing two copper Earth Cures, taped in their exact proper place, at a 90-degree angle and when dowsing is complete, the ring can be removed.

Now, I know this sounds fascinating, yet over the years not only, have I felt the shift in the field, but so have my clients. All of a sudden, they feel unburdened of their heavy social and familial relationships, as they delight in "giving the energy to the ring" in those few moments and throughout the completion of the dowsing. Elizabeth accepted the invitation to stand with me around the ring, and closed her eyes, internally expressing her worries, concerns, or ongoing issues with the adjacent landowners, as well as any new issues that needed to be given to the ring, within the portal of light. What happens here is one of the most potent moments in dowsing. This act of giving and surrendering allows for a powerful alchemy to happen within the individual and the circumstances at hand. We are not putting the person acting out into the ring, we are inviting the cause of their suffering to be healed and transmuted. With the first negative vortex concluded, we found a second negative vortex, which was located in Elizabeth's art room.

Placing a smaller ring under her desk, which was where the center of the energy was the strongest, together we called in the spirit of the land and again honored the Ancestors. After asking for clarity and guidance, the other subtle energies were cleared. Elizabeth commented that the house felt like a sanctuary. She felt free, stronger, and had the light-hearted feeling of purpose being restored.

As with any dowsing, one never knows how things will shift, yet something inevitably transforms for the greater good of all. In this case, a few weeks later Elizabeth's email confirmed how happy she was, and I learned that just a few days after her house had been dowsed, she was ecstatically engaging in her artwork once again.

This dowsing on the top of the hill ignited within me an increasing reverence for, and enhanced my love and connection to, this ancestral land. I was coming home to my wholeness, as I worked with people and was no longer questioning my role. A deepened sense of humility, and growing appreciation for this gift developed.

Standing on her treasured land after dowsing, the smell of freshly spread mulch satiated my senses. I remembered a time when I had tended a small garden plot in Marblehead, Massachusetts.

Each day I felt the call to go into the garden and put my hands deep in the soil. Scrunching the soil in my hands, I honored it, as if it were a holy sacred act. It was a part of my healing and enhanced the needed balance in my life at that time.

Before leaving Elizabeth's home, I took one more peaceful walk around her colorful landscape garden, connecting with the Nature spirits, plant beings, and stone beings and I stopped in silence offering my gratitude to the Ancestors for the opportunity to work as an emissary of light and love.

Chapter 7: The Mountain

The Aboriginal Sunrise Ceremonies are very special to our people. It starts when the sky is black, beautiful black. When the sun's yellow circle arrives, it turns the sky red. This is why the Aboriginal flag is half red, half black with a yellow circle in the middle. At the Sunrise Ceremony, I meditate and ask the Great Spirit for direction. My hands fill with electricity. I touch you and you feel it, too. I heal people this way. My Grandmother did that, too. I learned all about that when I was a young fellow. Umbarra, the Black Duck, is the special totem of our tribe, the Yuin. We learn to respect the elders who hand on the Law. The elders guard the Law and the Law guards the people. This is the Law that comes from the mountain. The mountain teaches the dreaming.

—Guboo Ted Thomas[35]

After my glorious healing time on Scotland Island in the Northern Beaches, I was back living on the houseboat with Heather and her boyfriend, Chris, whom I now affectionately called Chriso.

Picture the three of us living on a small houseboat, surrounded by houses hidden in the upper landscape in McCarrs Creek, a community about 2.5 miles north of the small town of Mona Vale. The land was auspiciously shaped in the form of a crescent moon and it was encircled by rich bush land that butted up against the Ku-ring-gai Chase Reserve near the headwaters of the Pittwater, the waterway separating greater Metropolitan Sydney from the Central Coast. It was a magical place.

---

[35] Antero Alli, "Interview with Guboo Ted Thomas," *Paratheatrical*, https://www.paratheatrical.com/guboo

Songline of the Heart / Shelley Darling

The Kookaburras far in the distance would begin their serenade at sunrise, and their comrades would take up their call along the line of the hills that enclosed the little houseboat. It was a glorious symphonic chorus. What better way to wake up than to hear these birds laughing? My heart sang each morning, knowing this daily immersion in hearing and feeling the vibrant rippling joy of the Kookaburras' song allowed quicker healing.

Sometimes, Heather and I would swim to the waterfall at the lower end of the Ku-ring-gai Nature Preserve, keeping an eye out for any of the massive jellyfish that might have entered the cove during the night.

We would walk the local paths high up to the flat plateau of the Ku-ring-gai, where the 10,000-year-old rock art carvings would take me back in time.

Strolling past Old Man Banksia and passing my first Scribbly Gum trees, I became upset as I looked at them and asked Heather, "how could someone scribble such graffiti on these trees?" Heather laughed as she saw the look on my face and realized I had no idea this was Nature's own artwork.

Trekking through this primordial land I startled when I heard an unusually wild and wacky sound. Out from behind a tree appeared a bird that looked like a roadrunner. Heather whispered to me that it was "Liar Bird." At that moment, I screeched a resounding "Noooo..." and covered my eyes, not wanting to be reminded of my experience with my dishonest husband. We both laughed hysterically, surprising the bird, and watched it scamper off. Standing in the bush, Heather explained more about this wondrous Aboriginal animal totem and spelled out its name. It was called a *Lyre*bird!

As we continued climbing, we passed a cave, and we stopped when we reached a place with a stone cairn high above the waters of McCarrs Creek. Looking out below the stone promontory one could see the magnificence of the Northern Beaches coastline.

We could just about see Heather's houseboat anchored in the serene blue cove below.

Later that afternoon, I instinctively opened my Australian Animal Dreaming Oracle Cards Guidebook by Scott Alexander King[36], and investigated the Lyrebird totem. Though feeling quite at home and relaxed in this paradise, the moments would arise where my mind would scoop me up for hours, feeling the betrayal. This was one of those times.

Heather read the last paragraph aloud: "Lyrebird crossing your path means you are being primed for a time of great remembering. The Ancestors are calling to you from the void, to remember a connection shared or a lifetime you had in a period long ago. Such effort will provide deeper understanding of relationships and responsibilities you have right now, enabling you to put them into context, creating greater clarity and personal direction."

Glimmer of Hope

Sanna listened attentively as I voiced the changes that had begun to occur since my previous session.

She continued addressing the Divine Masculine, as she saw how—even with all my training—I continued having a fear of separation and longing for personal safety. She spoke about activating the lower body with the stimulation of the blood and its "*Jing, Jing,*" the vital life force.

She reiterated that if we don't focus attention on the lower body, our energy contracts, and becomes depleted.

---

[36] Animal Dreaming Oracle Cards by Scott Alexander King, Lyrebird-Spirit Animal https://www.quietwriting.com/lyrebird-spirit-animal

When we open to the Divine Masculine, our energy fields naturally expand. This resonated as dowsing had awakened in me a wondrous process of exploration that included understanding the auric field of energy that surrounds a person's body.

Two people can stand face to face, about 15 feet apart with their dowsing rods in hand.

The first person asks the rods to show the outer edge of the other's Heart Chakra or energy field. Slowly, walking with the dowsing rods towards the other person, the rods will open outward the moment they came in contact with the person's outer perimeter of energy.

The Lyrebird

Through its ability to remember the forest sounds of over 200 years ago, lyrebird supports the concept of genetic memory. Flawlessly mimicking repetitious sound, the older birds pass on to the young birds the sounds they were taught by their parents, thus literally handing on sacred lineal knowledge to the next generation...lyrebird invites us to ponder the thought that these experiences passed on genetically are for us to access and to learn from in our current lifetime. Within every individual cell that collectively makes us whole, reside the keys to the unlocking of the memory of past experiences passed from one generation to the next. Such memory is inherited and genetic in nature. Genetic memory represents all that we have ever experienced, encountered and understood. It could be said that our body remembers the memories of everything ever witnessed by us since the beginning of time.

—Scott Alexander King

To experience how the energy changes, the person whose energy field is being measured may think of a time when they felt separate and alone. Inevitably the rods won't open for the person measuring the energy until they find themselves much closer to their partner's body. When we are feeling impassive or have the feelings we are not seen and loved, the field naturally contracts, mirroring our state of mind and heart.

I happily explained this to Sanna and she nodded in acknowledgement. She said our energy is actually meant to extend at least 10 feet beyond our body. She spoke of how energy diffuses out in circles beyond our body, beginning with the color red, like a volcano, in the area closest to our physical body. Then at about three feet, the color becomes a combination of red and yellow and orange, and as it goes further out it becomes more diffused.

In addressing the Divine Masculine and its application to the planet, Sanna asked me to visualize the center of the Earth, as the red-hot magma of the planet. Focusing to the center of the magma, I felt a deepening connection to Nature:

"The realization and healing of the Divine Masculine is so dynamic it can change your life. It can activate and awaken the sleeping serpent, sometimes spoken as the experience where the energy in the body rises like a spiraling snake, opening the energetic body while activating a unique type of enlightening transformational experience.

Physically, the energy spirals up through our spine, igniting any obstacle that has been lying dormant as unfulfilled potential. When we live authentically, aligned with Source consciousness, the light shines from within, as a beacon, [and] there is a physical shift in our awareness. Integration happens, comparisons stop, and we are able to stay present with our feelings, immersed in the truth of who we be. We next get to a point where we reach up and tap into our soul; concurrently, the soul reaches down and pulls us up into the Divine Feminine.

I became aware of an energetic pull, and a feeling of my roots deepening into the Earth. Just as a tree root system interconnects to the other trees near its base, my energy field, too, was radiating outwards. Immediately I felt filled with hope. At the same time a strong shiver rippled up my spine, releasing what felt like old victim energy. I then giggled and Sanna, who was smiling, said, *"that's when then real laughter happens, and laughter is Spirit!"*

Seven Mile Beach

Away from the stress of my home situation, I had the space to explore a growing connection with the ancestral land of Australia. Working with a naturopath allowed my physical body to begin healing, while allowing for a new relationship with my inner Divine Masculine to develop.

Heather, seeing my happiness, suggested a camping adventure. Her first thought was to go West to the Blue Mountains, a rugged region where the mountains themselves emit a mesmerizing bluish hue. As I was an avid sun lover, I instead proposed going to the Southern Beaches, located a few hours south of the booming metropolis of Sydney. Having never traveled down to the southern coast, Heather conceded, and, in her excitement, she turned up the music in celebration. We both relished the spontaneity and freedom of the moment.

With not a thought about where we would land, we set out, mother and daughter, giving ourselves to the winds that would carry us. The beauty of the Australian coast is hard to describe. Driving south I was astonished as I saw how closely the highway edged towards the water. Even in Sydney, with its famous Opera House, people can walk for miles along the ocean pathways. The water is held with deep respect here, with no one privately owning the seashore. It allowed for many miles of stunning landscapes with outstanding vistas. Heather showed me the closed-in ocean swimming pools that were built right on the beach to allow people the freedom of swimming in the ocean surf while being protected from the threat of sharks.

We surrendered to the beauty of the day, letting go of any thought of our destination, and found simple happiness in the journey itself. Growing up in a family that loved to travel, I relished these moments of riveting freedom. At one point, after we finally got beyond Sydney proper, we pulled over to watch some Paragliders, clad in worn sneakers running nose to the wind and sailing off the immense jagged cliffs above us. Heather murmured how she wanted to do this someday with her mate. I shuddered at the thought of jumping off a cliff and felt paralyzed watching an older woman, who we guessed was in her late 70s, flying off the edge attached to and assisted by a muscular young gentleman.

We had driven more than two blissful hours down the South Coast Highway, past the large blow hole in Kiama that spews water 25 meters in the air, when Heather's blood sugar levels dropped, and her need to find her some food quickly took over. For some reason, the thought of tea and scones filled our senses. Clinging to this vision, we drove on. In desperation, we continued to drive south. Choosing to stop in a charming ocean town called Gerringong, we finally pulled over at the sight of a vegetarian restaurant called "The Perfect Break." Heather's energy and patience were waning, so I ran in to see if this was indeed the perfect place for us to eat. Walking in I realized in disappointment that I was going to have to tell Heather that although it was an organic breakfast restaurant, the "Perfect Break" didn't match our dream of scones and tea, and therefore really wasn't so perfect.

Hastily opening the door to the car, I was shocked to hear myself say, "If you could just wait a few minutes more, about three-quarters of a mile down the road we will find just what we are looking for…" I was stunned by my own words, although Heather was in no way wary of my intuitions; she agreed to keep going. Down the winding road, past a roundabout, was a large white sign looming in front of an extensive view of the ocean on which were written the words "Gerroa." Turning left after the sign, we continued down the windy paved road, finding, with total elation, the wondrous "Blue Sea Haven Café." I gave a shout as I looked down at the odometer: *exactly, three-quarters of a mile!* Just as I had said, there before us, was an eclectic bakery and breakfast café with outdoor seating on a beautiful small wooden deck facing the ocean. The panoramic view gave way to a stable aluminum walking bridge over the Crooked River, where a huge white pelican was swimming in the estuary, slowly meandering out to the sandy white Seven Mile Beach.

Radiating Beacons of Joy

Sitting on the hand-built deck now ecstatically drinking our tea and polishing off our scones, we were radiating beacons of joy, mesmerized by Gerroa's enchanting magic. The landscape reminded me of a movie called *Brigadoon* I had loved as a child. Heather listened intently as I recaptured the story of two men in Scotland becoming lost in the woods and happen upon, Brigadoon, a miraculous village that rises out of the mists for one day only every hundred years. If any of the villagers ever try to leave Brigadoon, the spell would break, and the village would vanish forever. As the story goes, any outsider wishing to stay must love someone in the village deeply enough to accept the loss of everything he or she knows in the outside world.[37] For a moment, captured by the expansive view and smell of the ocean, I could sense how easily it would be to simply vanish in the pure magic and Spirit of this place.

Heather and I sipped our tea and reveled in gleaning the fruits of our collective intention. Although Heather had been at her edge, she had been willing to trust, stretch her imagination,

---

[37] Brigadoon, Warner Brothers, www.warnerbros.com/movies.

and allow this miraculous dream to come true. This was only the beginning of marvelous manifestations of synchronicities.

As we sat on the deck, enraptured by the view and the summer sun, a broad-shouldered woman with a tidy white shirt tucked into her black jeans walked by intent on heading to the blue-gray shingled house across from the café. Meeting eye to eye, and feeling a connection, we spontaneously both smiled.

Immediately, Lisa, who turned out to be the owner of this little café by the sea, struck up a conversation. After learning I was a dowser, she offered to drive us up to "the mountain" without even batting an eye.

The mountain? I was speechless. When I said goodbye to Sanna after our last session she had mentioned that her guides had told her I was to look for a mountain, and that there would be a drumming sound coming from the mountain. I had no way of knowing, at that moment, that I was to return to this mountain again and again. Still reeling from the synchronicity of my mountain appearing, we listened as Lisa shared her dream of opening a retreat center north of the small village of Berry, about 20 kilometers south and west of where we now stood in Gerroa. She owned 400 acres of land that overlooked mostly farmland and, ultimately, the sea. She spoke of an Aboriginal ceremonial place at the top of the mountain and wanted me to come check the energy.

She told us this place was secluded and hidden from view, and there was a track running along the highest point of the property that ultimately opened up to a panoramic view to the sea. And, what's more, when seen from above, the sacred spot she referred to was heart shaped.

Driving together to this magical spot, Lisa shared how she had come across the site by chance one day while hiking. She had been intrigued when seeing some stones set on the ground in circles. The original Aboriginals of the area were the

Wodi people of the language group Dharawal, and they had apparently been living on the land there for about 20,000 years.

Wooed by a magnificent view of mountain peaks, she boasted one could as far as Coolangata, a small mountain covered in bushland rising from Shoalhaven River Plain. This plus Moeyan Hill four kilometers west, Harley Hill with its lush greenery, and Kilajoa, were the high points in an area hosting Aboriginal sacred sites.

My heart quieted and my voice softened as we approached the mountain. The house was in a bit of disorder as Lisa was in the last stages of fixing it up. It had a large porch facing the land that extended out towards Gerroa, though it was the gargantuan banyan tree with a branch that was as wide, as I was tall, that caught my eye. It was the biggest one I had ever seen. It spoke to centuries of growth, and its splendorous vibration rippled out as a melodious song, which brought tears to my eyes. I ran up to the tree, laughing and greeting it as if we had been friends for years prior to my arrival that day.

Jumping into the back flat bed of Lisa's battered old 4-wheel-drive farm truck, we bounced along the dirt road until Lisa stopped to open the upper cattle gate. My eyes widened at the gorgeous expanse of pastureland that stretched out below to the farmhouse belonging to Lisa's mum. In a sharp turn of the wheel, the scenery changed dramatically. My skin hairs, as if blown in a strong wind, stood on end. In front of us, high above the 400 acres, was cut into the land a seemingly endless assemblage of high-tension power lines. Not wanting to offend Lisa, nor worry her I breathed quietly, and shifted my gaze.

Deep Awe Took Over

Passing through one more cattle gate, we entered a plateau, and had to continually duck under the low-bending trees that hid a jaw-dropping eastern view over and above the valley.

Songline of the Heart / Shelley Darling

I was aware of an energy shift, as a deepening awe took over. Bypassing an old, dilapidated caravan, my senses heightened; the spirit of place here was strong. Passing a giant hole dug into the earth, holding tight to the metal bar, I began stamping my feet and knocking on the truck window. Lisa stopped abruptly telling us it was made by a wombat, the world's largest burrowing marsupial. It looks like a cross between a porcupine and small bear. Apparently, wombats are highly intelligent and gentle, yet when provoked can become nasty and dangerous.

Finally, we arrived at a natural wooded area, clambered out of the truck and walked quietly, sensing the sacredness of the space, my dowsing rods held ready to tune in to the energy. I could see there was a mound where the earth had been heaped up, and the stones, though partially hidden, had been intentionally placed in a circle.

"In 2006 I brought an Aboriginal fella, up to the site," Lisa explained. "He was from the north coast." She noted he believed the site was an ancient ceremonial stone circle. "We did some vision work around the land, and he drew a little map, with pathways going in and out, demonstrating how it would have looked. With a few friends I brought out a canvas and did a painting. The questions the Aboriginal man asked us to consider included, 'What is the land asking for? Are you listening to what the land wants?'"

My dowsing rods were spinning wildly, reflecting to us the high positive energy of this sacred site. It was here at the top of the mountain near this sacred space that Lisa had expressed her dream of building some small retreat cabins. Silence took over as she lifted her drum, and Heather and I communed with the spirits of this magical land. It was a profound and powerful moment.

Slowly and in silence we made our way back to Lisa's house, stopping only once to see a stand of ancient turpentine trees, which can grow up to 60 feet tall. We found a small waterfall that dropped thousands of feet below the rust-colored stone over which it poured. We circled, invoking a prayer of gratitude for the Ancestors of the land, and for the wondrous gift of our new friendship.

Later, as the sun was setting, Lisa and I walked up the rocky dirt road just above the house as she introduced me to the understanding of Aboriginal Songlines.

Songlines

Traditional Aboriginal culture holds belief in a creation era and creation ancestors. These ancestors traveled across the country creating the landscape, the animals, and the law under which human society was to live. The journeys of these ancestors across the country make up a songline. They're the long creation story lines that cross the country and put all geographical and sacred sites in place in Aboriginal culture. These ancestral sacred stories are passed on as large song cycles.

In Aboriginal terms the kinship lineage of the ancestral people from that country, or the custodians, had control over that songline. It was their duty to uphold the obligations of passing the song on in perfect form to the next generation. In the initiation processes within Aboriginal culture each generation is taught the entire package of their culture over a series of stages of knowledge. Through these song cycles people gradually learn the entire cultural story of their people.

– David Wroth

The brilliant sunset light captured the huge old banyan tree in its rays. It reminded me of the Garden at Gethsemane, which is where the New Testament says Jesus prayed before His betrayal. (Mark 14:32-50). Our friendship now anchored, Lisa invited us to stay on with her a little longer at her beach house. She left for work early the next morning, and Heather and I walked across the narrow bridge over the river to the soft white sand beach. Heather invited us to stop for a few yoga postures about a quarter-mile down the beach. At that moment, with my bare feet on the soft sand, the sun blessing me with its light, and a sense of peace seeping through my body, I heard an ancient voice echoing deep within me. To my surprise, I found myself speaking out loud: "I could live here." [38]

Aboriginal Songlines

Heather and I felt compelled to stay at the beach house. I found myself zealously researching the Aboriginal Songlines, and their used as an ancient navigational tool for the Aboriginals. As a dowser with an insatiable curiosity, I wondered how these lines related to leylines, the electromagnetic lines that circumnavigate the Earth.

Travel writer Bruce Chatwin asserts in his book *The Songlines* that language started as song, and that in the Aboriginal dreamtime it sang the land into existence. "As you sing the land, the trees, the rocks, the path, they come to be, and the singers are one with them," he explains. Chatwin explores the Aboriginal mythology surrounding the sacredness and the creation of the world, and the energetic "songlines" that cross the landscape. He says these songlines were "the labyrinth of invisible pathways which meander all over Australia and are known to Europeans as "dreaming-tracks" or "songlines;" and to Aboriginals as "Footprints of the Ancestors" or "The way of the law."

In his book Chatwin shares with us that, "The Aboriginal people of Australia believe that the land is alive and that to keep it alive, they must sing to it. In fact, they can navigate the landscape of Australia by singing songs about the sacred landmarks that traverse it... Also known as Dreaming Tracks, [these lines] supposedly trace the route of ancient creator spirits from the Dreaming Time. The songlines are themselves a powerful memory aid to navigation over the Earth

---

[38] David Wroth, "Why Songlines Are Important in Aboriginal Art, https://japingkaaboriginalart.com/articles/songlines.

and to the location of essential resources, as well as providing a continuing rehearsal of cultural history."[39] In my research, I was enthralled by the relationship between the Australian Songlines and the European Leylines, and in China what are called "dragon lines or paths." In western traditional cultures, leylines are known to cover the globe in a triangulated grid.

Traditional pilgrimage pathways to sacred sites are commonly associated with leylines. Lung-Mei or Dragon Paths[40] were energy lines discovered in ancient times by the Chinese. Unlike leylines, which are natural phenomena, songlines are straight lines that may traverse the country or run from the territory of one clan to the next.

Some authors believe the songlines represent oral archives of Indigenous history and hold the stories of the people and the eternal spirits who inhabit them. The songlines or tracks transcend language groups, and if you know the song the songline represents, you can navigate along it.

Pennick and Devereux, in their book *Lines on the Landscape: Ley Lines and Other Linear Enigmas*, conclude by saying that the songlines themselves suggest that the straight-line ley is a universal concept, an archetypal one. "The straight line in the landscape, is the result of another kind of human awareness, interacting with a differently perceived environment, and that we have forgotten about our inner life; we have forgotten that the land is sacred, and we have forgotten the interaction between them both[41]." They speak of leylines and their associated metaphysical connections, as ancestral knowledge. Not knowledge of a particular people or tribe, but knowledge that *all humans once had*.

---

[39] Bruce Chatwin, *The Songlines*, 1987 (Franklin Press, 1987), p. 2.
[40] Linda J. Paul, "Dragon Paths," *Bella Online*.
[41] "Sacred Landscapes, *The Druid's Garden* citing Pennick and Devreux, https://druidgarden.wordpress.com.

Songline of the Heart / Shelley Darling

> ## What is a Songline?
> *A songline is therefore "a succession of sites" along a track, "vibrant with incident, power and meaning" allowing for a dramatic and aesthetic participation in the environment.*
> **—Yi-Fu Tuan**

Consider how we as a culture choose to vacation in natural, scenic places, feeling our consciousness shift as we listen to the rhythmic crash of waves, wonder at the magnificence of a waterfall, or hike a forested trail into the mountains. Upon leaving we feel whole, revitalized, restored, and nourished by life. Becoming aware of the ancient whispering of Spirit ignited a calling in me, as well as a need to understand and communicate with the subtle flows of energy that are ingrained in the landscape and held within the "songline of our heart." Embracing this non-visible state of awareness, pausing long enough to allow it to surface in our daily consciousness, evokes a sacred relationship or "songline" connecting us to the movement of all life.

The Beach House

Watching me dowse, Lisa was awed by the power of the two rods spinning. One morning she spoke of how she'd been trying to sell her beachfront property in Gerringong, a few miles up the coast from Gerroa. She asked me if I'd like to dowse the beach house where she had lived with her former husband before his passing. Apparently, the house had been on the market for more than a year-and-a-half with no bites.

Desperate to sell, she looked me straight in the eye and said if the house sold before the next two moons, she'd give me a round trip ticket back to Australia!

I quickly looked at Heather, as I felt it would be important for her to attend the beach house dowsing. Heather was a Doula, and I felt she could hold the space for Lisa as we worked with her lingering grief over the death of her husband, while supporting a gentle integration of her past, and a re-birthing into her present.

The next day we headed off to Gerringong. Driving to the house, we learned that Lisa's husband had loved playing his Didgeridoo, and it still lay wrapped in newspaper in her storage shed. In fact, it hadn't seen the light of day since his transition. I immediately asked how she felt about us stopping at her storage shed to retrieve it, so we could take it with us. Years earlier, at a summer music festival with Bamboo Charlie, I had sold handmade bamboo "didges," and had taught myself how to circular breathe. This technique is used with wind instruments to create a continuous sound without cessation.

I had to do a bit of soul-searching around the idea of bringing the didge with us as in Australia it's a tradition that only men play the didgeridoo. I'd been very diligent about honoring this long-established custom. Prior to this journey, I had met a few masterful women didge players in the US and felt the power of its resonant, otherworldly call. However, given the circumstances, I quietly communed with the ancestors, and made the choice to listen to my intuitive feeling that this was a needed part of Lisa's healing; I trusted the energy guiding me to bring her late husband's didgeridoo to the house. Although I was there specifically to dowse this house, it was important to share with Lisa my desire to work with the Feng Shui of the home to make sure the energy was moving directly towards it.

I offered Lisa my short meditation, the Sacred Golden Ray Attunement,[42] which helps ground and support opening one's consciousness as we energetically open the home. The Sacred Golden Ray Attunement, I went on to explain, experienced once daily at a minimum, will create a powerful

---

[42] Sacred Golden Ray Attunement by Shelley Darling. Receive your free download: www.evolutionarydowsing.com/free-resources

connection of your awareness with your heart allowing you to access your higher consciousness. This helps to balance the left and right hemispheres of the brain, while enabling the body to act as an open trans-receiver. Present in a state of "embodied resonance," the dowsing information is received succinctly, with clarity and direct knowing. This allowed her to feel the interconnectedness of the land, her home, and the energy of what scientists call, the Akash, or Unified Field. Upon arriving, my attention was immediately drawn to the fact that the "For Sale" sign was blocking the view of the front door. I explained it was important to have a clear line of sight from the door to the road, so the universal energy could find the house!

A miraculous moment occurred during the dowsing assessment after I discovered a very large negative vortex in the home. Following the guidance of the rods, and with Lisa behind me, I tracked the energy of the rods and walked slowly through the dimly lit main room, finally making a U-turn through the hallway towards an area by the far window of the sunroom. Lisa looked like she had spotted a ghost when I walked toward the open area where the negative vortex was situated.

Peering through the wide glass window, I was awed by the sight of a beautiful hand-painted oceanic mural on the outside wall facing the window illuminated by the sun. Apparently, one of Lisa's friends had offered to create an ocean painting for Lisa's husband when he became ill. It lay 15 feet beyond the negative vortex. Inspired by Lisa's husband's love of surfing and sea, the friend had painted whales, dolphins, and fish swimming freely in his beloved ocean. Lisa's husband died directly on the spot where the dowsing rods were now pointing.

I was called to place two large copper tensor rings in the form of a Vesica Pisces on the directed spot.[43] In the prevailing silence, we gently moved to the floor, and sat in a small circle. As the energy shifted, we unwrapped Lisa's

---

[43] "Vesica Pisces," *Crystalinks*, http://www.crystalinks.com.

husband's Didgeridoo. As mentioned, the relationship between a person and their home often has an ancestral component. Sometimes the house and the person have chosen each other, and the house has a message that will assist in the owner's evolution. In this case, the house was still holding the energy of Lisa's husband's death and Lisa's heart was still in need of healing. There was no way either the house, or Lisa's attachment to it, would energetically allow the house to be sold.

Lisa hadn't been able to let go and the undercurrent tides of Earthly connection to her beloved had yet to come to rest. Heather, with her skill as a loving Doula, stood by my side, and held steady with her grounded Earth Mother energy. We all came into presence and opened our hearts for the healing to take place. Having asked on Lisa's behalf for the Ancestors' permission to proceed, I began to play the Didgeridoo. [44]

Two hours later, after a personal healing and the clearing of the discordant energy in the rest of the beach house, we noticed a definite energy shift. Lisa was at peace.

Called to walk around the house and offer a final blessing on the property, I met the others in front of it. With the ocean behind us, we said prayers of gratitude to the land, the elementals (also known as Nature spirits), and our guides, as well as to the light-bearing Ancestors who had assisted with this dowsing.

At Seven Mile Beach, Heather and I, began packing up for our return to Church Point and Lisa, in a celebratory mood, gleefully invited us to return the following week to stay as guests, for as long as we would like! This was an offer I couldn't refuse!

---

[44] Eileen Nauman, "History and Uses of the Vesica Pisces," *Walking the Land*, https://walkingtheland.net.

Chapter 8: Global Contact

"And above all, watch with glittering eyes the whole world around you because the greatest secrets are always hidden in the most unlikely places. Those who don't believe in magic will never find it."
–Roald Dahl

The town straight south of Gerroa in New South Wales is Berry, a small, rural, historical village. It is situated in the Shoalhaven region of the South Coast, which the Aboriginal people originally called Boon-ga-ree. They survived as skilled hunters, fishermen, and gatherers of berries and other wild foods that lay scattered along the coastal area. Today, Berry is known as a tourist stop filled with colorful local crafts galleries, antique shops, a bountiful offering of freshly baked goods, and a diverse selection of eclectic restaurants.

I was introduced to the owner of an iconic metaphysical book and gift store in Berry. The store owner was a colorfully dressed, radiant woman, and she was as brilliant as the array of crystals she had displayed around her shop. She invited me to dowse her store. Global Contact[45] carried a broad selection of spiritual books, healing music, and vibrant jewelry that seemed to call visitors close to their cases. As you can imagine, the energy of the shop was relatively high, given the number of crystals sitting under its roof. But as I neared the completion of the dowsing, I found myself questioning why the energy was not topping the charts, and why my dowsing rods were still indicating there was something there that needed attention.

---

[45] Global Contact Bookstore: https://www.globalcontact.com.au

Over the years, I'd discovered the energy of a location won't stabilize if the emotional, physical, spiritual, or etheric energy of the person(s) for whom I'm dowsing isn't in its highest alignment. Most of the time an individual's personal energy field calls for a vibrational tuning to support them to living in a resonant higher frequency. When the rods rotate clockwise at high speed, all is harmonized and balanced.

Placing a large tensor ring on the floor, the store owner stepped gingerly into the center, I invited her to close her eyes. Her body softened as the positive field created by the ring allowed for a shift to take place. Encouraging her to breathe and pay attention to the energy, I gently lifted the ring slowly up and down over her body, clearing away any remaining deep-seated energy. As always, the transformation miraculously resulted in an opening of the heart, and I was pleased to see her relax into a greater sense of presence and peace. This is a fairly common occurrence. Sometimes, an emotion or thought will arise that will bring on a direct awakening.

This mystical, alchemical side to dowsing opens us into the realm of moving from transformation to "transmutation." Transmutation is likened to the metamorphosis of a caterpillar when it moves through its chrysalis stage into its emergent butterfly form. A deep inner cellular shift is taking place. When complete there is a sense of freedom and newness. There is no going back to the former state.

Creating a safe space this Divine alchemical process can occur is a powerful skill which allows for the acceleration of the individual's trust in their own intuition and inner guidance. A ripple of grace flows, enlivening their whole inner eco-system. The discordant energy surfaces to be embraced, integrated, and transmuted into the power of loving presence.

Another miraculous result of dowsing is the shifting of conflicting relationships in the neighborhood around the property being dowsed. *"Wild!"* you say? It's true! The harmonic resonance created by clearing the geopathic stress in one space can directly impact, and influence, the energy in a neighboring home—depending on the source of the energy.

I saw this first-hand when I lived on Soledad Mountain Road in San Diego with my former husband. The couple who lived to our left were very loud and it was obvious they both drank a lot. They were extremely unwelcoming when we arrived, and they used to yell at us over the 10-foot-high fence that separated our properties. On the other side of us lived a man who kept bugging us to cut down our beautiful, healthy oak tree so he could have more sunlight for his swimming pool.

Just days after the dowsing of our home, the couple to the left began re-landscaping their overgrown hedges and lawn, happily bringing us plants; to my surprise they became warm and friendly. Meanwhile, the man to the right shared with one of our friends he wished he could join us for our salons, and never again bothered us about the tree. Usually dowsing will create a circumstance where the neighboring people will become kinder; or, if they are not ready to change their behavior, they will move soon after the dowsing.

I encourage people to keep a journal of any subtle or noticeable changes in their lives that occur after their house or office has been dowsed. They might experience greater health, new clients, better communication with family members, or unexpected income. As I shared earlier, existing neighbors may become friendlier, or troublesome neighbors might move away. The dowsing activates a deep inner heart resonance, which lends itself to greater coherence in our daily life.

On rare occasions a client will feel uncomfortable or concerned their life is chaotic after a dowsing. This is not a cause for despair, but rather a good thing, as it indicates people are shifting out of old survival patterns that have kept them trapped in the past. Dowsing harmonizes and raises the frequency of a property and it's a welcome gift to oneself to allow some time for recalibration. The decision to dowse a property is a courageous one and it is sometimes recommended to have a private Heart Resonance Mentoring session to assist the body in adjusting to the newly raised frequencies on the property. Heart Resonance Mentoring[46] (HRM) sessions allow for a shift in body consciousness. When used in tandem with a dowsing, this experience helps to transmute any remaining fear-based limitations, supporting our return to wholeness.

No Horsing Around!

The store manager felt such a change in the energy of the store that she inquired if I could come dowse her house the next day. On arriving at her home, I searched the car for my large copper tensor ring and I was shocked to learn I had left it at the store! Trusting the circumstance, I asked her to drive me home, a trip that would take us about 20 minutes each way. Now, a new dowser might berate themselves for their oversight, yet over the years I've learned to stay calm and alert, knowing there is a reason this is happening. Remaining relaxed and present to what might need to happen, as we returned to Lisa's home, she began openly expressing her suppressed fear about the dowsing. With this discovery, we were able to use the driving time for clearing her concerns, allowing her consciousness to rise to meet her desired intention for the dowsing.

Fears resolved, I literally dug into the dowsing. Imagine crawling under the porch amongst spider webs, trying to reach the spot where a negative vortex was located—a gritty, dirty experience if ever there was one! Her daughter's room was located above the negative vortex and apparently ultra-sensitive to it. Three hours later we completed the dowsing and after miles of smiles, she gratefully dropped me back in Berry at Global Contact.

Swinging the large copper energy ring over my tired shoulder I entered an exceptionally quiet store. Then I noticed a

---

[46] To receive your free 30-minute discovery session, please contact: connect@evolutionarydowsing.com.

tall, thin woman with thinning dark brown shoulder-length hair who was standing with her back turned to me. Still in a zone from the day's dowsing, I was quite surprised when she whipped around quite suddenly, looking quite shocked to see me holding a 28-inch copper ring on my shoulder.

She didn't say hello or introduce herself, but rather spoke intensely, *"Where did you get that ring?! Do you know Peter Carson?"* I replied that, no, I didn't know the man she was talking about. She continued. "He's a horse trainer and uses these rings on his horses." I looked quizzically at her as she continued pointing and staring at the ring. "Are you sure? This ring?" I asked. I swung it off my shoulder and now placed it directly in between us at face level. "Yes, yes, yes," she said, and suggested I should reach out to him.

What she couldn't possibly have known was that I was in a serious pickle. I had been doing so much dowsing that I was out of the large copper tensor rings I used for my dowsing work. Prior to my journey to Australia, I had purchased them from a Light-Life Technology[47] distributor in Colorado. Yet the shipments to Australia were taking too long, and at an exorbitant expense.

In Search of the Wizard

The slight bodied casually dressed woman let me know Peter Carson was a racehorse trainer and lived about 15 minutes from the store, 25 minutes from where I was staying in Gerroa. In my mind's eye, I imagined a tall, well-dressed man standing in front of his fancy barn arms arms-crossed in a prideful stance.

Boy was I ever wrong! It was not easy finding him and I spent a good half-a-day looking for his phone number. After quite an extensive Google search, I finally found his name in a racehorse article that trumpeted the fact that his horses had won some trophies. His name was listed in the horse trial directory

---

[47] Light-Life Tensor Rings https://www.lightlifetechnology.com.

and I jumped for joy when I finally found his number. Peter cheerfully answered the phone right away, warmly greeting me in his deep Australian accent. He encouraged me to come visit with him and his wife, Cathy, at their horse farm.

Finding his home was no easy quest. I borrowed Lisa's car and headed South down the coast road, still not accustomed to driving on the left-hand side of the road. I encountered my worst Aussie driving nightmare: having to enter and move out from a roundabout! Round and round I went holding fast to the center eight times until I finally found the courage to pull off the roundabout to ask for directions. I released my fear when a friendly face smiled upon me and told me Peter Carson's farm was just past a small airport a mile down the newly paved road I was on.

When I arrived, there was no one to be seen anywhere—not at the front of the barn, nor out on the far horse track. Looking past a white wooden fence with a roughly tied rope holding an old metal gate shut, I felt at home seeing the old rustic colored reddish-brown barn. There was a small brick house attached to it that reminded me of what I might see in countryside of Maine or Vermont. There were no horses in the weathered barn, so I stepped cautiously through the opening, my feet thudding quietly on its packed dirt floor, and walked out to a circular cement horse-training arena. The uncut grass outside the barn was thigh-high. Finally, I sighted horses walking round and round a circular contraption in brackish knee-deep water.

Stretching my body, I found Peter, who, unlike my vision of him, was a small jolly, dervish of a man, with wild, wispy, whitish-gray hair, and an extraordinary gregarious smile. He was as eager to hear about me, as I was to hear about him, instantly striking up a rare friendship in minutes. In fact, his eyes twinkled when discovering we were born on the same day, December 19th! His wife, Cathy, strong willed and open-hearted, was the rider and trainer of the trotter ponies, as well as an animal communicator.

My mind racing, I kept wondering if Peter looked more like a gnome or a druid. If he had had a tall purple hat on, I would have called him Merlin. In fact, this beautiful softhearted man indeed had the qualities of a wizard. I was not surprised to hear he was a dowser, and he soon blew any old beliefs I had about magic right out that barn door. He showed me around as he talked to me about his biodynamic flow-form system and the small storage barn that held the biodynamic greens he grew for the horses. Inspired by mountain streams, a man by the name of John Wilkes had introduced the concept of Flow-forms in the 1970s as a way of naturally purifying water. The vortex principle, introduced into biodynamic agriculture by Rudolf Steiner, helped Wilkes create a series of water features that used water itself as a force for change.

The woman I had met in Global Contact had been correct; Peter had a plethora of copper tensor rings available for sale that were exactly the kind I had been looking for. Here he was, only 25 minutes away from my temporary home at Seven Mile Beach—what were the chances of that?! Not only did he have the tensor rings I needed, but he had other tools developed by the late metaphysical cowboy Slim Spurling that I had only ever heard about. He openly shared how he stopped taking his horses to a vet, 15 years earlier, once learning how to use the tensor rings.

Slim Spurling

I read Slim's book sitting up all night and immediately took on a distributorship. I acquired a few different Acuvacs, Environmental Harmonizers, all his high-powered tools. After buying more rings, I flew from Australia to Erie, Colorado, for a seminar, where they make the rings. Been using them ever since.

—Peter Carson

Peter and Cathy's skill in healing horses was well known, and people from all over the valley brought their sick racehorses to Peter and Cathy's for treatment. Peter's cousin, Bernie, often joined the couple to form a masterful trio skilled in administering another metaphysical healing modality called Liquid Crystals.[48]

Apparently, Bernie—who was a well-known Australian Kinesiologist, and a Neural Organization Technique Instructor—had discovered Slim Spurling's book through a client who had cancer but hadn't responded well to Bernie's treatments. One day, Bernie visited him to discover that the cancer had cleared. The reason? He had bought and placed one of Slim Spurling's environmental harmonizers in his home. Bernie became fascinated by Slim's wisdom and shared it with Cathy and Peter.

Cathy and Peter were working primarily with Standard Breeds, harness racing horses that compete as trotters or pacers. They have also been asked to bring their energy healing modalities to dressage and Olympic horses, sporting horses, and ponies. Cathy's passion lies in facilitating a trotter's training camp for children, right there at the farm. Drinking tea amidst numbers of flies in the makeshift outdoor kitchen, she told me how she taught the kids to be gentle and kind while racing the ponies. She stressed how important it was for the children to understand the emotional well-being of horses, and that these animals were brilliant healers. I was awed when she told me how she has a pony for every emotion that needs healing in a child. "Occasionally," she smiled, "If the kids are playing it up, and they get injured, I use the rings on them, but primarily they are used on sporting horses, trotters and ponies."

Cathy spoke of how she and Peter worked with the horses. "We tie them up and place the large energy ring around

---

[48] Liquid Crystals http://www.theliquidcrystals.com.

their necks, so the energy flows right through their body. Then we use a "Light-Life" acupressure tool on them to open up all the points in their body. We made a rug with [pockets] on the outside [and] we can place all the 1-cubit rings in the pouches, leaving them on for an hour. It takes all the stiffness and soreness out of their body and loosens their muscles. Prior to using the tools, we were going to the vet's quite a lot, and had a lot of other people doing bodywork on them. This is the most successful methodology we have found, and we get the best results by using the tensor rings and the rugs."

We spent hours together that day, speaking about dowsing and how we use the Light-Life tools. Peter showed me the room where he worked on clients using the Liquid Crystals, tensor rings, and harmonizers. The Liquid Crystals were new to me. Curious, I learned they are geometric vibrational remedies made from the Earth's metals, minerals, and crystals.

Peter was a man of his word, and I was awed by his deep insights and wisdom when working with these potent tools. Standing in the healing room I had a dizzying feeling of Déjà vu, of having been together with him in another life.

As the sun was setting, we decided to stop, and we all gathered around the table for a "cuppa." In a humorous moment, the door opened wide and tall stately man joined us. It was Peter's cousin, Bernie, a man well-known on the South Coast for his healing abilities. People drove two hours from the city to see him, and he only worked two days a week. His kind eyes rested upon me, as if he were seeing through me on a cellular level. He gently smiled as we were introduced.

A Severe Block in My Body

As I had come to Australia to heal and was still weak, I couldn't help but tell him a bit of my story, as I was still experiencing a severe blockage in my body. If I tried to move forward too quickly, I would experience a density that stopped me cold.

I felt awkward, yet with Peter right there I had to ask if he could help me. He came over and began touching points on my head. He had me close my eyes as he worked. Within minutes, he had me stand up and move my eyes back and forth. Then he told me he was done. I was totally astonished that he had me walking with ease within minutes.

Relieved that I no longer needed to try to ship the rings from the United States, I could now offer a way for people, to directly receive them without any additional customs charges.

Peter supplied me with tensor rings for my expected two-month stay in Australia, and he gave me the largest gage copper ring I had ever seen. It was called a Lost Cubit Ring[49] and it was spectacular.

The ring had been made by Slim Spurling after the discovery of the Lost Cubit length by inventor Hans Becker. He spoke of ancient times where knowledge such as this was only for royalty and kept from the public.

This unit of measurement is slightly larger than the Sacred Cubit and has a natural resonant frequency of 177 MHz. The Lost Cubit Ring is reputed to operate at the metaphysical level, specifically working with mental and emotional problems or distortions in a person's aura.

I had been feeling the need for a stronger energy ring to work with yet hadn't known about the qualities of this particular Slim Spurling Light-life ring.

Peter handed the ring to me saying, "this is the one for you, you need it now." As it was getting late, I excused myself, knowing I would be back. I could hardly stop from talking to myself all the way home. *Had it been a surreal dream?* If so, it had been one I could have never imagined.

---

[49] Lost Cubit Ring https://www.lightlifetechnology.com.

Chapter 9: White Buffalo Calf Woman

Love is the highest coherent emotion generated by humans. It is our potential to experience the emotion of love continuously on all levels of consciousness. Love sets up a harmonic field that cascades into the actual cells of the body and into other consciousness levels of one's being.
—The Hathors[50]

Standing on the rectangular wooden deck the next day I stood and stretched my back after meeting with Peter, Cathy, and Bernie. I looked out beyond the perennial garden to the vast flat white sand beach feeling calm and balanced.

I put on my worn blue jogging shorts and a pink V-neck tank top, quietly singing as I stepped off the deck. About 100 yards or so from Lisa's place the long metal galvanized bridge glistened above the slow-moving river.

To my delight I spied a large white pelican paddling around in the estuary and stopped to watch him proudly move through the water as he completed his morning inspection of his territory. I followed my usual route across the small white sand dunes, tracking alongside the shallow water.

I was awestruck. Instead of my normally slow pace I was now running; in fact, I was now gleefully cantering along the beach! There was no longer a dense wall of energy stopping me. My breath was no longer shallow and, glowing with gratitude, I reviewed my previous day's healing with Peter.

---

[50] Tom Kenyon, "Who are the Hathors?" *Tom Kenyon*, https://tomkenyon.com/who-are-the-hathors

I jogged past surf camp newbie surfers, learning how to stand on their boards and laughing as their cascading bodies slipped off into the gentle blue waves. Jogging further, I saw a handmade driftwood teepee made of tree boughs arise out of the sandy landscape. I felt called to stop and I sat down to meditate until summoned out to the gentle cresting waves.

Gliding into the glimmering ocean, I sang a blessing of gratitude as I spiraled in the water, completing the ritual by diving under the waves in the warm summer sun. To top off the morning, an ecstatic current of delight flooded my system when I saw five riders on horseback trotting down the beach with white powdery sand flying out beneath their dancing hoofs.

Exuberant and chatty the following morning, Lisa invited me to a special yoga class that was to be held at the Berry community center. Following the sultry smell of the sandalwood incense, we made our way inside. Scanning the carefully set up space and seeing its wide, white natural wood floorboards, I watched in wonder as many middle-aged Aussies greeted each other with warm laughter and smiles.

Learning the teacher was a devotee of Swami Satchitananda, I was whisked back to a far distant memory in my late teens when I had met this soft-spoken guru while living in New Hampshire. My body was relaxed and open, and my mind rested in the background. Towards the end of class, the teacher invited us to lay in Savasana,[51] a position where we lay down, palms up, in a fully restful position for a closing visualization. Savasana is a fully conscious pose aimed at being awake, yet completely relaxed.

---

[51] Karson McGinley, "Why Savasana is the Hardest Yoga Pose," *Chopra*, https://chopra.com/articles.

The teacher proceeded to lead us on an inner journey, gently inviting us down a path where we might meet our native animal medicine totem. I was a bit concerned that my visualization capacities were not in full swing, as I thought of myself as a feeler, not as a seer.

Falling immediately into a state of altered consciousness, I found myself standing a few feet away from the flapped open door of a teepee. Observing something moving towards me, my eyes strained to see, as the white vision was blurry.

Luckily, I knew enough to simply let it go, trusting the vision would make itself known if need be. Afterward, women yogis dressed in all leggings of all different colors stood in a circle and chattered like buzzing bees about meeting at a local coffee shop in town. Lisa agreed to have a quick cuppa' with them but said she'd need to head off to work soon after.

Still in an alternate state from the yoga class, to my wonder, the white blur standing outside the teepee kept fluttering through my awareness.

Feeling a bit indecisive, I felt compelled to walk into the coffee shop, though quickly changed my mind knowing this was not the right energy for me. Leaving the chitchatting women, I walked down the sleepy street past the closed boutique windows. In a bit of a stupor, I slowly slipped past some luscious fresh baked goods sitting in the open window of a bakery, and made my way to Global Contact, the last place I had dowsed, with an intention of only saying hello. I softly moved past the front counter where the owner stood busy at the cash register dressed in her bright pink silk shirt and matching pink glasses.

Unseen, so I thought, I seamlessly moved towards the back of the store near the books. The owner turned, looked past the display of tarot cards and gave a shout: she wanted to introduce me to two women who were now standing in front of her at the cash register. Sauntering over beside them, I quietly said hello, although their names simply vanished into thin air.

The Lives of Native Americans

Returning to the back corner of the store, I bypassed decks of medicine cards, and spied the coffee table photography book, *The Vanishing Race* by photographer and ethnographer, Edward S. Curtis. Born in 1868 in Wisconsin, USA, Curtis spent decades chronicling in photographs the lives of Native Americans as part of a project commissioned by banker J. P. Morgan. Curtis had for many years felt Native American culture was vanishing, and so he dedicated his life to recording the tribes and their natural world visually, before, in his mind, they disappeared forever. It was such a surprise to find this book here in this modest metaphysical store in Berry, of all places!

My connection with Edward Curtis went way back and for the moment I allowed my mind to meander to a time when my first boyfriend, Mark, better known to me as "Zip," introduced me to one of his friends, who was a collector of Indian artifacts. Close friends of theirs had discovered Edward Curtis's glass photographic plates, which had been missing for more than 50 years. They were trying to find an investor to help them purchase an original set of Curtis's photogravures that were up for auction at Sotheby's.

This was a time before the world was fascinated with Native American Culture. No one would give them the time of day. I was 16 at the time and when I told the story to my father, he agreed to meet with Mark and his friend. My dad, who was an entrepreneur, was always looking for a new venture in which to invest, and he loved their story. Upon hearing they hadn't found anyone willing to risk their money, my dad looked directly at them, put his outstretched hand into theirs and, with a strong binding handshake for both, with conviction handed them a blank check to purchase the Curtis Set.

I was heading down a wormhole of thoughts, lost in remembering how, at the time, I had believed that after all was said and done, I would marry Mark, in the end. The older woman I had just met approached me.

Our eyes met, and seeing her face and white hair, though still in a bit of a dream state, I had an immediate epiphany. Looking at her, I saw my blurry white apparition shape shift into a white eagle and realized the reason I couldn't see my vision clearly in the yoga class, was that its wings were moving! Looking closer at this woman, I was at a loss for words. With her white hair, long nose, and blue eyes she looked exactly like an eagle. To make matters even more wild, her friend in the same exact moment pulled a book off the shelf and handed it to this eagle woman whose name was Lynn Pearce. The book was titled *White Eagle*. I was not one to embrace the idea of intergalactic occurrences, yet with all my senses acutely present, in the synergy of the moment, I was captivated by the energy of this elder woman. I could not help but pour my story out to her, sharing the vision I had had just 30 minutes before, as well as my whole history with Edward Curtis.

Apparently, that very morning, Lynn had a visitation from Spirit, telling her she needed to drive to Global Contact, located an hour or more down the coast from her home in Wollongong. She said she had no idea why she was going, or who she was supposed to meet. She didn't drive, so she called her friend, who agreed to take her. Lynn and I instantly became friends, and she invited me to come to her house the next day, with the offer of a private session. In most circumstances, I would be interrogating a person who made such an offer, curious to know what modalities they practiced and to get a sense of what I could expect from the experience. Yet, oddly, on this day, in the quietude of the moment, though I was used to synchronicities in my life, this topped my experiential ceiling. Available and curious, I agreed, and asked no other questions.

Returning to Seven Mile Beach, the evening sunset stoked the burning fire in my heart. As the pastel colors reflected in the water, I, too, sat on the beach in the calming stillness. Lisa was driving up to the mountain house and after listening to the day's events she invited me to stay overnight. Her eyes revealed to me the excitement she felt about the dowsing her small rambling house. Her winding dirt road branched directly off the highway and it took a lot of "chutzpah" to meet the oncoming trucks that still used the old Berry Highway. We stopped to open the locked tarnished metal cattle gate, where I had to get out and wait patiently as her truck passed through before locking it up again afterwards. I was speechless when I spied a 15'-high cement sign on the hill. How had I missed this the first time we had driven up here? "Eldacanova," it said.

Gazing at the sign, an uprising inner voice took hold in my consciousness and sent out an alert. Lisa seeing my disturbing look realized, as did I, that the sign still had the last property owners' family name on it. Our eyes sparkled as we glanced once again at the sign, knowing that for the land to hold Lisa's highest intention, it was time to liberate it from the energy of the past owners. The name "Eldacanova" had apparently been derived from the first two letters of the names of the owner's children. This is an example of the beauty of how Feng Shui and the dowsing work hand in hand. The two modalities enhance each other, bringing about a greater synergistic change. Knowing Lisa's dream for the Mountain, I immediately asked her to pull out some tools, with the grand intention of right there and then shifting the energy. Laughing boisterously, we began madly scraping away some letters from the old cement sign.

Finding El Nova

When we were finished the sign read: "El Nova!" We looked up the definition of the word "Nova" in the dictionary and giggled as we discovered that in Latin "Nova" means new, but also means "a star that suddenly increases its light output tremendously!" We both nodded in delight at how the energy of the sign now perfectly aligned with Lisa's intention.

Lisa's attention was now fine-tuned from dowsing and applying Feng Shui to her ocean house. She knew she needed to clear and create a pathway leading up to the front door. Two wooden steps, blocked by a bushy plant, led up to an old porch with a vast expansive view out to the ocean and yet it did not feel inviting. Once inside the house, we had to walk through a dark hallway to the open living area. The side room off the hallway gave me the heebie-jeebies. The biggest problem with the house proved to be a negative energy vortex in the side room which expanded into the main bedroom.

It was evident, too, that geopathic stress was negatively affecting the huge Banyan Tree on the hill outside. I placed a brass tool from Slim Spurling in an open area in the tree to balance the energy and used my "Earth Cures" to remedy the geopathic stress zones. Earth Cures are made out of 18" copper-coated steel rods and are extremely conducive to holding intentions and activations at the highest level. These rods, when placed in a home or in the ground, will stop any discordant stress lines, such as geopathic stress, and negative vortexes, from entering the home or property. At this point in my dowsing career, I had not yet explored how to set up a unity field with a crystal Merkaba[52] around the house, but this solution worked well, nonetheless.

The Merkaba

The Merkaba, or Star Tetrahedron, is one of the most powerful of Alchemical symbols, symbolizing the union of Spirit and matter, the above and the below, the masculine and the feminine. "Mer" means Light/rotates around itself. "Ka" means Spirit. "Ba" means Body.

Songline of the Heart / Shelley Darling

That night, sleeping soundly on the couch facing the great banyan tree, I had a lucid dream and vision. In the vision I was being shown a group of indigenous people standing tall on The Mountain. I heard and saw the words "Gathering of Nations" and knew I was in some way creating or taking part in this gathering. What struck me was that the hordes people who had gathered below at the base around the mountain, facing the indigenous elders with reverence, were now standing alone on the ridge line above their people. Awakening from this dream, my inner detective was on the loose, so I opened my computer and discovered a "Gathering of Nations" Powwow was taking place that very weekend in New Mexico.

I hurried the next morning to catch the train to Wollongong where I was to dowse the home of Lynn, the white-haired woman I had met in Berry. I had felt compelled to carry my large, 28" Lost Cubit Light-Life energy ring. Holding the ring on my shoulder, I stood on the platform outside the old yellow brick train house with a few others and waited for the next train. People looked at me curiously, though no-one asked about the large metal "Hoola-Hoop" I was carrying. With ring in hand, I boarded the train north to Wollongong. The trains in Australia are spotlessly clean and provide a great platform from which you can see above the green hills out to the ocean. If it's the right season, you can even spot a whale or two breeching.

Lynn's house was like walking through a portal of vibrant purple. The lavender rug, hosting a dark purple velvet couch, was aligned with and hugging a great purple wall. There were amethyst crystals and, to my astonishment, violet stained-glass lamps. This color frequency was not new to me, as I had in the past researched its association with the Ascended Master Saint Germain from the book *Seven Sacred Flames* by Aurelia Jones, a favorite of mine.[53]

---

[53] Aurelia Jones, *The Seven Sacred Flames* (Mount Shasta Light Publishing, June 27, 2007).

Lynn nodded with a soft twinkle in her eye, when she saw the ring. She guided me up the slightly worn purple carpeted stairs to her healing room, which, of course, was decorated in different shades of purple. Even her massage table was covered with a soft velvety lavender blanket. Lynn had me carry my ring to the far end of the room, place it on the rug, and instructed me to step into its center.

> ### Saint Germain
> *The ascended master Saint Germain is the chohan of the seventh ray and is a master alchemist of the sacred fire who comes bearing the gift of the violet flame of freedom for world transmutation. As chohan, or lord, of the seventh ray, Saint Germain initiates our souls in the science and ritual of transmutation through the violet flame. Saint Germain and his consort Portia deliver the dispensation for the seventh age and the seventh ray—the violet ray of freedom, justice, mercy, alchemy and sacred ritual, creating a new life, a new civilization, and new energy.*
>
> **—Aurelia Jones**

Before I knew what was happening, she began an incantation, chanting as she circled the ring with burning sage, and brushing hawk feathers over and around me. She spoke of the ring as the Sacred Hoop, and she referred to my relationship with White Buffalo Calf Woman. I was stunned.

    White Buffalo Calf Woman had come into my life when I had been working with clients in Mill Valley, California, prior to moving to San Diego. On one client's first session, I experienced an unusual earthy smoky smell when I walked into one of the rooms in her home. I knew it wasn't sage, and I felt befuddled: no incense was burning. I looked up and on the wall I saw a magnificent painting of an indigenous woman dressed in a beaded white leather dress. She was holding a peace pipe and standing in front of a white buffalo, which seemed lit by a heavenly light. The same thing happened every time I entered that room, and that room only. Eventually, I met a spiritual woman in Hawaii who told me it was normal for the women who communicate with White Buffalo Calf Woman to undergo these exact experiences.

I also learned of an ancient legend which tells how the people of the land had lost their connection to the Creator and White Buffalo Calf Woman was sent to teach the people how to pray with the pipe. Seven sacred ceremonies were offered for them to follow in order to ensure a future of harmony, peace, and balance with the Earth.

New Energies Coming In

As I stood in the center of the ring in Lynn's home, I found myself even more surprised when she directly addressed the cessation of my relationship, even though I hadn't told her anything about my marital woes. She called forth the power of the new energies coming in. Finally, in a reverent soft voice, she introduced me to "Morning Star," an indigenous spirit who was protecting me and who said I could call on him at any time.

In his book *Black Elk Speaks*, author John G. Neihardt tells the story of the Oglala Lakota visionary and healer Nicholas Black Elk. Neihardt quotes Black Elk as saying:[54]

> *"Power of the World always works in circles, and everything tries to be round . . . The sky is round, and I have heard that the earth is round like a ball, and so are all the stars. The wind, in its greatest power whirls.*

---

[54] John C. Neihardt, *Black Elk Speaks*, Ch. 17 (University of Nebraska Press, 1979).

Birds make their nest in circles, for theirs is the same religion as ours. The sun comes forth and goes down again in a circle. The moon does the same and both are round. Even the seasons form a great circle in their changing, and always come back again to where they were. The life of a man is a circle from childhood to childhood, and so it's in everything where power moves. Our tepees were round like the nests of birds, and these were always set in a circle, the nation's hoop."

The idea of the Sacred Hoop—or Medicine Wheel of Life—originated in Native American traditions as representative of the sacred circle of all life. Each of the circle's four directions is a gateway to an aspect of knowledge and life learning, and each of the directions aligns with certain animals and their associated elements. Over the years I created for myself the aggregation of what I call the "Universal Prayer of the Heart," which honors the Four Directions of the Sacred Hoop, and is inclusive of Mother Earth, Father Sky, and the Heart.

As in all life, it is understood that the circle has no beginning and no end, and simply expresses the nature of the cycles we all move through as spiritual beings choosing to be on our earthly journey. I wished I had been able to record our session: I knew it had cemented my relationship with the Earth. Feeling her ground my energy through her movement around the ring, and hearing her incantations, I felt a renewed strength. Although we didn't know it at the time, my life and Lynn's were to be indelibly bonded until she transitioned in 2012.

Calming Horses

In the first Dowsing with Shelley, we had a huge shift with the horses that day. Horses when they first come to the farm are skittish, sometimes having had a bad time with their previous owner, and any noise spooks them. Since we did the dowsing, they are all very calm. They are a lot quieter; the dowsing instantly calms them down.

—Cathy Carson

Songline of the Heart / Shelley Darling

Universal Prayer of the Heart
Honoring the Seven Directions of the Sacred Hoop

ARISE Spirit of the East, to the turning of the new day, to the golden light within and without. To the golden eagle, illumination, and clarity of vision. To the East stargate: element of air to new beginnings, and change. We call for your presence, power and Spirit to come in.

ARISE Spirit of the South, to the child within, to trust, innocence and balance. To the Whitetail deer, mouse, and to the GOOD Road home. To the South stargate: to the element of fire; transformation, inspiration, and creation. We call for your presence, power and Spirit to come in.

ARISE Spirit of the West, to personal truth, strength, and the deep waters within. To the power places between the worlds seen and unseen, to the black bear, brown bear, Raven and the medicine way. To the West stargate: to the element of water our holy source of all life and healing. We call for your presence, power and Spirit to come in.

ARISE Spirit of the North, to the ancestors, past, present and future. To the wisdom council, the mountains and our return wholeness. To the White Buffalo, Snow leopard, moose and beaver...To the North stargate: to the elements of earth, death and rebirth. To grounding our light, power and love; while humbly receiving life's abundant gifts. We call for your presence, power and Spirit to come in.

To Mother Earth for your nourishment and compassion for all beings. For the two leggeds, four-leggeds, winged ones, cetaceans, and to all those that swim. We are all children of the mother.

To Father Sky for the vast limitless star nation, for universal and celestial information and energy.

To the Center, where the six directions meet in the sacred space of the heart, a limitless source of inner joy, energy, light and love. We ask for your guidance and grace.

May Divine love nourish our hearts, so that we might see an illumined world, as we express our essence and wholeheartedly embrace one another, while co-creating an effervescing shared vision and expanding resonant field of love. We open to receive the blessings of this day with gratitude. May we live with continued curiosity, courage and trust in the great mystery.

- **Universal Prayer** (content drawn from a plethora of sources).

Songline of the Heart / Shelley Darling

Before I left, Lynn handed me a pink sheet of 8.5" x 11" paper with an invocation from White Buffalo Calf Woman and she told me about a group of women for whom she was facilitating a 12-month experience aligned with the moon cycle, in accordance with *The 13 Original Clan Mothers,* a book written by Jamie Sams.[55] Jamie was a member of the Wolf Clan Teaching Lodge, and her teachings offered a potent method for integrating native feminine wisdom into our lives to guide us in cultivating our personal gifts, and our sacred relationship to all relations on Earth.

Sitting quietly in a stupor by myself on the return train, my heart jumped two feet when I heard a woman's voice from behind me loudly crying out, "Isaiah, Isaiah, come back here." Not only was this name unusual, it also just happened to be the name of my son. Shifting my position so to see what was happening, I saw a young dark-skinned boy about the age of five, heading quickly back down the middle aisle towards an older Aboriginal woman, who I guessed to be about 70 years old. I assumed she must be his grandmother. She was sitting with a multitude of colored bags of various sizes. My eyes quickly darted away when I felt her gaze back at me. Surprisingly, though, I felt the energy of her loving presence taking hold of my heart.

It turned out we were both transferring trains at the same stop. Turning once again, I watched as this stalwart elder steadied herself and stood up to get off the train. I was appalled that no one near her thought to help her with her cumbersome sized bags. I immediately rose out of my seat, and ambled back to help her, Isaiah now at her side with his wide eyes staring, looked curiously on. This time we looked directly at each other as she graciously allowed me to take her largest bag. We walked together with Isaiah between us and waited side by side

---

[55] Jamie Sam, *The 13 Original Clan Mothers* (Harper San Francisco, June 1993)

for the next train. I spoke to her about my son, who shared the same name, as the boy who I now learned was her grandson.

Auntie Jean lived in a community called Booderee in the Wreck Bay Aboriginal Community. It was located just south of Berry and Nowra in Jervis Bay. I was later to learn that in the Aboriginal *Dhurga* language of New South Wales Booderee meant "bay of plenty" or "plenty of fish."

As the train rolled into my station and our delightful conversation began to come to a close, she kindly invited me to come to her home and meet her family. My heart had filled with joy at our meeting and I let her know I would be seeing her soon. A few days later, Lisa and I headed off for a visit, and I was thrilled to see Auntie Jean again. As we learned from the Aboriginal Ranger at the park gate, Auntie Jean, was the well-known and highly respected matriarch of the village. I discovered her personal invitation to come to her home was extremely significant, as it was not a regular practice to invite strangers into an Aboriginal community. Lisa and I were welcomed with open arms as Auntie Jean, dressed in her colorful dress introduced us to her family, who were all excitedly standing by, Isaiah, giggling at her side. Stories were told, as she pointed to the many photographs and children's paintings on her walls. The family followed us to Lisa's truck as we said our goodbyes, making our plans to stay connected. We were genuinely taken aback when Auntie Jean pointed to a cooler on the ground, and had her son load us up with the fresh fish he had caught just that morning! We felt enormously honored and embraced each other as family. The natural kindness and love from this first nations family was, indeed, humbling, although I had no idea I would never see Auntie Jean again.

Sacred Tree Day

A few weeks later, Heather drove back down from Churchpoint to pick me up in Gerroa. Lynn Pearce had invited us both back to meet her for lunch in Wollongong. Hidden from sight on the backside of a small mountain in the woods, was a sacred Aboriginal track where Lynn showed us a hidden power spot. Inviting me to lie down on a wavy spine-like rock—which was apparently a known positive vortex—Lynn shared she had been guided by the Ancestors to teach me a chant. I then fell into an altered state, receiving this guidance without asking questions. Lynn's directions were very specific: I was to repeat this chant daily. Afterwards, this Four Sacred Element chant—the "El-Ka-Leem-Om"—became a powerful addition to my morning ritual, and remains so, even to this day. My experience has been that, when said slowly, and with a conscious breath in between each repetition, the vibrational tone takes root in our consciousness creating a deep resonance within the body.

It wasn't until three years later, while teaching a dowsing course in California, that I discovered where El-Ka-Leem-Om—originated. I had gone out with a few of my dowsing students for lunch and while chatting about the chant, I saw one woman literally wriggling in her seat. Barely able to contain herself, she blurted out that she knew this chant, and it was from Ancient Egypt. She spoke to me about a man named Tom Kenyon who worked with a group called the Hathors, a group of inter-dimensional, intergalactic beings who were connected to Ancient Egypt through the Temples of the Goddess Hathor. Tom, I discovered, is one of the most respected sound healers in the world and was at that time a practicing psychotherapist involved in brain research.

In the late 1980s Tom had been "contacted" by the Hathors during a meditation, and they began to instruct him in the vibratory nature of the cosmos, the use of sacred geometry to stimulate brain performance, and in the use of sound to activate psycho-spiritual experiences.[56]

---

[56] More on Tom Kenyon: http://tomkenyon.com.

According to them, these sounds approximate the words they have for the four elements. This is based on the ancient practice of alchemy used in Ancient Egypt to denote, honor, and appreciate the four elements:

> El—Earth
>
> Ka—Fire
>
> Leem—Water
>
> Om—Air or Space

These elements were understood as a living consciousness. They are the foundation of our existence on Earth and offer us the precise sustenance we need. For example, without water there is no life; fire cleans and creates replenishment for the ground so new seedlings may flourish. These elements are expressed in our biology and our physiology, and in the food we eat, the air we breathe, and the Earth upon which we walk. In today's world, most people have forgotten their connection with these four elements. Using this mantra—inwardly in meditation or outwardly by uttering or chanting it—reminds us of this sacred connection. Working with this mantra has opened new levels of balance and presence, gratitude, and appreciation for me.

In his book *The Hathor Material*,[57] Tom states, "It is as if these sounds open the doors of perception and allow you to move into a resonant field of Consciousness—the archetypal realm, the primordial force, the underworld of all matter—where the elements are alive. Staying here for a while allows you to shift consciousness and perception in such a way that you sense the profundity of the physical world and its place within the continuum of Consciousness."

---

[57] Tom Kenyon, *The Hathor Material* (ORB Communications, 1996), Chapter 8 pp 77-80.

El-Ka-Leem-Om (Chant of the Elements)

To use the chant, as shared by Tom Kenyon—in the way it was meant to be used—it's important to send the feeling of appreciation and gratitude to the external elements of your body first, and then move to the internal elements. Then move back to the outer elements and back to the inner, and so forth. Each cycle of the chant is used to send appreciation/gratitude to either the outer or the inner elements.

EL—KA—LEEM—OM	
Outer Elements:	**Inner Elements:**
EL: Earth KA: Sun/Fire LEEM: Oceans/Waters OM: Air/Space	EL: Bones KA: Solar Plexus LEEM: Blood / Fluids OM: Lungs/breath

So, for example, when you chant the sound "EL," direct your appreciation and gratitude to either the outer or inner element of Earth, depending on where you are in the cycle. When you hear the sound "KA," direct your appreciation/gratitude to the outer or inner element of Fire. When you hear the sound "LEEM," direct your appreciation/gratitude to the outer or inner element of water. And, when you hear "OM," direct your appreciation to the outer or inner element of air or space.[58]

"The Hathor Chant will clear the auric field through the four lower elements all the way down to the earth. It allows you to clear and expand your pranic tube while connecting to Mother Earth. The pranic tube extends down through the center of our body, and it is this we need to focus on to increase the flow of prana or energy throughout the body. It connects us to

---

[58] Tom Kenyon, "Chant of the Four Elements," Tom Kenyon, https://tomkenyon.com/chant-of-the-four-elements.

both Heaven and Earth. These are basic exercises which will help immensely to strengthen our life-force. The Kabbalist Chant will clear the field through all the dimensions, all realities, all the way back to God and it is good for clearing emotions."[59]

As you continue to direct your emotion in this manner, an inner bridge of awareness is established energetically between your body and the outer elements that can profoundly alter your awareness.

I eventually found a recording of author and spiritual mystic, Maureen St. Germain's[60] version of El-Ka-Leem-Om, which I play while engaging in an ancient exercise called the Five Tibetans[61] and following a protocol for conscious breath work.

The Five Tibetans gives the practitioner an experience of grounded physical balance, clarity of mind, and an evolved spiritual connection to higher Consciousness. Tom Kenyon notes: "I have made use of this mantra for many years and find it to be a most potent tool not only for remembering and honoring this sacred connection, but also for grounding. One can enter the archetypal realms in which they exist, which has transformational effects that can be quite powerful."[62]

As Lynn guided me through this process of engaging with the elements, I had a clear and sparkling revelation. Years before, I had been introduced to the book *The Magdalen Manuscript*, which had been written by Tom Kenyon with the assistance of his wife, Judi Sion.

---

[59] Iona Stewart, review of *Hathor Material* by Tom Kenyon and Virginia Essene, www.goodreads.com.
[60] Maureen St. Germain, https://maureenstgermain.com/ .
[61] "The Five Tibetans," https://www.healthline.com
[62] Tom Kenyon, "Chant of the Four Elements," *Tom Kenyon*, https://tomkenyon.com/chant-of-the-four-elements.

In the book, Tom had written about an encounter he had had with Mary Magdalen, who he described as "this magnificent being." He reported in the book that she had insisted her name be spelled without an "e" at the end, to distinguish her from the misrepresented character the Church had falsely presented to the world. She had announced to Tom that she was both the wife and tantric consort to Jeshua Ben Joseph, commonly known as Jesus.[63]

Tom's book claims Mary Magdalen was trained in an alchemical process known at the time as "sex magic" that was taught in the schools of Isis. Tom reports her as having spoken to him of the alchemy that occurred in the rising energy of the initiates and how the dross becomes clear, allowing what needs purification to come "painfully" into focus.

For me this brings to mind exactly what happens in dowsing. Sometimes the clearing of the house and land may trigger emotions the client may feel are slightly chaotic, unsettling or challenging. As I have said before, this catalyzes a "quickening" in the client's consciousness that creates a need for clearing any lower body frequencies or obstructions from their true essence and evolutionary path.

In other words, after a dowsing takes place, anything other than what is in true alignment—and in resonance—with one's soul, comes up to be unconditionally loved and transmuted.

In *The Magdalen Manuscript,* Tom Kenyon says the Magdalen also explains the term "initiate." As Tom puts it, "The term initiate refers to one who has decided to live upward in consciousness, one who has decided to leave behind the mundane life and to enter into an adventure of Consciousness."

---

[63] Tom Kenyon, "An Introduction," (to The Magdalen Manuscript), *Tom Kenyon,* http://tomkenyon.com/an-introduction.

This is precisely why I ask people before a dowsing: "Are you ready?" The bottom line is, are you willing to let go of the old beliefs, habits, and ideas of who you think you are, and embrace the profundity and truth of your authentic nature?

Lynn's presence in my life was indelibly imprinted on my heart. I saw her as a down-to-Earth priestess with a native soul, who worked in accordance with the laws of Nature.

She fully trusted her guidance, and she was connected to and tapped into a field of knowing that spoke of truth, love, and the quiet care of all relations. The ritual of the Sacred Hoop I was given was a blessing and a gift, and a reminder to honor the ancestors of the land.

Chapter 10: Sacred Buddhas

The key turning point, to me, in the dowsing was when the rods started spinning, I thought, 'what can do that?' You can't make that up. I didn't know what that energy was. All you know was that it was something bigger [than] yourself and you [are] connected to it.
—Dave Bambach[64]

Enraptured by an endless sea, and mesmerized by my experience, I was pinged by Ange, a new potential dowsing contact who lived in Mullumbimby, a town about 10 hours north in the Byron Shire area of the Northern Rivers region of New South Wales.

Researching the history of the area, I discovered the land was once inhabited by the Bundjalung people. Apparently, there had previously been a lot of fighting on the land. The main geographical feature was a mountain sacred to the Aboriginals called Mount Chincogan. It looked like a tall camel hump, although it was actually a minor lava plug created when magma, the source material of lava, hardened within the vents of an active volcano. The plug had come from the now-extinct Tweed Volcano. To the East stood Mount Warning, the sacred Aboriginal site that is the easternmost point in Australia and is known for receiving the dawn's first light.

Ange had heard about my dowsing from a mutual friend in the United States and she wanted to have her family's new house dowsed. They had recently purchased and moved to a property that had previously been owned by an alcoholic

---

[64] Dave Bambach Bio-Optic Holography www.uniquelyyou-boh.com

couple. Prior to that, a group of Harley-Davidson bikers had lived on the property. Feeling into the past history of this home, it was clear the energy of the land was calling for healing.

Emailing her the simple pre-dowsing form I ask all people for whom I dowse to complete, I requested she return it to me before I arrived. I also asked her to send me a drawing of the house and the property, as well as the names of each of the family members, including the children and their animals.

The pre-dowsing form would furnish a baseline for the upcoming dowsing experience. Ange trusted the process, providing me with bullet points that clarified what was not working optimally in her life. I am grateful to Ange and her family for giving me permission to share their story here, as it's a powerful example of how dowsing works, and what can happen as a result. Ange's answers to my questions began the process of our dowsing. While the dowsing helps to raise the energy in the home, sometimes, as the frequency rises, my clients will eventually forget about the original underlying issues with which they had been grappling and think nothing had really happened as a result of the dowsing. The pre-dowsing form reminds them of the transformation they have gone through, and it invites them to celebrate the changes. [65]

Ange knew that the whole family was to be present in the morning, so we could "open the house" together. Although some women might be concerned about their husband's response to the dowsing, Ange was not the least bit worried, even though this would be a new experience for him. After a lovely meal together the evening before the dowsing I explained how the dowsing was not only about restoring the house and the land, but it's also creating the conditions for

---

[65] Pre-dowsing Form: Starts the process for an optimal shift towards greater health, wealth, and harmony. For your free consultation and form: connect@evolutionarydowsing.com

people to remember who they truly are. The dowsing can open a portal for a return to their essential self. The energy is elevated, and there is a deepening of resonance activating a sacred, renewed sense of custodianship of the land.

The kids showed their curiosity by asking me if they could see and use the dowsing rods. Ange, present to their desire, immediately purchased on the spot, three sets of rods. Their curiosity deepened as I showed them how to use these tools and they were excited about the next day's dowsing. The three children, an older boy and two younger girls, ranged from eight to 11 years in age. If they had been younger, I might have suggested they not be there, although whenever possible I delight in the presence of children. Not only does it give them the chance to enjoy using the rods, but it is a way for me to share with them this ancient science. Children love working with energy and can easily connect with the rods. They can often see energy, even though the adults themselves may have seemingly lost the ability.

I returned to the motel where I was staying in Mullumbimby, and early the following morning I gathered my Earth Cures and two large copper tensor rings. Sanna had recently given me a beautiful Australian crystal necklace with an attached Buddha pendant. Hearing Ange driving into the parking lot, I quickly placed it over my head.

Ange and I spoke on the ride over to her house about the possibility of dowsing the children's school. Apparently, the children's teacher was having trouble with the class and was so frustrated she was ready to quit. I giggled as we drove straight through a deep gully of creek water towards the house before traversing down Ange's long flat dirt driveway. We passed a small "caravan"—what we in the USA call a "camper" and which the family was calling their "gypsy wagon" —parked in front of the family's house. It was delightfully painted with a huge, bold, blue woman hula dancer. There was an expansive lawn on one side of the property and large oak trees wound around the backside of the house alongside a bubbling stream that passed behind the gypsy caravan carving the shape of a crescent moon around the property.

Looking Inward

As we walked toward the house, I saw two stone Buddha heads sitting on either side of the stairs in front of the door. These sacred guardians represent enlightened wisdom and knowledge. Their eyes were half-closed in meditation, and they were looking inward. They each had an outer dot in the center of their head, illuminating the Buddha's supernatural vision. Ange passed by the guardians and headed into the house. I was startled as I walked closer when I realized these Buddha heads were exactly the same as the amulet I was wearing! There are many representations of the Buddha and for me, the synchronicity was uncanny. The children, excited to see me, bounced off the trampoline. In syncopated movement, they ran up the three steps leading to the front door of the house, passing the Buddha Heads on the way; I followed close behind.

Stopping for a moment as I placed my foot on the first painted step I looked around, noticing it was hard to determine which door was the front door. At the top of the steps to the left was a small pair of white doors, and to the right was a large sliding glass door. Following the children, I chose the sliding glass door to the right but froze in shock the second I entered the house. In the exact moment I stepped over the threshold, the string of my new crystal Buddha necklace broke and fell off my neck. The glass beads and Buddha Head hit the floor, shattering and scattering.

What was going on?! There had been no pull on the necklace from anything, nor had the string been coming apart in any shape or manner. Hearing the glass pieces drop, everyone turned, and I knew I was in for an extraordinary dowsing. Not even Ange's pre-dowsing form could have prepared me for the

Songline of the Heart / Shelley Darling

strong, dense energy I was experiencing. Ange's husband, Dave, later shared the following with me:

> "*I do remember when your necklace [broke] where the two negative vortexes were...I hardly slept at all [that night], worrying and wondering what was going on. I was watching you and the rods were spinning, and we were standing around the ring, and all of a sudden you became really overcome. I saw you physically, as if you got really woozy, something really powerful was going on. That was what told me that particular spot was very powerful. Something was really overpowering you.*"

When things settled down, and we had cleared the pieces of my necklace up off the floor, I placed myself in the center of the home and began the assessment. I explained the relationship between geopathic stress lines, the home, and our bodies. Ange looked on with amazement as she remembered all her family's past health issues.

The rods revealed that there was a QI line, and it was specifically for Dave. A QI line is a dynamic field of energy, neither positive nor negative, that is identified by the movements of the dowsing rods. It indicates to the dowsing specialist a specific item or place in the home or office that is acting as a conduit for an individual's personal transformation. In other words, it brings a personal message from the house so the individual, revealing their attraction to the home.

At the same time, it is a direct link to any unresolved spiritual or emotional blocks a person has that need to be resolved and integrated to allow for the evolution and full potential of each family member's clarity of purpose. The object or location identified by a QI line reveals a message to the person connected with it. They are invited to pause and feel into the experience, and to allow an inner revelation to arise. The process of finding a QI line may raise up old memories that have been keeping the person stuck in an old pattern. In addition, upon resolution, the energy usually dissipates, and the individual experiences an insight, as they stand taller in the truth of their being.

QI lines are among my favorite occurrences as they require me to directly implement my knowledge of emotional integration with the dowsing. Dave's QI line would be one of the last things we would address over the two days of dowsing.

The children became more comfortable as I explained what I was doing with my dowsing rods. My attention was called to Ange and Dave's son, who was sitting cross-legged and silent. I asked the children if there was anything they wanted to share. Lifting his head, the boy began quietly sharing that ever since they had moved to this house, he had felt there was a ghost chasing him. He said he was worried that if he didn't move fast enough the ghost would come into his body.

Completing the Dowsing

Given the size of the home and the work needed with the children, I realized I would not be able to complete the dowsing in one day. This is not unusual. I have learned from experience, for example, that if someone is elderly or ill it's generally important not to try to finish the house in one day. The dowsing rods will confirm what's needed for each case. In the end, I only closed the negative vortexes and cleared the geopathic stress on the first day, as that would be enough of an energetic shift for the family to integrate. I was not surprised when we discovered there were two negative vortexes exactly at the spot at the door where my favored necklace had frightfully shattered.

It was a joy to work with Slim Spurling's copper tensor rings, and I was thrilled I could easily get them in Australia thanks to Peter, my new wizardly friend. After completing the curing of the geopathic stress lines, I left my two rings in the shape of a Vesica Pisces at the front door overnight. Back at the hotel, I felt a nudge to call my friend, Nikki, who lived in Bay View, in the northern beaches area of Australia. We had met in a synchronistic way a year earlier at a workshop in California. She had flown in from Australia on her way to England to see her family. Nikki was a friend of my first client, who lived in San Diego.

By a wild set of circumstances, we all decided to go to a weekend workshop focused on healing Post Traumatic Stress Disorder (PTSD). When I learned there was a woman coming from Australia, I felt lured by Spirit to meet her. Once again, "magic" unfolded as I discovered she lived in Bay View, five minutes from where my daughter lived in Church Point!

What I hadn't known until I called her was that Nikki was a medium. When she answered the phone, she immediately asked, *"What's going on with the dowsing?"* I was stunned, as she shared with me how the night before the spirit of an Aboriginal boy came to her for help finding his dad, that he was stuck, and wanted to go home. Apparently, she worked with him and helped him go to the light. He revealed to her he was going to leave me a gift. He shared something about a bone.

At that moment, I had an intuition that the Aboriginal boy who had been looking for his father and the ghost chasing Ange's son, were one and the same. *Was it possible he had just been trying to get the attention of Ange's son?* I shared what had happened in the dowsing that day and told Nikki I was feeling some anger was still being held in the land. I had done some research and knew there had been fighting before the time of the two previous owners, when the Aboriginal people had still been residing there.

Heading back the next morning I wasn't sure what to expect. Happily, I found the energy seemed to be calming down, the kids were playing peacefully, and everyone seemed to have had a good night's sleep. There was one more thing to focus on and that was Dave's QI Line.

A keen sense of awareness, skill, and intuition are necessary to allow the information to be revealed when working with a QI line. No cures are placed, but a high level of embodied integration work and experience is necessary to fully support people who, like Dave, have a QI line in their house. And all parties need to allow time for the information to rise in the individual's consciousness before it can be healed.

Exploring Dave's QI Line

Inside the family gathered around the open glassed-in living room. It had a 12-foot bookshelf along one wall that was filled with books and pictures. Dave stood a bit to the side, near the kitchen, with his hands crossed above his heart. He was alert and had an inquisitive look on his face as I described the process.

Asking my guides to show me the whereabouts of Dave's QI line through my rods, I was immediately directed to the bookshelf. Some QI lines may take me up and down stairs, but here there was no sense of question or query in what they were telling me.

Simply following the rods, I walked towards the middle of the bookshelf, *but to what?* Amidst all the books, the pictures of the kids, and a few artsy items, the rods kept pointing to a stately trophy, standing alone. I slowed down and allowed space for everyone in the room to breathe. I scanned the shelves, turned to the onlookers and asked whose trophy this was.

Dave smiled and spoke out, acknowledging it was his. He was proud of his trophy, which he had received following a championship rugby win for kids under the age of seven. I then I asked him if there was anything else on the shelf that belonged to him. His arms dropped open, and he came in closer as his body energy contracted slightly. He shook his head and sheepishly responded "no."

Everyone waited quietly for me to continue. On the shelf, there were pictures of everyone else in the family, but none of Dave. He was a dedicated man with a big heart, though as I found out, he subconsciously didn't feel he was living his life purpose. The guidance from the rods spoke of his need to take up more space in his family and they pointed to the opportunity for him to step into his power. When I asked him how he nurtured himself, he couldn't answer.

Every dowsing is totally confidential which creates a safe space. Dave felt safe to share that he was unsure of his own spirituality, and he said he had in the past had a spiritual experience, yet had felt so uncertain about what it meant that he chose to keep it to himself. After a pause, which allowed him to drop deeper into the space, I asked him what brought him joy. Immediately his eyes lit up and he said, "Surfing!"

On the spot, we could feel his energy begin to shift. I now encouraged him to seek out that which was meaningful to him, focusing on the need for him to create the space for his joy, amidst his family life. I also urged him to consider having a private session with Sanna in order to nurture his relationship with Spirit. Unbelievably, one week later, I learned Dave was taking up yoga with Ange, and had decided to get up at sunrise each day to have some alone time to surf.

As the dowsing was coming to completion, I checked the smaller room the two daughters shared, and helped remedy a few last issues. The kids gingerly followed me from room to room, as we completed the final step in the dowsing protocol, which involved lifting the large energy tensor rings from floor to ceiling, thoroughly energetically brushing clean the corners of each wall. I invited the children to think of a color they would like to add to the home, explaining a bit about the relationship of color to its energetic frequency and how they could amplify the energy by visualizing pillars of light in the corners of their home.

Over the years I had learned the power of color frequencies, reading my favorite book, the *Seven Sacred Flames*, and working with my dear friend, Ellen Epstein,[66] a visionary artist and an Emotional Freedom Life Coach. After a profound personal experience swimming with dolphins, she had begun creating images and stained-glass sculptures designed to uplift humanity. She uses unique color-coded geometric mandalas in her work to awaken Spirit, raise Consciousness, help people remember their true nature while enhancing their wellbeing, and activate joy in the world. Ellen had kindly shared with me a knowledge of color frequencies I now apply to the dowsing of a home. She continues to intuitively design stained glass sculptures that create a balanced, high vibrational energy flow for the home and outdoor landscapes.[67]

Returning to the living room, I explained how family members can energetically alleviate any remaining obstructions in their physical and emotional body by lifting the large tensor rings over their heads and bringing it down over their body.

The tensor ring creates what I love to call a "portable positive vortex" that can sense where there are energetic obstructions. When used in this manner it may become noticeably heavier. Holding it steady will, within a short amount of time, alleviate any dense energy, allowing one's body to rebalance and harmonize itself. This is a wondrous experience for a dowsing practitioner as the ring will feel heavy and won't seem to want to move when it reaches a place on a person's body where emotions are being held. Holding the ring in that area causes the energy to shift, and the individual will sense a feeling of upliftment. Most often they will take a large breath or sigh as a result of the physical relief they feel.

---

[66] Ellen Epstein, "My Journey," *Living Supernaturally*, www.livingsupernaturally55.com/about-ellen..
[67] Global Glass Scapes and Global Joy Garden, *Global Glass Scapes*, www.globalglassscapes.com.

Catalyst for Change

The first thing in the context of time, to share is that we were in the process of healing our son who had a form of Autism and we were working with the Sunrise program in Massachusetts. He was the catalyst of change for us. It was a stressful time, and we had the realization that there was much more to life than what we were planning. When Ange invited you, as always, she knows when something is right, so here, too, I trusted her implicitly.

When I first met you, Shelley, I lived behind the scenes. When Ange invited you, I trusted you right away. I remember that day you came, at that time I had my own business [and was] working very hard, almost my default function; it was safe, and I was producing things a bit behind the scenes. That day I was planning to greet you and let you do your thing. I had always been sensitive to the world and always aware of spirits around. I realized we are sharing the space with energy we can't see, and it was energy I couldn't see that was the scary part, because it was very real. Now I am aware and I'm just as sensitive, but I understand more what's going on. I guess you were one of the first people I met that was living in this other world, and who lived a life of connection to the Field.

Before the dowsing I was contracted, managing my world, and controlling my experience and maybe [it] was so frightening [that] I couldn't control it, [that] I bunkered in; in many ways, not every way. The moment I saw the rods spinning, it was almost physical evidence [of] let's call it 'the field' for now. And when the rod did point to that trophy on the shelf that belonged to me, it was absolute truth for me. The way that you put it, how big I was being in my family and how big I was being in myself. I have always believed I was not demonstratively big, yet I was very powerful even behind the scenes in that contracted state, I was still doing lots of meaningful work within my family, powerful although not demonstrative.

—Dave Bambach

Songline of the Heart / Shelley Darling

Sitting on the porch alone after the dowsing, integrating the experience, I found myself looking out to the distance, far beyond the house to an upper meadow. Ange was dismayed as contractors would soon start building a plethora of new houses in the field above her home.

In the far distance, I was overjoyed to see a horse standing, switching its tail back and forth. Having a great love of horses, I jumped up and ran out to the fence that separated Ange and Dave's land from the large field.

As I got close, I was perplexed in discovering that in fact there was no horse…only a giant dark gray, metal barrel. I was stupefied, as I knew I had absolutely seen a horse's tail moving back and forth, swatting flies, or so I had assumed. I stretched my neck out and looked up and down the fence line. From where I was standing, I saw something hanging from the barbed wire. Cautiously, I strolled down the tall fence, thinking that what I was seeing was a branch caught in the fence. I was dumbfounded when I got close enough to realize what I had sighted was the full tail of a horse.

I have seen horses moseying up to fences to rub their tails, and I know sometimes a few hairs get trapped in the barbwire. This was NOT that. I began to unravel it and almost passed out. Not only was there a full three-foot tail hanging from this fence but there was an entire four-inch chunk of tailbone attached. I took a breath and cleared the last wiry hairs from the fence, and then meandered back to the house to sit outside on the porch.

I held the old dry bone and shook as I felt a pulsing sensation coming from it. Not believing what I was experiencing, I quickly put it down on the deck, and picked up a nearby pen. No, it definitely was not pulsing. I reached for the horse's tailbone once again and shuddered: it was still pulsing with energy.

At that moment, I remembered my conversation with Nikki the night before. *Could it be this was the gift the Aboriginal boy was speaking of?*

Holding the bone up to the sun, I took a deep breath, and sensing the magnitude of the interweaving of dimensions, offered deep gratitude to the land and the elementals for the gift the boy had left.

Though I knew in my heart the tail belonged with Dave, I have to admit I wanted to keep this powerful talisman for myself. It brought back to me my relationship with horses, not only the physical connection, but also the fact that the horse was a spirit animal, or totem.

Some people consider a horse's tail to be a "magical charm," an energetic tool that has been used by shamans for eons. I believe it is imbued with a particular vibrational energy that holds a spiritual connection with the Divine. The pulsating object I held represented my connection to Spirit and validated for me the work I was here to do in the world.

Speaking Truth

Ange invited me to come back to Mullumbimby, one month later, to teach a dowsing class. Her friend, Najma—whose Aboriginal name meant "songline"—invited me to stay at her lovely home, which was situated just below Mount Chincogan, a place sacred to the Aboriginals.

Visiting back at Ange and Dave's, I was delighted as I could feel the radiating energy now exuding from Dave's body. His presence had shifted in such a short time, and he was so magnetic! I was deeply touched over how he had taken the whole experience of dowsing to heart.

After our time together, Dave experienced a personal empowerment training session with Sanna. Months later he said to me:

"I have been realizing how you can use language for your greater outcome when you start to consciously choose your words and speak only what you want to come into manifestation. Word patterns, such as, "I can't," or "I want," I simply never say...anymore. Want to me means, I don't have. Consciously choosing your words, you begin to use the muscle of choice in your life. You always have a choice, 100% of the time. Looking back at myself in the beginning, before the dowsing, I didn't have that clarity and conviction. Now I do and [I] much more easily speak my truth."

Dave's energy was now vibrating at a totally different frequency. Though fearful in the beginning, he had chosen to step into his power, wisdom, and joy. His presence and words that day were simple, yet astounding, and now he was committed to living from empowered choice, offering me something new to contemplate.

Chapter 11: The Divine Spark

What set the Cathars apart from other Gnostic sects was the ritual of the Consolumentum. This ceremony, a transmission of immense vivifying energy, was said to inspire those who witnessed it. This energy transmission allowed the spirit to continue its ascent towards the Light in safety, to evolve or, if the recipient was on the threshold of death, to make the leap into the cosmos. To not fear death was a crowning achievement.

—Judith Mann, *The Legend of the Cathars*

Returning to the Northern Beaches, I resumed my sessions with Sanna. I learned about a sacred rite referred to as the Consolumentum, which was a transformation-related practice offered in medieval France and performed by Cathar initiates called "Perfecti." It allowed a person's soul to reunite with the "Good God" and it was usually performed immediately before a person's death. Something struck home for me. I was captivated to learn this initiation had at the time been offered in limestone caves and it leveraged the strong "telluric currents"[68] therein found. Telluric currents, otherwise known as Earth Currents, are electric currents of energy that flow in the Earth's crust and mantle, and under the sea.

    Entranced by the Cathars, and divinely sparked by the depth of their devotional world, I humbly asked Sanna if it I could experience the Consolumentum before I left Australia. Sanna had dedicated eight years to the deeper knowledge and

---

[68] "Telluric Currents," Ancient Wisdom www.ancient-wisdom.com.

mysteries of the Consolumentum and it had been the prime directive in her daily meditations to continually ask her guidance to assist her to completely embody a true understanding of it.

Sanna researched and explored everything she could about the Cathar perspective on the Consolumentum. Almost nothing had been written about it, and so her understanding of it had come to her as an offering from Spirit, which she described as a transmission. I learned she had to obtain an advanced level of Spiritual maturity in order to offer this rite to others. The illuminating experience of my sessions with Sanna, and the inner freedom and joy that resulted from them, had helped me widen into my true nature. There was an integration of self and Spirit involved, and a transmission of love and truth. Sanna's commitment to assisting others in their spiritual evolution was a huge undertaking yet she had offered the Consolumentum to only one other woman I knew of at that point.

Sanna had started on her own spiritual path when she had been very young, when she had had a first-hand experience of Jesus. She had felt this experience was beyond her own understanding of Christianity, so she asked her minister one day what he thought had really happened.

Without investing any time in seeking the details of her experience, he told her she needed to read the Bible more. Frustrated, Sanna continued her search for understanding. Although she first chose to study the Bible as literature, she knew there was more to it than what the words seemed to indicate. She continued her inner questioning, exposing herself to other paths such as Buddhism and Hinduism. She eventually began experiencing a "felt" sense of Jesus that did not seem to be religious. She also experienced a visceral feeling of love that seemed to be communicated through a direct experience of guidance that she began to know as the Cathar energy; beyond that she experienced a relationship with Spirit as an active energy in her life, and the lives of all who sought it.

Being a student at heart, Sanna pursued more information. Along with other epiphanies, she had a mystical experience on a visit to Assisi in Italy. Sitting in silence she felt a direct awakening, where she realized within the silence that she knew herself as one, no longer separate from all that Is.

In our first sessions Sanna had hinted there was an opportunity awaiting me. After a few more sessions, and some time spent traveling, and "marinating in my own frequency," as Sanna put it, I was now standing in the frequency of my soul with a "flavoring of Spirit Consciousness." I was open and ready for the next phase of my spiritual development. Sanna noted that some people tend to stop seeking at this point in their journey. Sanna agreed to be my guide in the process of the Consolumentum, which would take place over three sessions. At one point, she spoke quietly and with a reverence my heart knew to be true. Though I didn't know what was in store, as if in preparing for a sacred ceremony, I felt the importance of taking some quiet time in Nature before our first session. Listening deeply, I took time to meditate and journal the thoughts and feelings that were arising. I had to earn it; I couldn't just arrive at it. I had to be clear and clean.

A Map into Awareness

Sanna went on to say that, "The Consolumentum is a map through and into awareness. Only the Perfecti offered the Consolumentum in the past. This frequency of love, that's the power point."

Honoring Sanna's request to keep these sessions confidential, I won't disclose the details of them here. However, I can say that the Consolumentum gently and powerfully expanded my experience of unconditional love, which I now refer to as "undefined love," a love without boundaries, a level of deeper intimacy, with what many call the beloved within. Rumi, a 13th Century mystic poet wrote,

"Your task is not to seek for love, but merely to seek and find all the barriers within yourself that you have built against it."

    I had never experienced anything like this before. My thoughts reeled as I considered meeting myself as the beloved and being met in a potential union with a significant other. It required me to open myself to the vulnerabilities, disillusionment, and fear that had kept me separated from the truth of my own being. It was as if I were refining silken threads of joy that had never been brushed to the surface of my Self. Something was softening within me as I experienced each session with Sanna. I felt a sense of equanimity, and felt cellularly lit, as though a hundred suns were shining through the luminous silky-smooth layers of what felt like the deepest love possible; I felt whole.

    With joy and gratitude in my heart, I was now ready to leave Australia and return to my home in California. I had recovered my strength, and I was thriving in the knowledge that the "songline of my heart" was the only navigational instrument I needed. Feeling empowered, and with joy as my compass, I was ready to move forward. I was, like Dave, "100% in choice."

    A week before I was scheduled to leave Australia, I met with Sanna, one last time. In our last few minutes, she looked me in the eyes and said, *"Look for the clues you left yourself."* I didn't fully understand at the time, yet her message instilled in me an inclination to watch for signals and listen to the guidance that had indeed been supporting the evolution of my soul. I knew that what we feel as chaos is actually the recalibration of energies moving into their highest order, although that is sometimes hard to see at the time. And I became ever more alert to the subtle movements of energy, which constantly dance in every moment, like sunlight sparkling on water.

    Sanna's pearls of wisdom continue to guide me even to this day...

Part III
A Shift in Perspective

The Sacred Golden Ray Attunement

Begin by bringing your attention to your heart.
Slowly take a few deep oceanic breaths...inhaling, breathing in fully, pausing, and exhaling gently and easily. *(Gentle being the key word. Your conscious inhale is your "YES" to the Universe!)* With your exhale, choose to release the bearing weight of mass consciousness. Take a moment to call in all aspects of yourself to be fully present. Soften your body as you open to receive all the Universe, God, has to offer.

Now bring your attention to your "Joy" Point (J-Spot for short), located a full arm's-length above your head, otherwise known to some, as your Soul Star or 8th Chakra. Envision a radiant crystalline, golden light energy flowing from above your J-Spot, down through the central column of your body, or Prana-tube, around your spinal column) Imagine seeing this sparkling light filtering through your cells, filling and expanding out beyond your entire body. Feel the activation of this energy as it shines forth as a radiant beacon of light.

Quietly, say to yourself, "I AM the Light; The Light I shall remain. I AM Here Now" bringing yourself fully present.
Imagine a violet flame moving as a spinning vortex field of light, spiraling up from the earth, clockwise, moving through the center of your body, simultaneously, coming down through the top of your crown, interconnecting within the sacred chamber of your heart. Feel this energy radiate outside your body. This violet flame has the power to clear negative energies, past life conditioning, or limiting belief structures.

At this time, request and connect with the Ancestors of the land, the Council of Light, the Angels and Archangels, your Dowsing Guides, Animal Totems, Elementals, the Deva of the land, and any other benevolent beings that you wish to call in. Honor and offer your gratitude for their presence.

Quietly request: If there is any information for the highest good of all, please bring it forward now..."
The Violet Flame is the integration of a Rose and a Sapphire Blue ray of light, so begin by visualizing a ray or bubble of Sapphire Blue energy around you. The frequency of this energy induces great power and strength, and acts as a protective filter for any disparate or discordant energy. Now envision a Rose ray, bubble or light around you, feel it expanding fully around your body and up and around the Sapphire Blue ray. See this ray expand out towards the cosmos. Open your heart to receive this frequency of universal love, compassion, and Divine connection.

Return your attention to your J-Spot and envision a Golden Merkaba, spinning three feet above your head as it gathers light and information from all directions of the Universe. Feel the magnificence, movement, radiance and showering energy of this light. Know in your heart that you are the fulfillment and joy-full manifestation of universal love, within and around you. Choose to Pause. Immerse yourself in the beauty of the silence, receiving any messages for the highest good of all.

To complete the Sacred Golden Ray Attunement: Connect the palms of your hands together, placing them over your eyes, as you feel the crystalline energy moving between your hands and head. This creates a full circuit and whole connection to the Universal force of Creation. Gently open your eyes, knowing you can reconnect to this field of resonance anytime, especially when dowsing.
– **Shelley Darling**

Chapter 12:   Call to Presence

> *Dowsing is an ancient science and evolutionary tool that allows us to gather information not available to our conscious mind. We may have an intuitive sense of not feeling comfortable in a particular house or place, but not be sure of the reason why. Golden Light Dowsing trains us to consciously differentiate the energies present and to harmonize these through copper, crystal, and intentional cures. This harmonization can resolve health issues, relationship conflicts, lack of heart resonance and issues of financial flow. It is a journey beyond the five senses that brings visibility to that which is invisible.*
>
> **—Julie Armstrong,** Canberra, AU

I prepared to bring closure to my three-month Australian journey. My visa was ending and, as I had already extended it a month; it was time to go home.

I was physically stronger and feeling emotionally stable, and—more than that—I had come to embody great joy and inner peacefulness. Following the breadcrumbs, or golden nuggets of my synchronized experiences, I humbly turned my gratitude inward. It is easier to offer our gratitude to others, and the gifts they bring to us, yet as important is the return of love to oneself.

Trusting my intuitive guidance, combined with the embodied knowing of the benevolence of God, the universal presence of love, regenerated my Spirit. I wanted to jump up and give a great shout out! Aliveness rippled through my blood. This communion with our body, this holy temple as a full circuit of health, was my greatest achievement.

Songline of the Heart / Shelley Darling

Through Sanna's supportive sessions, I had regained a sense of wholeness. Now feeling clear and focused, I was ready to return to meet the unresolved circumstances and the completion of my marriage. I felt a renewed power, and a growing joy in life. I felt spiritually supported and now, through the dowsing, I felt energetically connected to the Ancestors of this land. Continued gratitude and appreciation expanded my heart as I prepared to return to the United States.

As life would have it, literally the day before leaving for the USA, a good friend of Sanna's, Kat, requested I return to Avalon to dowse her home. Kat lived in a naturally landscaped, cape-like home in the far northern corner of Avalon, high above a cliff that angled down to a beautiful sandy cove surrounded by an expansive view of the ocean. The evening before the dowsing was to take place, I received an endearing call from a woman in Canberra named Julie. She had heard about my integrative type of dowsing and although she lived three hours away, she insisted I couldn't leave Australia without teaching her how to dowse! Although I kept telling her there was no way for this to happen, the delightful lilt in her voice and her sheer determination to learn moved my heart. She said she would do anything to learn and would even drive the three hours between us to meet me.

At first, I thought I could possibly squeeze in an hour-long lesson before I had to leave for Kat's place, but then an idea arose: I could ask Kat if she would mind if Julie audited the dowsing of her home. Kat generously agreed and Julie arrived the next morning within minutes of us starting. She was like a glass of champagne, bubbling over in delight, and smiling like a Cheshire cat, as she told Kat about our conversation of the previous day.

Julie explained she had had an initial experience of dowsing with a member of the Dowsing Society in Britain but she hadn't felt ready to do it herself.

"After a session with Najma Ahern—a notable cranial sacral therapist—she told me how excited she was because she had just met a woman named Shelley Darling who had just come from America and [she] had learned an incredible way of dowsing. Without hesitation, I said, 'I want to do it too!' When I learned Shelley was leaving for the US the following day I said, 'You can't leave until you teach me dowsing!'"

Standing all together outside at the front of Kat's house, we collectively attuned the house, a process I had used prior to dowsing every home or business in Australia. The Sacred Golden Ray Attunement[69] is one I had developed through years of meditation, dowsing wisdom, heart integration, and guidance.

The Golden Ray frequency features in a book I've mentioned previously, *The Seven Sacred Flames*[70] by Aurelia Louise Jones. I explained to the ladies that an attunement is used prior to a dowsing to charge and strengthen our personal energy field, so we become clear conduits for the energy. It also sets the frequency of love and protects us as dowsers, so we don't take on any of the unbalanced or negative energies that might be residing in the home or land we are dowsing. We use it to open a home and let the land know who we are and what our intention is, and to connect with the ancestral, elemental and Spirit of place.

I shared that practicing the Sacred Golden Ray Attunement daily will enhance your capacity to be fully present, balanced, relaxed, and connected. This is a spectacular way to begin your day, and you can add it to your other meditations, or simply use it to prepare yourself to dowse.

---

[69] Sacred Golden Ray Attunement by Shelley Darling
 Free download: www.evolutionarydowsing.com/free-resources
[70] Aurelia Louise Jones, *Seven Sacred Flames,* (Mount Shasta Light Publishing, June 27, 2007)

Songline of the Heart / Shelley Darling

The Sacred Golden Ray Attunement is used as an invocation to not only set your personal energy field, but also to bring luminous light into your home and the land upon which it sits; it can also be used for an office, school, or community environment.

With the completion of the Golden Ray Attunement, I invited Kat to state a clear intention for the dowsing. I watched as she looked at her home. She closed her eyes and stated, with focus, the intention to align her business with her heart's calling, while creating a peaceful, flowing relationship with her partner. Julie listened quietly as I shared with her the wisdom of facilitation required when working with an individual, a home, and the land.

We took a break for a few minutes so I could go over how to use the dowsing rods. I had Julie hold the brass rods at heart level and invited her to relax her grip while bringing her attention up above her head to what I call the "Joy Point." I coined this phrase after having an ecstatic experience while dowsing. From then on, I loved sharing the concept as it relieves any density and tension that might be in the space.

The ladies laughed hysterically, as I explained that, true, we as women are aware that we have a G-Spot, and isn't it wonderful that all human beings, including men, have a Joy Point, or as I like to bring attention to as the "J-Spot." Located just above the head, sometimes known as the Soul Star or crown Chakra—the Eighth Chakra point—about a foot-and-a-half above the crown point. Bringing our attention to this "J-Spot" while we are dowsing stops us from getting stuck in our mental mind and feeling so serious, all of which leads to the frustration of the dowsing rods not working. In a sense we are creating an energetic plumb line from the Heart of Heaven, down through our physical heart, to the Heart of the Earth. This alignment creates a full circuit of golden light energy as we become a clear flowing channel for the incoming information.

Songline of the Heart / Shelley Darling

Julie caught on quickly. I showed her how to hold the rods a few degrees below parallel, allowing them to move easily to reveal the answers to her questions. I moved to the center of Kat's living room to assess the house's energy. I discovered that Kat's energy was higher than that of the house, and explained how, inevitably, when someone was feeling stuck in life, there was a good chance the house's energy was extremely low. It's like there is a glass ceiling you keep trying to rise beyond: no matter how much training you do, or how many counseling sessions or workshops you take, you always end up coming home to your house...it will either enhance or limit your outcomes.

Over my years of working with people I have discovered that when a person feels their life is not moving in the direction they would like they blame themselves, and the energy backwashes. They wonder, "What's wrong with me?" One of the most profound realizations I had in my first year of dowsing was that about 50%-60% of the source of a person's stress is related to their house.

As we dowsed Kat's house, we found a major negative vortex outside and six geopathic stress lines in her office that radiated into her sun porch; there were more stress lines in her son's room. We also found a few negative Hartmann and negative Curry Lines. Kat curious, immediately asked for more information. I responded whole-heartedly that in the 1950s Dr. Ernst Hartmann and Dr. Manfred Curry discovered many energy lines that radiated from within the Earth, forming a magnetic field. The Hartmann Grid forms North to South, and East to West, whereas the Curry Grid flows from Northeast to Southwest, and from Northwest to Southeast. As the Earth rotates around its axis, it functions like a generator, forming a grid work of electrically charged energy lines. Places where these energy lines intersect—such as a fuse box, refrigerator, washer-dryer, or even our computer cords—can very often be sources of negative energy.

Although the electric company will tell you that smart meters are safe, years of working with them has convinced me they have a negative radiation output, which is not healthy for the circuitry of our bodies. Smart meters have a dramatic impact on our as well as what is known as "dirty electricity." This is an industry term for dirty power such as that derived from fossil fuels—coal, natural gas, and oil. These all have very serious and harmful consequences. In some individuals, the related health issues show up as insomnia, memory problems, and communication issues.

We headed outside past the closed-in porch and blossoming tree and then followed my rods to a point along the fence about midway down Kat's yard. We weren't surprised to discover a negative vortex there when we saw the tree growing at that spot was bent right over alongside the fence. We could see and feel the dissonant energy around the curving tree. Kat and Julie were awed by how the dowsing rods rapidly spun in a counterclockwise direction, indicating the area was being negatively affected by the energy. We set down a few clear quartz crystals, dug a round three-inch deep hole in the ground—big enough for the small 8-inch copper sacred cubit ring—and placed the crystals in it before covering and packing down the hole.

A year later, on my dowsing journey, I met Katherine Parker, now a dear friend, who through her book "*Resonance Alchemy*" I was introduced to Kum Vita.[71] This is an evocative universal language of Spirit, a sacred language where each syllable has many levels of meaning. It is not meant to describe objects, nor human concepts or experiences, but rather to evoke the omnipresent essence of Spirit. This modality includes the programming of crystals with focused intention through an invocation or an energy mantra in which sacred healing codes are silently repeated.

---

[71] K. Parker, Resonance Alchemy, www.resonancealchemy.com.

Julie tried to check the energy herself and after placing the crystal she was amazed at how her rods now spun fast in a positive clockwise fashion. We cleared the geopathic stress on the outside of the home by walking back and forth from the front to the back, wherever the rods guided us. And we made sure the copper cures were placed parallel to each other when we embedded them into the ground about three or four inches, making sure they wouldn't move in any kind of weather. I no longer use this methodology often, yet it was all I knew at that point, and it worked perfectly.

Problems in the Body's Nervous System

We headed back to the house to clear remaining interference lines and look for places where the Negative Hartmann and Curry Lines[72] might be causing disturbances. When these energy lines come in contact with electrical appliances or an electrical fuse box—or even the green power boxes, which feed a whole neighborhood—they create a negative waveform and can cause severe problems in the body's nervous system resulting in anxiety, panic, Tourette's Syndrome, or even Multiple Sclerosis (MS). The electromagnetic energy becomes polarized, creating dissonance where the negative Hartmann and Curry Lines intersect each other.

Stopping in Kat's office, I took some extra time to share some golden Feng Shui nuggets. Kat's office desk faced a window, which meant her back was to the door. I encouraged her to move her desk into what's called "the command position." Sitting at her desk, facing the door, she would be available to receive the energy as it flowed into the space and this would now allow for a significant positive shift to come into her life.

---

[72] Earth Medicine Alchemy Phase 1 Manual 2013-2021 by Shelley Darling,. Learn More: www.evolutionarydowsing.com.

Moving into Kat's bedroom, I saw her bed was blocking the energy of the door. As I scanned the sunlit room, I noticed there was no headboard on her bed to support her. I began by clearing the interference lines and placed copper Earth Cures in the appropriate places. Next, I calculated Kat's Personal Energy Number (Kua Number[73]) looking to find the best supportive placement of the bed. The Kua number is an additional modality practiced in traditional and classical Feng Shui to help align the energy in the best direction. Kat's bed needed to be moved to the wall opposite its original position. She understood, happily leaving the room to bring in some colorful pillows to act as a headboard until she could find something to her liking. Although I have studied various types of Feng Shui over the years, I continue to consult and work in partnership with Feng Shui Master Deborah Harnett. She honors the Black Hat Sect Tibetan Buddhism School of Feng Shui (BTB) founded by Grand Master Professor Lin Yun.[74] In 1999 she was one of the first Americans to be certified in his protocol in the United States.

Sitting down for a "cuppa" I reminded both Kat and Julie we needed to keep drinking a lot of water during the dowsing process as it helps the body integrate changes in the energy field. This is important: the vibrational frequency of the environment being dowsed rises as a result of the closing of a negative vortex and a mitigation of geopathic stress, interference lines, and negative Hartmann and Curry lines; your body needs to relax into this higher vibration. For example, someone who lives in a home where there has been a death or a lot of abuse will be accustomed to being on high alert, and their adrenals will likely be drained. If they move to a more sanctuary-type environment, it will take time for their body to relax and integrate the sensations of being truly safe. I remember this being true with foster children who came into

---

[73] Kua number; https://redlotusletter.com/resources.
[74] Deborah Harnett https://www.cinnabardesign.com.

our home when I was growing up. At first, they were in a state of high alert, and it would take at least a month, or more, for them to feel safe.

Julie had now filled her notebook, and I was enjoying her fascination and delight with every discovery she made. She asked myriad questions about dowsing and thanked Kat and me again for allowing her to be part of the experience.

During the break, I was thrilled to get to know Julie and learn that she was a dedicated student of Rudolph Steiner,[75] the founder of Waldorf Education and steward for the biodynamic approach to agriculture. I was impressed, when I learned that sometime in the late 1800's Steiner professed that western civilization would gradually bring destruction to itself and the Earth if it did not begin to develop an objective understanding of the spiritual world and its interrelationship with the physical world. Julie also shared she had taught handicrafts for years at a Waldorf School; she lived in Canberra, the capital city of Australia and through her both Kat and I found out the city of Canberra had been built with the understanding of Sacred Geometry.

Apparently, Canberra had been designed by American landscape architect Walter Burley Griffin and his wife, Marion. Both had originally lived in the United States, and, like Steiner, they believed in living in harmony with Nature. Walter was an advocate of design in harmony with Nature, while Marion was an accomplished artist influenced by mysticism and spirituality. I listened intently as Julie described how the capital had been built on land that was riddled with caves, sink holes and large earth mounds. Walter Burley Griffin once said, "I am what may be termed a naturalist in architecture. I do not believe in any school of architecture. I believe in architecture that is the

---

[75] "Who Was Rudolf Steiner?" Biodynamic Association, https://www.biodynamics.com/steiner.

logical outgrowth of the environment in which the building in mind is to be located." [76]

Julie also spoke of geomancy which, according to Alex Stark,[77] is the study of the energies of the Earth. The word is derived from the Greek words Gaia, meaning the Earth Goddess, and manteia, meaning study or divination.

Traditionally associated with sacred craft, geomancy today takes many forms, from the simple pursuit of dowsing for underground water to the highly complex sacred ritual techniques employed in the enhancement and cultivation of the Earth's subtle yet vital force fields.

Of all the geomancy traditions around the world, perhaps the best known is Feng Shui, although geomancy features prominently in the architecture of ancient Britain, Greece, and the Roman Empire. There is some evidence geomantic principles were applied to the layout of newer cities like Washington, DC.

Julie asked me to clarify the difference between Feng Shui and dowsing and I explained Feng Shui is an ancient art and science, developed more than 5,000 years ago in Asia. It's the study of Nature as it influences our life. Translated into English, it means "Wind and Water." The universal principles provide guidelines to harness the powerful connection between our own personal energy and that of our environment.

As Deborah Harnett notes, Feng Shui, "is a 5000-year-old Tibetan method of managing one's life thru conscious awareness. [Western] BTB Feng Shui's energy creates new beginnings; repairs existing challenges and delivers balanced positivity by adjusting our environments and adjusting ourselves. It awakens a clear view of what is needed by

---

[76] Anonymous, "American Designs Splendid New Capital for Australia," New York Times, June 2, 1912.

[77] Alex Stark, alexstark.com/services/geomancy.

understanding our surrounds as a perfect expression of our spiritual and psychological states."[78]

Feng Shui and dowsing are two very different ancient arts, yet they both work to harmonize the energy in our environment, complimenting and supporting one another. They both work with visible and invisible energy, yet each works in specific ways. Feng Shui manifests and heals the flow of energy as it moves around and within buildings. It creates balance with a focus on prosperity, health, happiness, and fortune. Evolutionary Dowsing not only works with stressful Earth energies affecting our homes and land, such as geopathic stress, interference lines and negative vortexes; as a whole-system modality, it is inclusive of personal transformation as well as the larger planetary realm of unseen energies such as entities, faeries, and elementals. As I said before, Feng Shui and Dowsing *"woven together create a portal to heaven!"*

Heavenly, Human, and Earthly Fortune

Classical Feng Shui believes in a trinity of elements—Heaven Luck, Human Luck and Earth Luck—affect our destiny. As a Feng Shui consultant, I felt the word "fortune" clarified how dowsing, combined with Feng Shui, affects what I like to call the manifestation of Heaven on Earth. By "Heaven on Earth," I mean the ways in which we can enhance and amplify greater harmony and balance on Earth.

Heavenly Fortune is the spark we are granted at birth. It speaks to our potential and the innate gifts with which we transition into this life. It relates to the placement of stars and planets at the time of our birth and connects us with our Human Destiny. We can connect with this aspect of ourselves through Meditation, Prayer, Inner Journeying, and Chanting. Exploring our relationship to our Heavenly Fortune can link us with the golden thread of our Soul's Purpose.

---

[78] Deborah Harnett, Cinnabar design, www.cinnabardesign.com.

Human Fortune governs a person's virtues, education, and actions and it can be influenced through positive thoughts and embracing our feelings and responses through our actions. It is the element we can have the most control over to become more resonant and positive in our current and past lives. Human fortune can be developed and elevated through empowerment practices, education, conscious breathing, yoga, and exercise.

Earth Fortune refers to factors represented by the forces of Nature. Consider that we are gifted with all the resources we will ever need to survive here on Earth. What's more, given we understand that the nature of life itself is always evolving into its highest potential, we also, have the potential to thrive as a unified community.

Our bodies are subject to Earth energy influences, and both natural and artificial stressors. When we build our homes without understanding these energies, we create containers that can either support or deplete our life force. The form of dowsing I practise can optimize environmental energy, creating a sustainable and harmonious habitat involving Nature outdoors and our inner landscape, as well.

With Julie satisfied and smiling, I moved to complete the dowsing of Kat's house. I checked back in with the energy of the house, and Kat and Julie's jaws dropped in the final checking of the energy, as the rods spun wildly positive with no hesitation; the energy in the house soared! In laughter, celebration, and joy we danced at the shift in Kat's home.

Julie had a few more hours available before she had to leave, so we decided to drive around the peninsula, through Mona Vale and past Church Point to the Ku-ring-gai Chase National Park. The preserve is the Aboriginal site of the Ku-ring-gai people and provides access to wondrous Aboriginal rock engravings.

> **Ku-ring-gai Chase National Park**
>
> *As you come in from the main Elvina Track, the path forks into two trails, both of which lead to the engraving site. If you take the left-hand fork you'll find a pair of wallabies engraved in a rock across the path, which, it is said, is a warning that you are approaching a male initiation site.*
>
> *If you take the right fork, then when you reach the main site, you will see a giant whale to your right, and an emu and the Baime/Daramulan creator spirit, together with his emu-wife, to your left. Walking down the sheet of rock, look for shields, wallabies, fish, eels, and other shapes that are not easily classified. On your left, you'll see a line of rock a few centimeters wide, which is presumably natural, crossed by several lines, which appear to be manmade. Its been suggested that this is a lunar calendar.*

As we approached the engravings, we worked a bit more on Julie's dowsing as I demonstrated how to use the rods for land healing. For Julie, this represented the awakening of a memory, and her ancient connection to dowsing. At that moment, she had an "Aha" realization and exclaimed: "Wow, this is my work! I feel such a clear sense [that] this is something that is really important in my life, and although it has been such a brief time together, I feel the dowsing is really important."

Julie passionately continued practicing her dowsing after I left Australia and I was in awe watching how she seemed to be called to clear what she called "massacre sites." The truth was that this was the beginning of a long-time friendship between us. At that time, she was one of my most dedicated students and we bonded, continually sharing our dowsing experiences in service to the Earth and humanity.[79]

---

[79] Ku-ring-gai Chase National Park; www.nationalparks.nsw.gov.au

Clearing Houses

I couldn't wait to [dowse] peoples' homes, [and] in some ways, I was a little bit over-enthusiastic and probably dowsed [the] houses [of people who] weren't ready for it. I just couldn't wait to clear everyone's house...In that journey it has been so fascinating because every house is so different.

In terms of dowsing, I feel like for me it's opened up this connection that was there...and really tapping into energies that we are not conscious of—but subconsciously I think there is an awareness—and...you start to connect with the land, and feel the living energy, and pay respect to the elders and custodians, and be aware of the guardian spirits of place. Once you start...with practice you can feel a shift and there is an alignment and openness, and there is a conversation that starts to happen, [with] this world of aliveness and connection, that is so amazing. It's so amazing.

I created a great big art piece called "See the Land is Dancing," based on the dowsing I had done on each of the mountains surrounding Canberra. It was so exciting discovering that they each had different energies.

I would go to the different places, and ask "show me your energy, show me the positive vortexes." Oh crumbs, I had no idea this was happening. Then I would say "show me where the ley lines are, and where do they connect to?" In Australia, there are books about the Aboriginals following the Songlines—these leylines are the Songlines—and they're very ancient pathways. The Aboriginals were very aware of that energy. So, in many ways, this created a bond so much stronger to the land, and in some ways to indigenous connection.

—Julie Armstrong

Chapter 13: Compass of Joy

We are beginning to see the entire universe as a holographically Interlinked network of energy and information, organically whole and self-referential at all scales of its existence. We and all things in the universe are non-locally connected with each other and with all other things in ways that are unfettered by the hitherto known limitations of space and time.
—**Jude Currivan**

I knew in mere hours, I would be returning to the United States.

Sitting quietly with Kat and Julie on the small ledge behind a parking lot facing out towards Scotland Island, I thought it was fitting I found myself back where I had first begun my healing journey.

Looking out at the calm waters of the bay under a blazing sun, I closed my eyes, as my hands naturally extended out, palms open in gratitude. I slowly clasped them together and cupped my heart. I sensed a genuine warmth arising, and felt my body integrate my journey, through long deep breaths. I reveled in the sense of peace and joy I was feeling. I reveled in remembering the myriad of ways kindness had been bestowed upon me while I had been in Australia.

This journey to wholeness had unfolded in tandem with my growing capacity to be present. I had begun to trust and act on my inner knowing, and to practice bringing my awareness, without judgement, to whatever showed up in the circumstances that came before me. No longer was I in doubt, pain, and confusion.

I knew my journey forward was to listen deeply and make conscious choices aligned with my heart, while standing in the fullest expression of myself.

Now ready to fly back to the States, I was grateful for this time of reflection and pause.

I honored the Ancestors and rejoiced in the awakening my journey had stirred. I felt strong, emotionally grounded and open to the glory of a newly established presence and power. The internal questioning that had almost driven me mad in the beginning of my journey now felt resolved. I knew heading home to face my impending divorce would be challenging, yet I had truly found my compass of joy.

I was sad to leave Heather. Our friendship had grown and taken us far beyond simply mother and daughter, yet I knew I would come back to Australia in the near future. Finally, I slowly sauntered down the boarding ramp, with *The Book of Love* packed away in my suitcase, and boarded the plane. I placed my medium Balance and Harmony copper tensor ring behind my back to help with the man-made Emfs I would be experiencing over the next 14 hours of travel. Taking out my journal, I heard a whispering of questions arising, which seemed to induce a transpersonal state of awareness. I quickly began to write down what came to mind:

What is it that really brings you joy?

What is it that truly nourishes your whole being?

What happened in your life to make you feel and believe you can't have it all?

... And what if joy was meant to be your compass, your guide to everything you ever dreamed of?

The plane taxied down the runway, gathered momentum, and lifted off. At that moment, within the liminal space of what felt like a prolonged pause, I heard, "I am the Resurrection and the Life."

In his two-volume commentary on the New Testament called *The Second Coming of Christ: The Resurrection of the Christ within You,* Paramhansa Yogananda[80] wrote, "When Jesus stated, 'I am the Resurrection and the Life' he means 'I am Christ Consciousness in which Souls rise from a lower state of Consciousness to a higher state of inner development.' When Jesus says, 'I am the Life,' there is no egotism in his voice state of realization, 'My life is one with the Cosmic Life within everything, whereby I feel all living creatures are born out of me and sleep in me.'"

Sitting in contemplation, and listening intently to the subtle whispering of my heart, I reveled in finding the green light to move forward. My journey to Australia, enriched by the reciprocity of connection with the Ancestors, had accelerated the healing and unification of my own life-force with the fecundity of the land.

I had awakened to the very nature of my own knowing. What I now realized, was that working with dowsing and land healing—combined with my sessions with Sanna and influenced by the wisdom of the Cathars—I had experienced an embodied "quickening" of "Christ Consciousness." I was being called to embody my own light and live "The Way of Love."

My life had flourished as my relationship with Spirit Consciousness—supported by my growing trust in the natural world—deepened.

When I looked at it all from this perspective, I found myself asking, "Are our lives really separate from the Nature that we see and participate in every day?" The storms, the calms, the natural formation of gas, which we see as clouds, the rain, and then the sun…This web of life, and the movement of these foundations of energy had been held with the utmost reverence by our Ancestors.

---

[80] Paramhansa Yogananda, *The Second Coming of Christ*, Vol. 1 (Self-Realization Fellowship, 2008), p. xxi-xxvi.

Songline of the Heart / Shelley Darling

They had been described by past civilizations as magical happenings. Were they primitive or did these people understand how to live in harmony and balance with the creative forces of the Universe?

I allowed myself to wander back to the vision I had had years earlier, when I had beheld the crucified Christ over the hot pool at Harbin Hot Springs and then 30 minutes later saw, with unobstructed awareness, His fully resurrected body. Over the past few months, I had experienced an awakening of consciousness, being resurrected from the messy soup of shame, blame, and betrayal, and now feeling like an illuminated butterfly, experiencing a spiritual state of golden emergence.

The City of Angels

After a long flight from Sydney, we landed with a buoyant thump on the tarmac in the City of Angels, Los Angeles. I was ready for the next chapter of my life, one which I knew would feature the official dissolution of my marriage. I strode bravely through the winding path, of the customs line, and was shocked when I saw people in line insanely pushing one another to get through. They had no consideration for the people in front of them. A tall man in a dark coat turned and gave me a disdainful look as I reorganized my luggage in the hope of not being called over by the customs agents. I searched long and hard for the warm smiles I had seen upon landing in Australia but found nothing but grim endurance and misery. For one moment, my head lifted hearing a familiar uplifting lilt of dialogue as two Aussies conversed, and my heart soared.

Driving South to San Diego I would stay once again at "Archi's Acres," the farm belonging to my friend and former dowsing client, Karen. She had kindly invited me to stay in the small apartment above her barn after I had discovered my husband's unfaithfulness. Karen had fiercely supported me then, and I was grateful for her support now.

Songline of the Heart / Shelley Darling

Ready to face the challenge of finding closure with my husband, I invited him to meet me for dinner. I had no expectations around how things would go. I had been away for four months and in my return to wholeness, I was ready to embrace the truth with crystalline clarity so I could move into the next phase of my life. I still had personal belongings in our house and, given my husband's decision to take the business we had built together, I needed to clarify my next course of action. When he had first made the unilateral decision to take over the entire business, I was too sick to think about what to do, and I hadn't been capable of even considering hiring a lawyer. I had been in survival mode and, to the dismay of some of my family members, my need to heal had taken precedence over everything else.

My husband and I planned to meet at a nice restaurant in an attempt to have a peaceful dinner together. Prior to my departure from Australia, I had called to negotiate the use of our car upon my return only to hear him unemotionally and unabashedly tell me I had no car: he'd taken the car we'd been sharing over the years since we'd been married and transferred title to the woman who was now his significant other.

We pulled into the parking lot at the same time. He was driving our green Honda SUV, and I was driving my friend's old station wagon. He was dressed in his usual jeans and a light-colored cotton shirt. Greeting each other somewhat cautiously, we walked in silently together, following our hostess to a round table with a white linen tablecloth situated in a quiet corner of the dining room. Surrounded by dark maroon velvet curtains, I placed my white linen napkin in my lap, as my husband hastily ordered us each a glass of red wine.

I had only one question.

Once the glasses of wine were placed on the table, I calmly asked, *"Do you feel it was acceptable and above-board to place the car in your girlfriend's name?"* His response, without any contemplation, was a definitive "Yes." With that, he excused himself and stopped the Maître d' to ask the way to the bathrooms. Taking an extended breath, I knew, in the magnificence of that moment, I was complete. Unreservedly, and downright *done*. I knew I was no longer willing to give up my joy, not for him or anyone else, ever again.

So how does one sit through a casual dinner after that?

I noticed his hesitancy upon returning to the table. He slowly lowered himself to the chair with barely any eye contact. There was nothing more to say. The stale smell in the air created by the half-moon antique red curtains seemed to get stronger, and sharply stung my nose.

To be honest things became a blur and I do not remember whether we finished ordering or not. My life had taken a turn and the only way was moving forward with grace and dignity. Slowly walking out the door to the parking lot was a stretch, the air hung heavy as we nodded and said good-bye. Picking up his pace, he gingerly headed towards the SUV, and with my back to him I stiffened as the old station wagon door creaked open.

Later that night, after returning from dinner, I sat alone and honored the mystery and magic of my journey. I took out my journal and effortlessly wrote what was moving in my soul. I was neither radiantly happy nor sad. Simply present.

A tumultuous nine months followed my return to California as I devoted myself to preparing for my divorce. I travelled between my home in San Diego and Sarasota, Florida, where my parents—as well as my single daughter, Nina, and two of my grandchildren—lived.

When I had come back to my home in San Diego, there were rent payments overdue, yet I was still hoping for an amicable divorce assisted by a practice of mediation that would serve us both. I spent three entire months studying and getting all the paperwork together to prove the business belonged to both my ex and I, and not just to him.

Point of Presence

Slow down, relax, and always choose love.
Make it your commitment,
No matter what is swirling around you.
Keep your eyes WIDE open
There will be lots that you see,
Engage only with what lights up your Soul.
TRUST with every micro cell of your being
There is heavenly support,
Ask for guidance daily with gratitude.
Express fully with courage and care
Your capacity and skills are expanding every day,
Believe it.
Create with wild enthusiasm
Beauty, love, and grace are your golden essence,
Keep tending the fire.
Joy is not the result of the journey,
It is the process and the way,
Be it.

—**Shelley Darling**

Like Sherlock Homes, I was prepared for the courtroom. I had asked a dear friend to be with me and on the day of mediation we sat together in the waiting room outside the courthouse. Scanning the grayish-green painted cement hallway, we looked at the depressed faces of people passing by, looking eye-to-eye we quietly called in the angels to bring the light and love to this environment.

The entire case came down to one moment: I was alone with the presiding judge, an older man in his late 70s or possible even his 80s, and I had the paperwork to prove my ex-husband had not told the truth to the judge. The judge pushing the papers aside, would not even look. He kept scanning anxiously towards the clock hung high on the opposite wall. Finally turning to me he said saying, "Dear, everyone lies to the judge, don't you know that?" In a hurried manner, he then asked me to make up my mind whether I wanted to take my husband to trial.

I was shocked and asked him for five minutes. I went outside to sit on the icy stone bench with my friend. Months of healing in Australia passed before my eyes, and I remembered the strong feeling I'd had the few days before leaving where nothing mattered more than the imperative of "following my compass of joy." I had learned to listen, trust this evolutionary force in my life, and track this "home frequency." I took a deep breath, turned and nodded to my friend.

Walking back through the door, I was clear and in that final moment, I knew my joy was the only thing that mattered. I paced myself slowly past my husband, whose hands held tight to the edge of another bench a few feet away. His eyes seethed with anger. And with crystal clarity, I let it all go. My life forward was what mattered, and the years it might take going to court to prove my worth to others was, in no time done and dusted...

A few weeks later, having my early morning cup of Jasmine tea, I was exuberantly surprised when I opened my computer and saw an incoming email from Lisa in Australia. She was writing to let me know the beach house had just sold, and there was a round trip ticket waiting for me: I could return to Australia anytime.

Chapter 14: Living Resonance

"I believe humanity is a force of nature whose very makeup is shifting because of a change of heart. As coherence moves from an occasional human state to an enduring human trait through conscious choice, humanity may evolve from being a natural force... to embodying a natural power that restores wholeness."

—Claudia Welss[81]

Being in San Diego allowed for a powerful recalibration of my past as a wife, teacher, and co-founder of the "Mastery of the Heart" training business I had birthed with my husband. For the next few months, the challenge of staying present was at times excruciating. I was geographically close to my former beloved, and I was grappling with the question of how to bring closure to our shared history while finding a peaceful way forward.

Thanks to my Australian journey, I was able to sustain the experience of living in heart resonance and felt the power and grace of walking in alignment with my authentic self. My choice daily was taking quiet time to listen and track what I now called the "home frequency." I felt ecstatic in a greater communion with Nature, and the synchronicities that abounded were a testament to my internal happiness. I continued to privately dowse and responded with joy to the invitations to teach dowsing to groups. I felt privileged seeing how the information transmitted during my clients' dowsing was indeed enriching their lives, and giving them a roadmap to living in empowered choice.

---

[81] Robert Atkinson, *Our Moment of Choice: Evolutionary Visions and Hope for the Future* (Atria Books/Beyond Words, September 2020).

A powerful shift came when I began learning about Quantum Physics and the Unified Field. I had been living with my daughter, Nina, and my two grandsons in Florida when, through myriad synchronicities, I learned about a leading-edge speaker who had written the book *Emergence: The Shift from Ego to Essence*.

My heart strings struck home, and after a three-month online course designed to help me become an Agent of Conscious Evolution, I flew back to LA and began a yearlong mentorship with this woman.

Mentoring with Barbara Marx Hubbard,[82] marked a turning point for me. Barbara was a futurist and global ambassador for conscious change and she had been nominated for the vice-presidency of the United States on the Democratic ticket in 1984. At the time, she proposed a Peace Room in the office of the vice-president to scan, map, connect, and communicate what is working in the world.[83]

Barbara was a visionary, a social innovator, and an evolutionary thinker who believed global change happens when we work collectively and selflessly for the greater good. She often referred to problems as evolutionary drivers, and she felt that "crisis precedes transformation." This viewpoint gives us all a new way of seeing and responding to our global condition.

The Law of Resonance

The Law of Resonance states that, in a harmonically tuned system, anything that is not harmonious cannot become resonant. Thus, all frequencies outside the resonating frequency of the initiating body remain ineffective.

---

[82] Barbara Marx Hubbard: www.barbaramarxhubbard.com.
[83] Evolutionary Leaders: www.evolutionaryleaders.net.

Songline of the Heart / Shelley Darling

I participated in Nassim Haramein's[84] Resonance Science Foundation's first delegate program. With voice rising, I found myself speaking passionately to others about the understanding of Conscious Evolution— and dowsing—that inspired me to call the type of dowsing I offer "Evolutionary Dowsing." I was continuously in awe of how simply allowing a gratitude pause while focusing our loving attention on the Earth resulted in a resplendent feeling of heart coherence. My partnership with Spirit and Nature grew, and as I raised the vibration of people's homes, businesses, and land through dowsing, I saw how an aperture of new possibilities seemed to open where there had been none previously.

Traveling internationally offering presentations about dowsing had shown that Evolutionary Dowsing, as a whole-living system, does indeed powerfully support the optimization of our sacred connection to ourselves and the Earth. Evolutionary

Dowsing was the aggregation of 30 years of spiritual work that began with the guru I'd worked with when I was 20. He had awakened in me the understanding that what I was looking for was already within me. In my 30s, I left my first marriage after nearly dying of a hemorrhaging tumor inside my spinal cord, and I began working in the field of emotional integration. After diligently doing my own work, a doorway opened assisting others to shift their self-limiting core beliefs. I applied practical processes opening new neural pathways that assisted me to anchor in my clients beingness the experiences of inner freedom, unconditional love, and empowered choice.

I'd created a 20–30-minute home assessment and as I applied fundamental dowsing techniques clearing the dissonant energy caused by the geopathic stress, Negative Vortexes and Interference Lines (EMF's) affecting people in their homes, I became aware of something astonishing: my clients were able

---

[84] Nassim Haramein: www.resonancescience.org.

to quickly bridge a dimension of unknown territory within themselves and move forward in their lives with greater momentum. I felt compelled to explore the visible "quickening" that was taking place in people's lives. They seemed to experience a revolution in their consciousness. Working one-on-one, I saw that clearing the stagnating energy of someone's home gave rise to them finding the courage to stand taller in their sacred authority.

As I worked with individuals to de-stress their environment, I saw a remarkable transformational shift in them. Trusting their intuition led them to walk with greater confidence, in ways they hadn't explored prior to the dowsing.

As the foredoomed Tarot cards revealed, things had to dissolve between my husband and I. Now let me be clear, and do not fear, not all relationships dissolve with dowsing! In many cases, a relationship was already wobbly prior to a dowsing. Dowsing simply creates a pure, positive frequency, supporting the chances of people meeting each other in a place of truth and love.

Some individuals who are still living "under the radar," and lying to themselves and others, might simply not yet have had the courage or fortitude to stand in their truth. The dowsing creates a higher energetic vibration, allowing for greater resonance with the truth of who they are, and the potential for seeing and letting go of what is no longer serving them. Without judgment, I learned to allow the movement necessary to evolve towards a life of our soul's design.

Earth-Heart Resonance: Rollin McCraty Study

Dr. Rollin McCraty studied the interaction between the Earth's geomagnetic fields and the human heart and brain and he revealed how disturbances in these fields deeply impact our health and wellbeing and, conversely, how collective emotions can alter Earth energies as well.

About 1,600 members of the Global Coherence Initiative,[85] a science-based, co-creative project, have been participating in a long-running experiment to explore this idea, and a correlation was found between physical and psychological states and geomagnetic and solar activity.

Dr. McCraty reported that, "When the geomagnetic field is disturbed...we feel more anxious, more fatigued, and more mentally confused."[86]

He described geomagnetic fields as flux lines that vibrate at different frequencies—like guitar strings—depending on their interactions with solar winds.

These frequencies can overlap with those of the human heart, "so, in other words, the Earth is singing away at the same frequency that our heart and cardiovascular system operate on," he says.

Definition of Heart Field:

An electromagnetic field produced by the heart that can be detected several feet from an individual.

McCraty states, "Most people appreciate the feeling of a harmonious state—the feeling of hearts, minds and bodies united in a state of wholeness. When we are in such states, we typically feel connected—not only to our deepest selves, but also to others, and even to the Earth itself. We call this state of internal and external connectedness 'coherence.'"[87]

---

[85] Global Coherence Initiative: www.heartmath.org.
[86] Rollin McCraty, "The Resonant Heart," HeartMath Institute.
[87] Rollin McCraty, "Coherence: The Heart Connection to Personal, Social and Global Health", www.thescienceofpsychotherapy.com.

With that as background, it serves to know that we start an Evolutionary Dowsing experience with gratitude and a judgement-free acceptance of the client's circumstance. A safe container is created and from that point on the dowsing protocol generates a state of greater resonance, which in turn activates in the client a suite of heartfelt, positive emotions.

The feelings increase as greater coherence and harmony in the individual's consciousness synergize with the energy of the home and land. The individual feels empowered and experiences a growing interconnected relationship with Nature.

When individuals experience a safe field of love and trust they easily drop their façades and old fears. This evokes a sense of resonance and:

- deepens our bond with our self
- influences our families and circles
- catalyzes heart-based community interconnection and action.

The experience of heart resonance opens the way for people to feel in tune with the flow of the Universe. There is a sense of communion and belonging. We feel alive, connected, and whole, and therefore our expressions reflect and radiate this sense of presence, compassion and wholeness.

Resonance is vital and necessary at this time in our evolution. It allows for a conscious return to greater presence, positivity and loving power. Not power *over* but power that comes from *being in alignment* and following one's inherent design towards unity.

When we discover our true essence, and learn to track our unique heart's calling, we experience resonance with the nature of life itself. This evokes the flow of prosperity and wellbeing.

The Field is the Determinant Force

Lynn McTaggart, [88] author of *The Field* has said, "There is no "me" and "not-me" duality of our bodies in relation to the Universe, but rather is there one underlying energy field.

This field is responsible for our mind's highest functions, the information source guiding the growth of our bodies. It is our brain, our heart, our memory—indeed, a blueprint of the world for all time.

The Field is the force, rather than germs or genes, that finally determines whether we are healthy or ill, the force which must be tapped in order to heal."

Understanding resonance is the keystone for a conscious return to wholeness. In a curved stone archway, the keystone is the one at the top center of the curve and it holds the whole arch together.

The keystone is the most important stone, and that's why this word is also used, figuratively, to mean the most important part supporting the whole. The Merriam-Webster Dictionary defines[89] the word "keystone" as "something on which associated things depend for support."

My integrative healing experience in Australia, including having received the Consolumentum through Sanna, enabled me to ground and simultaneously expand my capacity to follow my compass of joy. This embodied joy became a navigational instrument, which allowed the clarity and conviction to let go of my past relationship, and courageously choose love over fear.[90]

---

[88] Lynn McTaggart: sit her website at: lynnemctaggart.com.
[89] Keystone: www.merriam-webster.com.
[90] "Lynne McTaggart, www.inspiringquotes.us.

> ### A Coalescence of Energy
> *Human beings and all living things are a coalescence of energy connected to every other thing in the world. This pulsating energy field is the central engine of our being and our consciousness.*
>
> **—Lynn McTaggart**

While studying with Barbara Marx Hubbard, I became aware of how seemingly unrelated circumstances were actually interconnected, always catalyzing a recalibration of life into its highest order. Some people call these synchronicities "miracles" and Carl Jung referred to them as an acausal connecting principle of two or more psychic or physical phenomena, which create new possibilities. They have always exceeded what I've thought probable or even possible and have always been part of what I term "everyday grace." Even today, people wonder how I travel around the world the way I do, and they ask what the key to this type of life is. It's just how I live.

As a voice for Conscious Evolution, Barbara noted, for the first time in history humans have the chance to be conscious of evolution, while evolution is happening. "Evolution by choice, not chance," I heard her say during one of our first mentoring sessions. As science and spirituality converge, we're becoming aware of our potential to progress collectively towards higher Consciousness, choice, and freedom.

Barbara addressed the same field of energy as Teilhard De Chardin, a Jesuit paleontologist who was also an eminent thinker and a mystic. He worked to understand evolution and the cosmos. He introduced the term "Noosphere" in 1922 and used it to describe a "thinking layer" around Earth that expands as we come into conscious connection with it. As Jim Campbell said in the magazine, *America,* a Jesuit magazine published weekly, "In his thinking and writing Teilhard studied the intimate relationship between the evolutionary development of the material and the spiritual world, leading him to celebrate the sacredness of matter infused with the Divine presence."[91]

The Unified Field Theory

Barbara's vibrant energy was uplifting and blew wide open within me a new love for science and spirituality as I explored this "Unified Field." The Unified Field theory—a term coined by theoretical physicist Albert Einstein—is sometimes called the Theory of Everything. It posits the interconnectivity of Nature and all matter and energy in existence.

In physics, a *field* is an area under the influence of a force, such as gravity or electricity. Dr. Will Taegel describes the technical definition of the field as a "region of non-material influence."[92] In the space around a magnet, the magnet influences other objects without coming into contact with them. The magnetic field is defined in terms of the force it exerts on other objects—it can only be measured by the *influence* it has on objects in its field. Thus, we understand a field only when we consider it as a space that relates to other objects.

The interconnectivity of all matter helps to explain the experience my clients were having during dowsing. As the house and land came into harmony, it directly influenced their capacity to receive information, instilling in them an experience of expanded consciousness.

Barbara introduced me to a model called the Wheel of Co-creation. It demonstrated that at the core of Universal Intelligence is an impulse to evolve. I and other students became excited when he understood that at the hub of Barbara's

---

[91] Find out more about Pierre Teilhard de Chardin here: www.ignatianspirituality.com.
[92] Will Taegal, "Quantum Prayer: Charting A Path Through Chaos," *Earth Tribe*, www.earthtribe.com.

Wheel of Co-Creation was "Heart Resonance,"[93] the vibrational frequency needed to create harmony with everything we undertake. The beauty of connecting through our hearts in one unified field is that new pathways open in our consciousness and continue to inform us by new thoughts, emergent ideas, and co-creative solutions to any problems we may face.

I was already expounding on the mystery of the "quickening" that takes place in an individual's life after their home and land are dowsed. I now grasped that "Evolutionary Dowsing" was unique: embedded with the skills of what I called, "Embodied Heart Integration," the process I developed and have been using with my clients for more than 10 years.

"Embodied Heart Integration" is a life changing approach to self-healing. It involves a set of specific processes I have used to find the cause of feelings of separation embedded in a person's psyche. Using a series of natural breathing techniques during a private mentoring session or an actual dowsing experience, I watch my client's body naturally integrate the emotional trauma with which they have been struggling, resulting in a complete cohesive change. They have an inner "awakening" and as the past trauma integrates, it also shifts in present time. This is a practical tool that opens a doorway for the evolution of their Consciousness.

While waiting for my divorce to come through I was called to travel, dowsing the homes and businesses of Barbara's students, the "Agents of Change," as well as the Mentors who were training with her. I began supporting these "teachers of teachers" through my dowsing work, which Barbara characterized as "taking the lid off." As I dowsed, I was always listening to what was arising or, as I liked to call the sensate experience, "the voice of the emergent Field."

---

[93] Heart Resonance: A Pathway and Practice Free Download
www.evolutionarydowsing.com/free-resources

Barbara once asked me, *"What would you be doing if you took the lid off your life?"* My response at the time was that I'd be dowsing her home – which came to pass a year later.

This universal energy, known in some circles as the "evolutionary impulse," is always moving us into our highest potential. Barbara would often say this evolutionary impulse is the energy that is driving humankind towards our next quantum leap. This generated in me a blossoming of the wisdom of dowsing as a viable evolutionary instrument. Over time I became acutely aware that Evolutionary Dowsing attunes and expands people's capacity for greater resonance with the innate intelligence of Nature's design, which in turn influences our co-creative relationship with others as a collective humanity.[94]

The Etymology Dictionary[95] notes the word resonance is derived from the Latin word "resonantia," which means "echo," and from resonare, which means "resound." We all love it when the strings of an instrument are struck producing a sympathetic tone, which in turn creates a feeling of harmony within us. Sympathetic vibrations create an entrainment between vibrating systems or fields; the field with the strongest coherence influences the less coherent, or ordered, field.

> **Resonance**
> *Resonance transcends the intellectual exchange of ideas, encompassing intuition, the intelligence of the body, and the energetic space between people…it taps into greater sources of intelligence than the individual and even the group can access alone.*
> —**Renée Levi**, Resonance Project

---

[94] Renée Levi, *Resonance Project*, www.resonanceproject.org.
[95] https://www.etymonline.com/word/resonance.

Songline of the Heart / Shelley Darling

Entrainment and Resonance

Entrainment is an aspect of resonance and it explains why one object's oscillations can set another object into motion if it shares the same frequency. For example, when you strike a tuning fork and bring it near another tuning fork that has the same resonating frequency, the second tuning fork will start vibrating, even though it has not been struck. The second fork will begin to vibrate and sound, merely by being in the same field as the first vibrating tuning fork.

A tuning fork will also cause a guitar string tuned to the same frequency to vibrate without contact.

One of my favorite examples relating to the vibratory nature of the Universe and resonance involves the idea of entrainment. Dutch physicist Christian Huygens, a 17th Century contemporary of Sir Isaac Newton, was the inventor of the pendulum mechanism we now see in today's "grandfather" clocks. He had a room full of these types of clocks, all varied sizes.

A story is told that one day he went around the room starting the pendulums of the clocks in motion at different times. When he left the room, the pendulums were all out of phase with each other. When he returned the next day, he found all were locked in step with the largest clock. This is an example of entrainment.

Resonance invokes a shared coherent vibratory state that intensifies and magnifies the original vibration. For individuals, the experience of what I call "heart resonance" fosters an internal feeling of connection and wholeness.

The experience of resonance infuses a state of presence where one feels in tune with the flow of the Universe. The body naturally relaxes, evoking a felt sense of innate unity and belonging.

When we align with our true essence, and follow our unique heart's calling, we experience "resonance" with the nature of life itself. Life synergizes within and around us, evoking feelings of "win-win-win."

Every challenge becomes an opportunity to return to center, recalibrate our thoughts and leap forward in empowered choice. Where there is resonance among individuals and groups, the field naturally unifies and creates greater coherence.

Resonance fosters the embodiment of power infused with love. The experience of heart resonance opens the field for greater clarity, peaceful relations, communication, empowered living, joy and prosperity.

How ideal would it be to experience the flow of prosperity that comes from the joy of living life on purpose?

The journey from ancient times, when the first people lived in harmony with the Earth, to the unfolding discovery of our evolutionary purpose has come with challenges, most of which have left their mark on our innermost being.

But as my dear friend Dr. Don Pet,[96] founder of the Peace Academy states, "We are Humane Becomings."

Resonance as regards dowsing allows for a positive high vibrational environment, which allows for much clearer communication and a shift away from criticism, blame or judgment; it opens the possibility for harmony, mutual respect, and connection between people.

While dowsing in Australia, I grew in my understanding that, indeed, love IS practical, and if one courageously opens and trusts this "Resonant Field of Love" the result is the promise of an exponential experience of synchronicity and joy.

---

[96] Don Pet: Peace Academy, www.peace.academy.

My perspective expanded as I began to consider dowsing as an exemplary pathway to navigating one's life with love. "The Resonant Heart" became a theme in my life as I cultivated the field through the process of dowsing.

Clearing stagnating energies was essential to expanding my capacity to navigate my life with greater wholeness, harmony, and empowered choice.

The invitation to return to Australia encapsulated in Lisa's gift of a ticket opened a channel that allowed me to feel the land calling me back. The vision to offer others a sacred dowsing wisdom journey back to Australia began to blossom.

I was ready for the next phase of this journey, which, unbeknownst to me at the time, was to involve meeting an extraordinary archeologist, historian, author and dowser in New Zealand...

Chapter 15: Tracking the Southern Serpent

There is always a moment when we can make a new start. The seed we plant is for our children and their children's children. And that seed honors promises made long ago...

—**Barry Brailsford,** *Song of the Old Tides*

An experience in Montecito, California opened doors in my life I could never have imagined. I was asked to offer an evening presentation on "The Art and Science of Dowsing" at the elegant contemporary home of a Frenchman named Michel, and his significant other, Mary.

I was taken by the elegance of a woman named Cheryl, dressed in soft ivory colors and embraced by a cashmere wrap, and sitting close to a big picture window that looked out on the vast Pacific Ocean. She patiently waited until I was complete with my evening program and then asked me to sit beside her. She pleaded with me to come to her home to dowse as soon as possible. We arranged to meet in the next few days.

Passing through the towering stone-bordered gate to her home I was captivated by the sprawling stone walls, extensive gardens, and huge overhanging oaks on her property. It was a compound of sorts, with three buildings altogether: an L-shaped Tudor home, a "Writer's Cottage," and a charming small stone hut.

I could feel Cheryl's heart and soul in this enchanted property. At any moment, I half expected a fairy, or an Earth Deva, to come out and whimsically offer me a tour!

"There was much to be done in this house," I heard, as I stood outside with Cheryl ready to begin the dowsing.

Connecting with the home was a bit disconcerting at first. The angled front door was blocked by a huge tree limb, a warning something was hidden from sight.

The unusual angle at which the front door met the front walkway was problematic from a Feng Shui perspective, as well. Upon entering the home one had to pivot to move into either the central sitting room to the left, or the kitchen and the dining room on the right. We chose to sit by the fireplace in front of a large elephant painting on the mantle as I continued with my assessment.

Although Cheryl had confided that her marriage had been bumpy for years, I could feel the hope she still carried in her heart.

My curiosity was pinged when we went into her husband's office on the main floor: more than seven computers connected him, at any moment, with people situated anywhere in the world. The energy in the room was dark and dense. I later found a book in the library that revealed Cheryl's husband had been a Chess Master at the age of 13 and then he had become a Master at Backgammon. He had an international reputation and had been written up in the book *Gambling Wizards: Conversations with the World's Greatest Gamblers.* He was also a passionate philanthropist and together he and Cheryl had funded organizations such as Tribal Trust, Green Peace, and the Sea Shepherd Conservation Society.

It took more than two days to dowse the entire property, with its various buildings and stone structures. It was a complex dowsing, yet Cheryl's presence was amiable, and she responded immediately to my suggestions, even arranging to lop off the large oak limb hanging in front of the angled door within minutes of understanding the need to liberate herself and the home from the energy it signified.

Songline of the Heart / Shelley Darling

Cheryl's Story (Part 1)

We were all were sitting in Michel and Mary's living room for a presentation from a Dowser, and she talked about feng shui, and ley lines, and Qi lines. I was listening to her and after she spoke, I said, "I need you; I need you. I need you. I live only five minutes away. Come."

I needed Shelley because I knew from therapy what was happening, and I needed things to get really clear, one way or another. I had been in a seven-year difficult patch, a roller coaster in my thirty-two-year marriage, and my husband was out of the country and returning in a few days. I was also going out of the country to pick up my grandson and bring him back. I had 17 easements on my three-acre property, and I knew there were a lot of lines conflicting. I wanted the house dowsed, I wanted the property dowsed and I wanted the clarity that Shelley could bring, right then, before the six-week visit from my grandson, because my husband and I were at a very low point....

When she came it took her a day and a half of dowsing because of the size of the house. It is a 6,000-square-foot four-bedroom house, on three acres. We began outside the house, facing the front doorway where there was an oak tree with a limb that was coming down low in front of the door.

Shelley told me: "Oh this will never do you can't have a limb crossing the entrance of the house!" I immediately called up my tree people and in 10 minutes they chopped the big bough off. Shelley said, that doesn't usually happen, that her clients, usually have to think about things, but I had already been in a seven-year journey and really wanted my marriage to last. These days I don't think I would feel the same way, because I have realized there is a lot more to life than having a long marriage.

—**Cheryl Tomchin**

Cheryl's Story (Part 2)

I followed Shelley around with my trowel and my shovel, digging holes for her to put in her copper cures and crystals, and then later added [a] ring up on the ceiling, trusting her wherever she felt there was static. We spent hours and she willingly shifted the furniture if it needed to be moved, or if there was a painting that had a water feature. I listened and moved it into the correct place, doing whatever she said, making sure it was done right then and there.

Shelley was intent on remedying the one bedroom that was my husband's room at the time, as it was not really connected to the rest of the house, being over the garage. It was connected only through a walkthrough area and after letting Shelley know I was ready for the shift, she connected that bedroom to the other bedrooms, by placing a copper ring in the light fixture. She said to me that she didn't know which way the dowsing [would] go, but within six weeks something would shift, and things would open up. I said, "I don't care which way it goes at this point," and I was so grateful to think something would open up and shift after all this time.

I went to England, picked up my grandson, came back and towards the last week of my grandson's visit, my husband was playing tennis on our court and he had a heart attack. At the time [we] didn't know what it was, so I drove him to the hospital, and after putting him through all the tests, they kept him overnight for observation and two days later he had a five-way by-pass. So, things did open, and his arteries opened up! He was living a duplicitous life and was doing a lot of other things to try to stay young, and he was definitely not being the man that I married, and he could no longer live those two different lives and so our marriage did end. When I looked back on the calendar it was exactly six weeks to the day that Shelley had dowsed the house.

—**Cheryl Tomchin**

Songline of the Heart / Shelley Darling

We don't always know how the energy will shift following a dowsing, but it always does. Yet I was surprised upon reading the email Cheryl sent me soon after completing the dowsing, which she has been kind enough to allow me to share:

Email from Cheryl:

"Last Friday my husband had a heart attack, and we didn't know what was going on. I took him to the hospital, thinking it was dehydration and an electrolyte imbalance.

Monday morning, he had a five-way bypass. This was four weeks to the day that I returned from England and six weeks after you dowsed our home and land. You said it would "open up" the possibilities.

He is in incredibly good shape and [had] played hard tennis for over an hour with the pro just prior to feeling "indigestion." His diet has been very, very good for 30 years.

But the stress of his workload and choices and genetics rendered his arteries clogged despite not [having] high cholesterol. He also smokes (electric) cigarettes.

The morning of surgery I called him and said, "You always said, anger kept your father alive... (His dad was a codger who lived to 93). When they open up your heart, release your anger. Whether we live together or not I hope you have a long life with more joy" He listened.

He comes home Friday. It will be a long road, but I am much lighter now. I am happy. Thank you.

His anger [at] being incapacitated is great, but I now know to step aside. Come back when you are in town.

Cheryl"

Songline of the Heart / Shelley Darling

Another email (months later - more disruption in Cheryl's life:

"What I had heard at that time was, typically a person that has open-heart surgery goes through lots of emotions, and that grief and rage are two of them, and so in the three months after, I was still hopeful he would find the generous loving person that he had been for twenty-eight years, just not the last seven.

Two weeks after he had the surgery, we had our second police raid at dawn, as it was still dark. The first raid was in the afternoon when I was taking a nap and the second one was all about online sports betting.

Imagine, he's on medications, has just had surgery, and they take him to jail, not given a bed for twelve hours, and doesn't have his medications. I mean it was brutal. As [he] is a very disciplined person, and he loves to fight for the underdog, in this case, he was the underdog, and he wasn't going to let them win the fight.

Cheryl"

One might look at this sequence of events and ask, "Why would I want to have my house dowsed if things like this occur?" I am not afraid to use Cheryl's story as an example. As she herself experienced, and I, in my knowing, *understand* that if a person—like Cheryl, in this case—is choosing to step into their higher purpose and stand in the power of who-they-be—as Sanna shared in the past—then the universal energy will respond by reorganizing the energetics of the circumstance that will allow this to occur, and anything other than the highest frequency will either shift or dissolve.

I might add, if there is any subconscious intention that would not be for the highest good for all persons involved during a dowsing, then, as the facilitator, I will pause and take time for greater clarification, resolution, and release of any obstructing energy that would inhibit the dowsing.

Personal empowerment coach Chuck Danes notes that "The Law of Resonance will provide you with the 'seemingly' hidden key of all the keys concerning the unwavering process of manifestation...meaning how each of the events, conditions and circumstances are drawn or attracted to you and created in every area of your life, whether physically, relationally, emotionally, financially or spiritually. Once understood, will provide you with a greatly enhanced ability to begin 'consciously,' intentionally and consistently attracting and experiencing more of the desired outcomes that you desire to experience and envision for yourself..."[97]

In Search of the Southern Serpent

As Cheryl shared in her letter, I did return a few more times, to raise the energy and create greater coherence on her property. Our dowsing connection catalyzed a long-term friendship that lasts to this day. In the beginning, I'd stay at her "Writer's Cottage," an enchanting stone house located below the tennis courts, which was decorated with beautiful Balinese antiques.

I loved looking out beyond the house, past a fruit tree orchard, to a large fig tree that stretched out over a dry stream bed leading to a small view of the ocean. My favorite experience was taking an outdoor shower in a beautiful spot, featuring smooth round stones set out in a spiral pattern. The outer spiral of the shower area connected to an outdoor hot tub with crystalline water kept clean by a mesh bag full of herbs. Cheryl had previously been a Chinese doctor and didn't care to use chlorine or any other chemicals in the water. The hot tub was situated so that in the evening, you'd be enveloped by the celestial movement of the stars overhead.

---

[97] Chuck Danes, "The Law of Resonance," *Abundance and Happiness*, www.abundance-and-happiness.com/law-of-resonance.

Cheryl happily invited me to stay for a week or two before I left for my second trip to Australia. I was looking forward to attending the "Birth 2012" event with Barbara Marx Hubbard being held on December 22nd of that year in Australia. It marked the beginning of the next 5,125-year cycle of the Mayan calendar. Barbara was the keynote speaker.

Two days before I was due to head back to Australia, Cheryl came to the writer's cottage carrying a delicious green smoothie for each of us and a very large coffee-table book. She insisted I read it before I left. I was resistant, and wondered, "what is she thinking?" Over and over again she nudged the book towards me. I stubbornly stated, "I can't read this whole book before I leave!"

Cheryl persisted, and smartly left the book sitting on the wooden table in the breakfast nook. The book, *In Search of the Southern Serpent*, had been written by a man named Barry Brailsford, a well-known author and archeologist, and his co-author, Hamish Miller, a top-notch dowser from England.

I finally surrendered and opened the large hardcover book. I was completely captivated and entranced after reading only one page. It was about the authors' story of dowsing as they traveled throughout New Zealand, learning and interacting with the Earth energies of sacred sites [98] and, for me, unearthing an evocative story of a confederation of people called Waitaha.

Of Stories and Dreams

When we lose our story we lose our dream, and when we lose our dream the spirit dies.

—Barry Brailsford

---

[98]Hamish Miller and Barry Brailsford, *In Search of the Southern Serpent* (Stoneprint Press May 5, 2006)

Chapter Sixteen: Tale of the Peace Trail

Within the confines of ordinary physical form exists the subtler conscious body, so called, because it is intimately connected with a deep level of consciousness. It is from the subtler levels that the potential energy of blissful wisdom arises, an energy capable of transforming the quality of our life completely... It represents the essence of who we are and what we can become.
—Lama Thubten Yeshe[99]

As is wondrously noted on his Stone Print Press website, "Barry Brailsford says his love of the land and the mystery of the past is his birthright. Born in Cobden, Te Aka Aka o Poutini, the ancient anchorage of the great navigator Poutini, and nurtured by the wild coastlines and forested mountains of New Zealand, he knew a childhood where his spirit had been free to soar."

He graduated MA (Hons) in History at Canterbury University, was a member of the New Zealand Archaeology Association Council and was a Principal Lecturer at the Christchurch College of Education. In 1990, he was awarded an MBE for his contribution to education and Maori scholarship.

Te Pani Manawatu, was the Ariki [Chief] of the Tuahuriri Runanga [Council] of Ngai Tahu, a South Island "iwi," the Waitaha word for tribe. Te Pani's request marked an unprecedented moment in the relationship between the indigenous people and the nation of New Zealand.

---

101 Thubten Yeshe, *Introduction to Tantra: The Transformation of Desire,* (Wisdom Publications, 1987), pdfroom.com.

The sacred knowledge Te Pani Manawatu was asking Barry to share had never left the tribe's Higher School of Learning before and now Barry, a white man whose European ancestors arrived in New Zealand only four generations earlier, was to be custodian of their greatest treasures of knowledge.

> **Carry Your Cross Well**
>
> *People will ridicule all the things you say and do in the name of Waitaha... it is a dangerous journey-it is a hard journey; you must walk it as a student.... Write what you learn and hear in peace and love...Carry your cross well for it is a heavy one that you bear.*
>
> **—Te Pani Manawatu**

In 1988, Te Pani Manawatu said to Barry, "You've been chosen to write the record of our ancestors and tell the story of Waitaha because of your skill and the awhi [support] you gave the people of Ngai Tahu during the Tribunal hearings. This is not the easiest of tasks because of the things that have been hidden away from the majority of the people." [100]

This decision to reveal the knowledge of the Waitaha Nation, kept secret for so long, was said to have been made possible by a unique alignment of the stars, an event that had been foretold some four centuries earlier.

As Barry has said "It was bound in prophecy. The stars freed them to share all they held sacred and to announce to the world that it was time for the people of peace to stand tall again."[101-102]

---

[100] Ngai Tahu Land Report: https://ngaitahu.iwi.nz
[101] Te Pani Manawatu, *Barry Brailsford*, https://stoneprint.co.nz/about-barry-brailsford.
[102] "Jaime Mathis: www.jaimemathis.com.

Songline of the Heart / Shelley Darling

The Ancient Peace Trail

Before the stories of the Waitaha people were told, Barry gathered a group of 12 and together in 1988 they walked over the mountain passes of the Southern Alps, to reopen Te Huarahi o Rongo-marae-roa, the Trail of Peacemaker.

The ancient mountainous trail with its steep vertical descents had in the past been guarded and maintained by women. It had been closed by the Waitaha for 130 years because, as I understood it, the gold miners of the time had been fighting over the gold and blood had been spilled in anger. The trail had become "tapu," or "sacred and prohibited."

Only when Barry's nine-day journey was completed in 1989, and the "tapu" was finally lifted, was the way open for the writing of his first book about the Waitaha people.

Accordingly, in 1990, representatives from 140 tribes gathered in Whangarei to decide how much of the old knowledge to release. After some time, they stood and said to Barry: "We support you to the death." The meaning of these words, in Waitaha culture, was, "We give you everything we have, our lives, our dreams, our prayers, and the most sacred of treasures, the wisdom gifted by the Ancestors." And with that blessing, Barry began writing *The Song of Waitaha*.

Our Common Language

"Humanity has a common language. We all walk - in our minds, on our feet; we all have sacred trails that we honor. Whether it is a path through nature or the morning race on Wall Street, we all carry a cadence that moves our bodies into belief. We all have stories that propel our lives and give them meaning."

—Jaime Mathis

Songline of the Heart / Shelley Darling

> ### The Story is Told
>
> "At last our story is told. Now the brave ancestors we have hidden for so long stand again for all to see. With these words the Elders of Waitaha tell us that their ancient and sacred lore is shared for the first time. Bound in secrecy for centuries, protected through the ages by those who gave their lives to keep it safe, this knowledge travels out of the past to be revealed in Song of Waitaha For years New Zealand archaeologists have been puzzled by a people who lived without weapons and created trading systems that moved industrial stone the length of the country."
>
> —**Barry Brailsford,** *Song of Waitaha*

With the clock ticking towards my departure for Australia, I devoured another of Barry's books about Waitaha, *In Search of the Southern Serpent*. I stayed up until 4:00 a.m. for the next two nights, madly taking pictures of pages I knew I wasn't going to have time to read.

With no knowledge of the Waitaha at that point, I found the information Barry shared about dowsing to be of particular note. I was most interested in how he spent five years guiding dowsers Hamish and Ba Miller around New Zealand researching sacred sites.

I was intrigued by their discovery of the power and signatures of the leylines and wondered at the meaning of what Barry calls the "power of place."

At one point he speaks well of Hamish: *"Hamish added a vast net of knowledge to our understanding of Earth energies, breaking new ground in his three-year charting of the Michael-Mary line in England, continuing that work on the Apollo-Athena line in Europe and gathering ancient traditional lore on the Capetown-Cairo line in Africa. Those who come to his work late will find he strides the pages of his books with an honesty and down-to-Earth quality that both teaches and inspires. We began in the dawn-time and greeted the rising sun. At each rock, where Hamish and Ba had explored the Earth energies, we gathered water from the sacred lake on the Peace Trail across the Southern Alps."*

Barry tells of the positive vibrational patterns generated by and emitted by stone tors and sacred sites, called a "signature." He and the team would measure the signature by walking around the stone with their dowsing rods, recording the energy pattern—the pulse of the Earth—as it resonates through these sacred sites. They were struck with awe when they returned six months to a year later to find that, although the site signatures reflected exactly the same pattern, they had expanded beyond the original signature.

After much contemplation, Barry, Hamish, and Ba met with a Maori Elder. It was revealed that the Earth is indeed radically changing as we bring more of our conscious attention to it. The information was electrifying. Over the past few years, I had learned, similarly to Barry and Hamish, that the Earth energetically shifts its vibratory field as it interacts with human Consciousness.

In my own dowsing experiences, I had begun to see a pattern. My dowsing protocol began with the clearing of any non-beneficial, non-resonant energy lines in the house and land.

As I dowsed, my clients by my side, we seemed to be witnessing an opening in the power of their home and the land upon which it stands, as well as an opening of a gateway in our consciousness. It was almost as if an experience and a transmission were being shared at the same time, and this allowed my clients to easily access their psyche, passion, and purpose. This naturally evolved into a feeling that they had a responsibility to live the inherent truth of who they were, and they felt called to fulfill their purpose.

Coming Home to Ourselves

Many of my clients have said during and after a dowsing that they feel as though they are coming home to themselves, and the dowsing has seemed to evoke a noble compassion for their family and the Earth. I, the dowser, am simply a conduit. My past work of emotional integration, combined with the dowsing, has literally represented an opening of the "Way of Love" for individuals, generating within them a renewed relationship with the sacredness of all life.

From the time I had left on my first visit to Australia to this moment on the verge of returning for my second journey to that beautiful land, I had continued teaching dowsing from the East to the West coast of North America.

I offered free dowsing presentations in each town or city I visited, and then dowsed many of the participants' homes. I had become acutely aware of how dowsing created what I called a "quickening," an empowered energy shift in an individual's life. In some cases, it also seemed to act as a catalyst for community connection.

If a few houses, offices and schools were dowsed in an area, the expansion of the Earth's vibrational frequency was measurable. This was similar to what had happened to the signatures of the rocks and sacred sites Barry, Hamish, and Ba had dowsed.

What's more, many of my clients repeated stories of how neighbors—who were not agreeable people—would change dramatically or would sometimes move after dowsing. In one case, I was visiting Nina Patrick, friend, and powerful community mentor, who lived in Highland Park, a suburb of Chicago. She was thrilled when I accepted her invitation to host, two days later, an evening dowsing presentation.

Songline of the Heart / Shelley Darling

Given that I had not dowsed her home, I woke up early in the morning to dowse prior to the evening's offering. After making her morning coffee, Nina joined me and sat on the couch as I began.

Unusually, the rods spun wildly, and I began to cry. I experienced nothing quite like the energy that was moving through me.

Realizing what was happening, I finally spoke, letting her know her mother, who had recently passed away, was in the room. It struck me with an enveloping sense of humility. The room became very still as Nina shared her wondrous relationship with her mother. Barely completing the assessment, her little dog Tulip bounded into the room, and to the astonishment of Nina sat down sweetly posing in the center of the large copper Tensor ring placed on the floor. I laughed, as I had seen this happen many times with dogs. The ring emits a positive field and light, and dogs love its energy field. Continuing, I left Nina and headed outside to resolve the geopathic stress lines affecting her home.

A few hours later, with the completion of the dowsing I took a few moments to myself, walking the streets admiring landscaped gardens and flowering shrubs, and I paid homage to the large Oak trees. As the evening sunset-light filtered through into the living room, I prepared for my presentation. I chose the area in the room that supported me as the speaker and laid my copper dowsing tools on the small nearby table, which held a few contemporary Lucite sculptures.

The room glowed, and the people circled in front of me smiled as I explained the practicality and power of dowsing and harmonizing their homes, lands, and businesses. It was a joyful time, and everyone left in appreciative awe.

After saying goodbye to most of the participants, I turned to see a youthful-looking tall blonde woman sitting waiting patiently on the stool, near to where I had been speaking. She shared her appreciation of the evening and asked if it was okay to tell me her story.

Unbeknownst to me, she was the next-door neighbor. Apparently, she had seen me out her window walking the property with my dowsing rods. She now understood what I had been up to and shifted her communication to the circular two-story tower-like room that directly faced Nina's house.

Her voice quieted as she told me about the room that her children—twins, aged four—would never enter. She said as soon as I disappeared around the corner of the house, for the first time, the children openly danced in the room and continued to play until bedtime.

She knew she had to come to find out exactly what I had been up to. Given her experience, she asked me to come the following day to dowse their very large Tudor home.

> ### Shelley's Dowsing
>
> *Shelley's dowsing was comprehensive and enlightening. Afterwards, I felt uplifted and supported by my home in a new way and have ever since! Even with its imperfections and inevitable messes, the whole of it now feels like sacred space.*
>
> *Shelley brought forth the true and pure vibration of my mom, so shortly after she passed. What a gift to know she was so powerfully present. At the very end of the day of dowsing we laid crystals under the moonlight around the perimeter of the property in the pattern of the sacred geometry of the Merkaba. It was sheer magic! My energy within and the house was transformed on many levels.*
>
> **—Nina Patrick**

Over the years, I've noticed how dowsing a home evoked a natural desire in my clients for greater connection and community. For example, Nancy, a petite bubbly brunette woman whom I met while mentoring with Barbara Marx Hubbard, became elated after dowsing her home in California. Nancy immediately, deemed herself an "Evolutionary Hostess" and promptly began inviting people to gather at her house. Elated with the experience she went on to become an Evolutionary Dowsing Specialist, (previously a Golden Light Dowsing Specialist) and is one of the best Energy Detectives I've ever seen! She has since then built an outdoor art studio and added a small teepee for people to co-create together.

Nancy's husband, cheerful though nonchalant about the dowsing, enthusiastically waved us on during the dowsing, although he did not wish to be engaged. Once again, as in the case of Dave in Mullumbimby, there came a moment when this changed. The assessment had revealed a personal QI line. He was a dedicated businessman, and to Nancy's dismay, would often travel for work and rarely be at home.

His downstairs desk was literally in the middle of a thruway for foot traffic. The family continuously walked through his space to go upstairs after parking their cars. A few days into my visit, he easily agreed to engage. I immediately found the blocked energy and with delight, he now became mesmerized by the dowsing rods and allowed the full transformation of his office.

We worked together for a few hours and finally the space was ready for him to stately take his place behind his desk. If you only could have seen his radiant smile! By the time we were done, Nancy, who I had told previously to stay away, came downstairs admiring the shift, yet nudging her husband to get ready to leave for the mountains. Gesturing towards his desk, he said he was in no way going to be taken away from the preciousness of the moment. He was beaming and loving his new home office. His candid remark, which I promised not to repeat, was so outrageous that we all fell to the floor hysterically laughing. To this day, Nancy is no longer complaining, as his home office is well inhabited!

As is often the case, the Field naturally seemed to be opening for greater awakening, collaboration, and community connection – similar to how ancient sacred sites such as Stonehenge and Avebury—at the intersection of two positive leylines—are natural gathering places for higher consciousness.

Australia Bound

I was beyond myself with delight at the thought of returning to Australia. Unlike the first time, I was healthy and strong and felt an urgency about my return, although I had no preconceived ideas about what would take place on this second journey to the land that spoke so deeply to my heart. It was truly the only place I've literally felt "home." It's hard to explain the connection I feel with this land. As a child I had traveled to Switzerland, the Bahamas, and Virgin Islands, and in my 20s and 30s I'd traveled throughout Europe and later to Israel, yet no place had touched my soul like Australia.

I flew directly to Sydney and then hopped on a Jetstar flight to Byron Bay, an ocean side town located in the far northeastern corner of the state of New South Wales. Ecstatic to be returning, I would join Barbara Marx Hubbard and some of the members of our closely-knit Mentors group for the Festival UPLIFT 2012, serving as one of the anchor hubs for Barbara's newly founded global event, Birth2012. We, as Mentors, were committed to Barbara's year-long training circle, and a few of us flew to be on hand to volunteer and support Barbara's vision.

Staying with Ange and Dave in Mullumbimby, the small town in the Byron Shire, I would be only five minutes from the auditorium. Najma Ahern, who had hosted me on my first visit to Australia, was thrilled at my return to her homeland. After fulfilling the dowsing requirements, Najma, too, became a certified Evolutionary Dowsing Specialist,[103] using dowsing as a modality for her Cranial Sacral clients, as well as for home

---

[103] Evolutionary Dowsing Specialist: www.evolutionarydowsing.com.

and land healing. Barbara's December 21, 2012, event marked both the Summer Solstice and the end of the Mayan Calendar. Barbara had written a narrative called *The Theater of Our Birth*,[104] which was to be unveiled at the Uplift Festival. It describes the next stage of evolution on planet Earth and predicts the birth of a new humanity.

> **Sacred Relationship**
>
> *Dowsing changed my life. I love using the dowsing rods. I used them yesterday and I used them this morning. When Shelley came to dowse, I was still in the process of building my studio. She placed the cures under the tiles before the floor got laid. The reason I continue dowsing, is so people can understand that they can expand, shift and be inspired in their sacred relationship with the Earth.*
>
> **—Najma Ahern**

This was a day that many people had expected to be a cataclysmic one, but in Barbara's eyes it was more about the birthing of a planetary consciousness on Earth than any proposed disaster. In her view, we were, in fact, waking up.

I was pleased to meet Karen Everett, a filmmaker who was in the process of filming *American Visionary, the story of Barbara Marx Hubbard*,[105] at a place called the Crystal Castle.

This was a magical sanctuary in the hinterland where some of the largest crystals I had ever seen had been set meticulously on a hillside. I was especially impressed by one huge clear quartz crystal that was at least 15 feet tall, and I found myself bedazzled and possessed by its radiance, surrounded, as it was, by gentle clouds and azure skies.

---

[104] Theatre of our Birth - Barbara Marx Hubbard, www.youtube.com.
[105] American Visionary: www.americanvisionarythemovie.com.

Two days later, after the festival, I visited Najma whose property I had dowsed some years earlier. She was excited to tell me she had discovered that the houses I had dowsed on my first journey to Australia were all dots on a line leading from Mount Chincogan, a triangular shaped mountain overlooking the town of Mullumbimby, the "biggest little town in Australia," through to Coorabel ridge which forms part of the southern spiral arm of mountains from the Wollumbin caldera.

This southern spiral continues to the ridge line that surrounds Byron Bay, Australia's most easterly point, and to Julian Rocks out to sea, which was once connected to the mainland via a land bridge. In Aboriginal mythology it is said that Mount Wollumbin captures the first light of day, which lights up the rose quartz at its core, and from there ignites the Earth's energy grid. This mountain, named Mount Warning by British explorer Captain James Cook in 1770, has been, and continues to be, a place of traditional significance to the Aboriginal people and today it is still the site of sacred ceremonies and initiation rites.

Najma went on to describe how she had created her own personal energy grid, an interconnected network of high vibrational energy sites, by connecting the dots between her home, Anna's house just down the road, Ange & Dave's place across the river in Mullumbimby, and the home of author Elaine Seiler,[106] who wrote the book, *Multi-Dimensional You: Exploring Energetic Evolution*.

Her home sits on top of a ridge in the area. These were all places I had been asked to dowse. Najma was sure I had been called to mend something in the land, as all of these properties were along a line formed along the highest points of the ridge connecting with Mount Wolumbin.

---

[106] Elaine Seiler: http://elaineseiler.com.

Songline of the Heart / Shelley Darling

Once again, I was reminded of the returning gift of being a teacher, when the student has far exceeded what they have been taught and makes and shares discoveries of their own. The circle of energy, like an infinity loop, seemed to expand and uplift us all.

Just as we were completing our time together, I received an email message from my friend Cheryl in Montecito, California.

Cheryl had met Barry Brailsford and his wife Cushla at Quail Springs,[107] a former cattle ranch in California's Cuyama Valley that was now a non-profit organization focused on education and land stewardship in Santa Barbara. At the time Barry was offering a three-day workshop on fire tending. The message read:

Dear Shell,

As much as I'm half-expecting you to be ensconced in the cottage and walking Bear-dog come February, I just got this email from Barry and Cushla in New Zealand. He is giving some workshops on dowsing if you read along.

I am well. I saw two movies this week and have had a marvelous ten days alone. My piles of messes are getting cleared. I am done with the wrangling of why and wherefores and onto relearning my center, whatever that means. Thanks for your assistance., Cheryl

Barry will be at the Sacred Voices Festival, Kawai Purapura, 14 Mills Lane, Albany, North Shore, Auckland 0632 Saturday 9th and Sunday 10th February Saturday 9th 2pm -3.30 pm. An Earth Energy Workshop:

---

[107] Quail Springs: www.quailsprings.org.

exploring the frontiers of consciousness with dowsing rods. Limited to 24 people.

Sunday 10th 11am-12.30 pm. A seminar: Ancient wisdom for modern times: discovering your ancestral lines. Using the power of place and awakening to the old rhythms of life.

Upon receiving Cheryl's letter, I adventurously stepped into the unknown, trusting my inner guidance, and I watched events in my life change seamlessly so I could easily change my plans.

I felt an incessant urge to meet with Barry and immediately sent an email, letting him know my intention of coming to the Sacred Voices Festival, at the Kawai Purapura Retreat Center in Auckland.

In reading about the event, I learned the objective was to bring indigenous wisdom, the wisdom of the land, and the wisdom of spirit, together. I felt its strong calling and knew an augmentation to this journey was about to begin. [108]

---

[108] Marcia Browne, "Wairua and the relationship it has with learning te reo Māori within Te Ataarangi," Massey University, 2005.

Chapter 17: Wisdom of the Ancestors

Knowledge stored in Whakapapa (genealogy) comes from a similar awareness, all things live, or vibrate, be it rocks or birds, people or trees, "physical phenomena and people are held to proceed from a common primal source. They are all interlinked through wairua, (quintessential energy) with each having its "own mana or psychic force."

Marcia Browne, Master of Educational Administration, NZ

At Cheryl's prompting I flew to Auckland where I was to finally meet Barry Brailsford on a traditional New Zealand marae—a sacred Maori meeting ground—during the Sacred Voices Festival.

Arriving a day early gave me the chance to settle into the small, shared cement bungalow I would be staying in and feel into the nature of this place.

I had come alone and knew no one. The entry space of the communal residence had a beautiful atmosphere and it led out to a large kitchen area with huge picnic-style wooden tables that allowed people to congregate easily.

Outside was a small meadow surrounded by native flora, a large teepee, and some small outbuildings. People of all ages began arriving with broad smiles.

Not realizing how chilly it would be at night, even in the heart of summer, I was grateful when my roommate from the UK arrived with an extra down vest, which she generously handed me to use.

Morning Welcome Ceremony

Small pods of people greeted each other warmly the following morning while gathering for the *Powhiri*,[109] the traditional New Zealand welcoming ceremony. The entire congregation of participants stood outside, as the indigenous wisdom keepers opened the way with a traditional Haka.

From ancient times, this somewhat fierce ritual has been conducted to determine whether a visitor is friend or foe. A warrior issues a wero (a challenge) to the *manuhiri* (guests), as he checks their intentions. Traditionally the warrior carries a *Taiaha* (a spear-like weapon) and lays down a token—a small, leafy branch, for example—never breaking eye contact. A guest picks up the token in an act of peace and goodwill.

An indigenous female elder standing at the edge of the bush, began her *Karanga*, a hauntingly beautiful chant whose cadence seemed to drive my consciousness into the deepest of silent spaces. At that moment I could feel her welcoming the Ancestors as well as the guests. It reminded me of the first time I had heard and felt the deep memorable soul-stirring cries and extensive moans of a whale's song. Another woman responded with another call, and afterwards she invited everyone to walk onto the land as a group and enter the meeting place where other indigenous elders had gathered.

Slowly, one by one, we entered the meeting house, which ran down a short corridor alongside the kitchen area. I watched in wonder as each person stepped through the glass doorways into the building's main room and greeted a line of elders with what is called a *"Hongi."* This ceremonial exchange appeared to involve just a simple touching of noses.

---

[109] Rachel Gerwig, "The Power of Music in the Maori Welcoming Ceremony," 2015 Butler U. https://digitalcommons.butler.edu.

Later, I was told the Hongi gesture was a sacred act of connecting one person's third eye to another's, and it involved an exchange of the HA, or breath of life.

There were many colorfully dressed guests and the greeting continued for more than an hour. I scanned the room to see if I could see Barry, though I couldn't remember what he looked like, having only "known" him from the picture in his book, which could have been quite dated.

After the welcome, the elders shared stories, and then invited people to come back the following morning, after choosing which of the many events available they planned to enjoy.

At sunrise the next day, I wandered through the sparkling dew-blanketed grass and stepped onto the large deck stairs near the kitchen. After eating a vegetarian breakfast, and hearing the conch shell blow, I headed to the teepee where several elders were gathered, most notably a man named Hirini Reedy and a woman, Makuini Ruth Tai.

Hirini[110] is a great orator and warrior of the heart, and he speaks of himself as a cultivator of Spirit and an engineer of human potential, supporting people in living their fullest expression.

I was joyfully surprised at the synchronicity involved in meeting Makuini Ruth Tai[111] at this festival. She is a revered New Zealand Grandmother and founder of Aroha Education.

A few years earlier, we were in communication about my vision of the "Ancestral Bridge Wisdom Journey," a travel odyssey for people wishing to experience the profundity of Australia. The intention was a sacred pilgrimage, which would complete its cycle on the North Island of Aotearoa, with a full

---

[110] Hirini Reedy: www.ourplanet.org/greenplanetfm/hirini-reedy.
[111] Makuini Ruth Tai: www.soulplacesmovie.nz/makuini-ruth-tai.

moon three-day ceremony facilitated by Makuini Ruth Tai. Little did I know at that time that a family crisis was to erupt that would delay this sacred journey a few years.

Praying for Guidance

The session in the teepee opened, as almost all Maori gatherings do, with a Karakia prayer for spiritual guidance and protection. Makuini and Hirini asked all 70 participants to stand and share who we were, and why we felt called to be there.

As always, I'd situated myself at the front of the gathering, and I counted myself fortunate to be sitting next to these two Maori wisdom keepers leading the experience.

After everyone was seated on the floor of the teepee, Hirini looked towards me to begin the sharing. I stood up and somewhat nervously rambled out my story of having been handed the book *In Search of the Southern Serpent*. I said I didn't know why I was there, other than to meet a man named Barry Brailsford.

We circled around the teepee hearing everyone else's story until there was only one person left, a man who was sitting by the opening. To my surprise he said, *"To the first one who spoke, I can take you to meet Barry, the one who wrote that book."* I could barely see the man through the ocean of people, as he was crouched down below my line of sight. And I couldn't believe my luck!

Finally, at the end of our time together, the teepee began emptying and I walked quizzically to the man sitting by the opening.

As I got closer, I saw a broad Cheshire smile on his face, letting me in on his joke: this was indeed Barry himself! We laughed, hugged, and honored my friend Cheryl, who had played such a key role in our meeting.

The next morning, I was back in the teepee to participate in Barry's introductory dowsing workshop. Barry called on me to be part of a demonstration and asked if I had the courage to stand there. His remark surprised me and struck a note deep within my core.

I listened intently as Barry spoke. I was stupefied when I discovered his manner of teaching was so similar to my own.

First, he opened with having people simply focus on their heart center, inviting the group to become aware of the shift in energy. I too, begin every session or event with "Heart Resonance," first connecting with our personal heart, then from a still place, connecting with the energy as it expands.

Reaching for his handcrafted dowsing rods, Barry asked me to stand still and become the tree. With a Cheshire smile, he walked with his dowsing rods, showing the group how to measure the heart chakra of the tree. There was a quiet murmuring as his rods moved when he was at the outer edge of its energy field.

Picking up a bundle of his handcrafted copper dowsing rods, he passed out one rod to each person so they could try their luck at dowsing. Requesting that we stand and meet him outside the teepee, we filed one-by-one outdoors. We stood and watched as Barry placed a large snake-like rope on the ground. He showed the group how to use their rod to find the rope's edge. It was wonderful to watch as people awakened to their new ability to dowse. It was the children though, that I watched in delight, as they joyously held their rods high, walking forward in trust and determination.

Wandering around the beautiful, serene grounds of the marae at sunset, I found my way to a path that led to a hidden amphitheater of trees. I was met by a spectacle of glow worms illuminating the woods. Surrounded by the magic of the glow worms' enchanting aura of light, my mind wandered, and I found myself ruminating on where I might go after this event.

There, in the sparkling light, I heard a whispering and imagined dowsing some sacred site with Barry.

Later that night, in the retreat dining room, I was filling a cup with some tea to warm my thin-blooded bones when a strange thing happened.

A woman who was an attendee, camping at the far edge of the festival grounds came up to the tea table and asked me what my plans were for after the gathering. Having no idea, I stuttered a bit, then sighed. I said the only place I was feeling called to go was the Temple of the Four Winds, a sacred site that had been mentioned in Barry's book *In Search of the Southern Serpent*. She stared oddly at me, then looked deep into my eyes before mysteriously turning around and abruptly leaving.

After a deep meditation the next morning, I slipped out from my small cave-like accommodation and walked through the lush garden to the gathering grounds where I found a Maori woman with a notable Moko (tattoo) carrying a hand-woven cloak. She looked at me oddly, laughed mildly, and with a tone of certainty, said, "it will all be revealed... let it unfold."[112]

I walked quietly down the dirt path to the small, shaded vending area, where I met Barry's wife Cushla. Her warm smile reached out to greet me as I approached the table where Barry's books were carefully aligned. I noticed a small book that came with a deck of cards. I immediately purchased them noticing the picture of what looked like a large gray-green lizard on the cover. The title of the book was *Wisdom of the Four Winds*.[113]

The story of New Zealand is vast and profound, and one can't share it without speaking about Tuatara, the gatekeeper. The Tuatara is unusual. Rachel Fritts in an article

---

[112] Barry Brailsford, *Song of the Old Tides* (Stoneprint Press) www.stoneprint.co.nz/product/song-old-tides.

[113] B. Brailsford *Wisdom of the Four Winds* (StonePrint Press, 1999)

about Tuatara states The Tuatara has retained some of its archaic traits harking far back to an ancient and intricate evolutionary branch that has been all but lost, making it a species of great interest to scientists."[114]

> ### Tuatara
>
> *When the ancestors came to these shores, they knew that Tuatara was both ancient and wise. And they saw in its power a path to the dreaming that is of the rainbow mind, for this wondrous creature had a third eye. He looks to the side with two eyes and uses a third eye to reach beyond space and time to define the boundaries that divide. The third eye brings us to the Dreaming of the Rainbow Mind.*
>
> **—Barry Brailsford**

His forehead has a vestigial third eye that responds to changing light. After reading the introduction to the *Temple of the Four Winds*, I became aware of how the spirit of Tuatara was guiding my New Zealand journey.

Opening to the spirit of Tuatara, as Barry stated, will guide you as you enter what are known as the Mana, Mauri, and Maui of this ancient, enchanted land.

Taking the time to understand the undercurrent of energies embraced by the indigenous people of New Zealand, I discovered Ginney Deavoll, a New Zealand artist, adventurer, and author, who describes these terms well: "All living things have Mana," she says. "It is our essence, our presence. Te Mauri is the excitement or energy, the life impulse, the movement, and change. Te Maui is the design that captures the energy and excitement and constructs the ever-winding cycles creating balance and wonder in the natural world. Follow the

---

[114] Rachel Fritts, "Tuatara: The Three-eyed Baby Dragon of New Zealand," *Earth Archives*, https://eartharchives.org.

clouds to the peaks where they dissolve into millions of snowflakes, watch the snow melt and run as a torrent through the valleys, over towering falls, all the way to [the] ebb and flow of the tide. The circle that has no end, for the end is but a new beginning."[115]

> **Water**
>
> *Water can be visible or invisible, so the Ancestors used it to describe the next child of Io. Its name is "Wairua." "Wai" means water, the life giver, and "Rua" means two. Think of the meeting of the two waters, the waters here and the waters unseen, the place of the Ancestors. Wairua joins the moment with all that has been, opens today to yesterday, and guides me into tomorrow to move me into the power of Spirit. It helps me to step beyond myself, to reach for the stars and, if I wander too far, shows me the way home.*
>
> **—Barry Brailsford**

Prior to my trip to New Zealand, I'd already learned of the "wairua" a Maori word that speaks to the quintessential life force, that exists in both birth and in death. The wairua, as I understand through my experience, is the spirit or energ, that's always moving us to our highest potential. It's the unseen energy that lives in all matter. Some call it the God force, others the evolutionary impulse. It vibrates and is the living current or flow of one's soul destiny.

In her thesis paper for Massey University (2005) Marcia Browne states "One of the carriers of spiritual knowledge or wairua is sound vibration, it links us to the deep

---

[115] Ginney Deavoll, "Mana, Mauri, Maui," http://ginneydeavoll.com.

beyond," and, " wairua present being the connective glue between each other."[116]

Te Miringa Te Kakara

During Barry's workshop, someone in the circle had asked him about dowsing houses. Barry had replied he couldn't answer the question as that wasn't in his area of expertise. I wanted to speak to the person who had asked, as this was exactly the modality of dowsing, I had spent five years mastering. But I didn't feel comfortable about speaking to this man, and in this place of ancestral wisdom, I felt a meandering doubt and unworthiness surfacing. Lying in bed, in the dark of the night, in the silence of the cement room after having met Barry and other indigenous elders, I felt so small. Even though dowsing houses was my gift, I began questioning my ability as a dowser.

In a dream-like space, I found myself reflecting through my past to the time in 1990, when the discovery of a tumor in my spinal column had prompted me to begin cooking macrobiotic food for myself in support of my healing. For months, I would carry the meals I had made (and was planning to eat) into friends' homes and restaurants. When people saw the meals, they would ask me if I would teach them how to cook them, and there were those who begged me at the time to cook *for* them. I was resistant to the idea, as I doubted my capabilities. I felt I had so little knowledge compared to the other macrobiotic cooks, who were true experts in the area.

While attending a cooking workshop, I shared my dilemma with a macrobiotic counselor. Looking directly into my eyes, she said, "You are here to share your experience to the best of your ability. You will attract just the right people who know less than you, and they will need your wisdom and skill." Finally, finding my "yes," I joyfully took a leap of faith and

---

[116] Marcia Browne, "Wairua and the relationship it has with learning te reo Māori within Te Ataarangi," Massey University, 2005.

created "Shelley's Café." I taught gourmet vegetarian-macrobiotic cooking and catered these specialized meals for people for the next 10 years. Now, here in my little room, I was searching for that "yes" inside once again.

The next morning, with the festival coming to completion, I was becoming a bit alarmed. I still had no idea where I was going next, and I didn't know anyone in New Zealand. I walked back into the large dining area and plugged in my computer to see where I might be called to go for the next 10 days. To my surprise, Jo, the woman, I had met at the tea station the night before, moseyed through the door into the dining room with a slight lift in her step.

Although she had appeared quite sallow the previous evening, her eyes were now bright and radiantly glowing as she made her way towards me. Jo said she had gotten an answer to her question, and she offered to take me to the Temple of the Four Winds herself. She explained she was very connected to this sacred site, as years earlier she had been adopted by the Maori family who owned the land, and she had needed to ask the Ancestors if she had permission to take me there.

After the closing ceremony, and before leaving, I found a few minutes alone with Barry and asked him to sign my newly purchased copy of his book, *Song of the Stone*. Deep in thought, he signed the book for me, and then looked up and spoke about the "Power of Place." He said that prior to writing *Song of Waitaha* he had been a multitasker. The elders had taught him the necessity of focusing on one thing at a time. This affected me deeply, as I always had at least five things happening at once. For a lifetime I have experienced over and over the inevitable results of scattering one's energies too widely. Although initiating brilliant ideas, I have not necessarily seen things through to completion. I was the multitasker of multitaskers!

Here I was learning how to ground my energy through slowing down and becoming present to whatever was moving in my field of awareness, which at times sure didn't feel easy.

I had spent a lifetime multitasking, skimming above the dark waters, and although I was optimistic, I rarely experienced the wild letting go of full-body belly laughs.

In the past I had not wanted to look at my suppressed grief, nor embrace the grief held within the collective. This journey, guided by seemingly unseen forces, was allowing me to alchemize my heartache and rise transformed and empowered. My capacity to stand as a generator of love and wholeness was expanding. Indeed, this was a resurrection of my being, the power of which I was just beginning to understand.

As Barry handed the book back to me, I told him I was being called to the Temple of the Four Winds, the Waitaha marae whose Maori name was Te Miringa Te Kakara. He gently nodded.

Te Miringa Te Kakara—The Temple of the Four Winds—had been known as an ancestral school of learning in the past, or a "Wananga." Its celestial story is linked to the Southern Cross and its name means "The Fragrance of the Heavens." Located near the town of Bennydale, in the North Island of New Zealand, it is known as a "Star Temple," a storehouse of ancient knowledge that honors all cultures. In fact, the elders speak of people of many colors settling in this land long ago.

The Temple of the Four Winds was built in direct alignment with the Southern Cross. This constellation seen in the Southern Hemisphere is made up of four brightly lit stars, almost in a perfect cross. Comparable to the Big Dipper in northern sky, the Southern Cross has a longer shaft that almost points exactly to the South Pole in the sky, used by navigators across the world.

The land at Te Miringa Te Kakara still holds the imprint of the cross-shaped building, which burned down—some people say through a fire that was deliberately set—in 1983. According to Martin Doutré's[117] research in 2001, "The Crosshouse of Miringa Te Kakara was not some form of "orphan" dwelling, the attributes of which are unique to New Zealand. It was built according to an internationally distributed parcel of astronomical codes" in accordance with a measurement standard that had originated in the ancient world and which had been carried across the oceans.

His article also states, "The most accurate, detailed plan ever made appears to be that of architect C. G. Hunt in 1958 for his 1959 article in the Journal of the Polynesian Society, 68: 3-7. Hunt's scaled plan has been used in the mathematical analysis of the Crosshouse.

The full analysis tests geometry detectible at the Waitapu standing stone circle in Northland, NZ, against similar geometry found in buildings at Rennes le Chateau in Southern France by former army surveyor David Wood and his team.

Careful work undertaken in the Languedoc region of France showed very clear trigonometric evidence of known British Standard measurements, surprising in a building considered ancient by today's standards.

Amidst the geometry detected at Rennes Le Chateau by David Wood and his team was a Grand Cross. Doutré goes on to say "This is also clearly in evidence at Miringa Te Kakara, where the width of each cross arm, designated by the extreme positions of the Crosshouse windows, is 24-degrees of arc…There are eight intersection positions on the eight-pointed star that clearly stipulate how the Grand Cross is constructed and how it overlays the eight-pointed star geometry. This cross

---

[117] Martin Doutré, "The Crosshouse at Miringa Te Kakara..." *Celtic New Zealand, December 30, 2001*, www.celticnz.co.nz.

remained prominent in the symbolism of many ancient Northern Hemisphere civilizations and developed into the Knight's Cross, and the Templar Cross."

After much deliberation, a new building was built next to the site of the original one. Only a few of the large outer posts have survived.

Miringa Te Kakara is known by many as the spiritual home of the Four Winds, where the spirit of Oneness is honored. It is the "turangawaewae" which means "the place where we stand tall and remember who we are." It is said that here we remember our connection to the stars through the stones. There are many sacred sites in New Zealand, yet this one had called me to it. How is it that from thousands of miles away something can capture your attention and kindle your "Knowing?"

The Way of Peace

Te Miringa Te Kakara, the sacred Waitaha school of learning was hours from Auckland. Happily, on our way as new traveling companions, Jo openly shared her love of hiking.

To our surprise we had both spent time in northern New England, reveled in the wonder of the Old Man in the Mountains, the Flume, a cascading waterfall path, and the many beautiful sites that Franconia Notch in New Hampshire had to offer. Before we could head further south, she told me we needed to stop in a small town along the way meet with a grandmother who was connected to Miringa Te Kakara.

Scanning her modest home, I was directed to sit and relax on the couch, as the two friends conversed. There was only one question directed towards me. "What do you see yourself accomplishing in the next 50 years?" the grandmother asked.

I was dumbfounded, and unable to give her an answer. I felt myself shrinking a bit, although I knew it was mine to carry this question into my journey to Te Miringa Takara. Hours later we arrived at a small wire gate leading onto the land that housed the star temple. There wasn't much to see here: just some tracks that led out past a small stream and through a field; there was a small hill behind it all. The way in was rough on the car, yet Jo drove with conviction through the mud to the final gate where I saw an octagonal wooden building.

As we got closer, I felt as though the site was beckoning me. Getting out of the car, I was immediately pulled out to the area where the original building had stood, awed that I was able to still see the cross made by the former building's posts lying in the grass.

The dedication plaque on the Temple of the Four Winds reads:

> *To the Ancestors who keep the dream of peace*
> *alive and carried it forward to this day.*
> *To all who walk the path of the gentle way.*

Indelible Memory

A large hawk flew into the branches of a large tree without leaves and rested in my consciousness. Beside her a small burnt wooden post spoke and shared her story.

—Shelley Darling

I was called to lie down and place my head on the land, and I immediately fell into a deep altered space where "Kahu," the hawk, came flying into my consciousness.[118]

---

[118] B. Brailsford, *Wisdom of the Four Winds* (StonePrint Books), Pg. 67

Songline of the Heart / Shelley Darling

> **Guardian of the Trails**
>
> *Kahu is the soaring hawk that greets us as we travel the land. It is the guardian of the trails that cross the mountain passes, and the messenger who joins us with the stars and ages long gone. Kahu is vision.*
>
> **—Barry Brailsford**

Still lying on the ground, and in somewhat of a trance-like state, I felt time dissolving as I considered the lineage of the Waitaha people and their dedication to living the "Way of Peace."

> **The Old Histories**
>
> *Few understand that the Pacific world knew peace for over 2,500 years. The old histories that cover those years speak of the days without conflict and say to take the life of another is to destroy your own. Archaeological excavations find no weapons of war in the sites of those times."*
>
> **—Barry Brailsford**

The history of New Zealand was not contested until the Waitaha elders, trusting the timing and correlation of the stars, in 1988 brought forth the knowledge of a story that had not yet been told. It was a story that spoke of a confederation of people called Waitaha, meaning "water carriers," who navigated the ocean currents with an understanding of the stars, the water, and the land, and who had lived the "Way of Peace" in Aotearoa/New Zealand, for more than a thousand years.

Early evening came quickly. Walking ever so slowly on this land aligned with the stars, I found myself returning to the beginning of my Australian journey when I had first learned about the Cathars from Kathleen McGowan's *Book of Love*. Kathleen had referred to the work of Jesus and Mary Magdalene as the "Way of Love." Immersing myself in

Kathleen's story and feeling into my journey with Sanna, and the experience of the Consolumentum, I felt the sacred transformation of love's union on a cellular level. Shifting my awareness to what little I knew of Waitaha history, and how they lived the "Way of Peace," I felt prompted to look at how these two seemingly disparate paths, Waitaha and the Cathar, were merging within my consciousness.

> **New Paradigms**
>
> *In the course of normal science, it may happen that anomalies begin to accumulate. Some of these may be set aside for future research. Some may be dismissed as irrelevant. But if a sufficient number of anomalies accumulate, anomalies, which resist solution by the paradigm or incorporation into it, a crisis develops.*
>
> *As the crisis intensifies, scientists begin to offer and promote new paradigms capable of accommodating the anomalies. If one of these paradigms attract the attention of a sufficient number of members of the research community, a scientific revolution takes place. The first step toward movement to a new paradigm is thus recognition of anomalies, of counterinstances to the current paradigm.*
>
> **— Martin Doutré**

I was intrigued and mystified by the unfurling experiences of my journey since I had left San Diego. Understanding the interconnectedness of life, I allowed myself the space to muse about the intermingling of internal forces that seemed to be guided by an innate intelligence. Over the years I had learned to trust the myriad coincidences that came my way. The question burning in my soul related to the Waitaha's relationship to the Cathars, who themselves similarly lived the "Way of Love."[119]

---

[119] Martin Doutré, "The Crosshouse at Miringa Te Kakara..." *Celtic New Zealand*, December 30, 2001, www.celticnz.co.nz.

The sessions with Sanna seemed to be catalyzing a union of my heart and mind, which seemed to open a portal to a matrilineal lineage of descendants to which I was inherently connected. In the journey of my return to wholeness, Spirit continued to lead me.

Was it possible the Cathar and the Waitaha people were connected in some way?

Many threads wove themselves wildly together as I lay on this hallowed ground.

Since my teenage years, I have known my destiny was somehow related to the pursuit of love and truth. I have long recognized that no matter what I am *doing*, it is a service motivated by love.

Love became the undercurrent of all my endeavors, whether I was the proprietor of a decorating store for children's rooms—called "Heartwings"—that I had started in my late 20s, or, later, the owner of "Shelley's Café," a thriving gourmet vegetarian café and catering business that had given me enormous emotional satisfaction and joy.

The energetic exchange of love with my clients and customers always mattered most to me. And that is what people responded to. I can still remember how my customers would say, *"You must love to cook!"*

With a smile, my answer was always "No, what I love is seeing my customers' eyes light up as they share how they can feel the love and the healing energy in the food I prepared, and then hearing them shout out how much better they feel."

For four nights, while living on the grounds of Miringa Te Kakara with Jo, I learned of the old ways. Her reverence for the people of this land was heartfelt and endearing.

Each night I slept on a makeshift platform bed and felt a current of electromagnetic energy coming from the Arika, the center post in the Crosshouse.

In the serenity of our last evening at this sacred site, we noiselessly hiked up the grassy landscaped hill of Te Miringa. I found myself assimilating the Waitaha's understanding of sacred geometry, the cosmic tapestry, and our souls' destiny as planetary Earth Keepers.

I stopped for a moment and closed my eyes, becoming consciously aware of my breath. Here in the evening light of the setting sun, at the Temple of the Four Winds, beneath the Southern Cross, I called out to the Ancestors to carry me back to my original *Knowing*.

The Divine Masculine and the Divine Feminine

After my divorce, there were moments when I had a *knowing* that I was charting a course for sacred relationship and greater intimacy; what hadn't yet become fully embodied was what Sanna had referred to in Australia as the "True Trinity."

Embracing and embodying the Divine Masculine, the Divine Feminine, and the Divine Essence, she said, was to walk in our truth, resonant with our inner "knowing."

I am present to this experience of "knowing," not as a "new normal" as I had been hearing from others, but as the "true" normal.

Standing in this place there is no separation, only a sense of wholeness and unity in direct relationship with the vital force of creation.

When we live from this naturally awakened state of "Knowing," life unfurls in the most wondrous ways as we begin to sense, attune, and track our personal songline.

Songline of the Heart / Shelley Darling

The Dreaming of the Rainbow Mind

In a story from the sacred lore shared in Barry Brailsford's book, the Song of the Old Tides, a man is speaking to his granddaughter, Emma, about "the knowing," a key concept of the Waitaha: "...the dreaming is not about sleep!" he says. "The Dreaming is not about drifting into a cozy space! The Dreaming is not about fluffy stuff without substance! Aye, The Dreaming is about waking up. The Dreaming is about awareness, no more than that, it is about the ultimate awareness that we call Te Wai Pounamu. And it is that awareness that brings us to the Rainbow Mind...Te Wai Pounamu, is a stream of ultimate awareness, and enlightenment, the altered state that brings us to the highest of minds."

The Knowing
Grandfather continues on, speaking of the Kuaka, the bird who follows the sun. He shares that, "The map for their amazing flight is not gifted in the memory of the egg. It is of the Knowing. In some the Dreaming lies dormant, for it cannot be reached by the closed mind. I'd like to begin our quest for Dreaming that is of Te Wai Pounamu, by bringing into this circle a power I call the 'Knowing.' *"The Knowing is of the hidden tides that serve the mind. It is seen in all creatures. Let us go to the bird people to learn of the Knowing. Hear the birds sing to greet the dawn or farewell the sun and look behind their songs to the cause. Each call affirms life and place. Each says, 'I am, and this is where I stand tall.' Those songs change in the winter months and again in the spring when they attract a mate. Together, they gather twigs and grasses to build a nest and its design is always unique to their kind and just right, for its shaped by ancient memory, the Knowing, that defies time. Some of the songs and rituals of the birds are learned, are gifted from parent to child, but many are not. Instinct is the word used to describe these understandings that are 'Known' rather than learned. I call them the Knowing, for they come from messages written into their lives.*

"Bird scientist have taken eggs from different birds, nurse and raise the chicks in isolation, discovering each bird knows how to build a nest of its own kind. Staying true to a family they have never seen they re-create their parent's nest design from an inner Knowing'."

—Barry Brailsford

Songline of the Heart / Shelley Darling

With the Cathars now an integral aspect of the wisdom I was carrying, I could tangibly feel a growing coherence with the evolution of my soul's design and the Songline of my heart.

We all have access to this vital force that guides our awareness into the slipstream of the experience of what some call the "I AM" presence. As we experience more and more synchronicities, and gain trust in our intuition, we feel a deepening resonance with this experience of "knowing."

As human beings, we have a choice to stay connected and present to what I am calling the "Songline of the heart." The Songline itself is a pulsing current of energy connected with the whole of existence. It is the flow and connection to a non-linear sensory awareness, and it vibrates aliveness in all beings, two-leggeds and four-leggeds alike. It's the same energy that flows through the sun, the stars, and all celestial bodies.

When we directly experience that energy as our "knowing" we notice a potent shift in our consciousness and a greater sense of aliveness. Our personal Songline is the unique golden thread that connects us to the vast tapestry of life.

Chapter 18: Navigator of the Heart

For the Tenth Pouwhenua: Song of the Rainbow Mind
"We are of the Dreaming, the Rainbow Mind that crosses the frontiers of space and time. Great power resides within paradox; the letting go that moves more than we can ever truly know; the letting go that frees us from expectation... and learns from every outcome; the letting go that takes us beyond judgment and into compassion; the letting go that cuts us loose on the river and trusts the journey; the letting go that admits the presence of a guiding Spirit within the flow."

—**Barry Brailsford,** *Song of the Old Tides*

Stone of Peace

A treasured emblem of New Zealand is Pounamu, the sacred Greenstone of Aotearoa. Pounamu is a jade stone known as the "Child of Peace." It is made from the same tectonic forces as the mountains themselves and master carvers know, the stone is not "found;" in right timing, it is revealed to the one who's meant to work with its energy.

When Barry Brailsford was called in 1989 to lead a party of 12 chosen people over the mountain passes by the Waitaha elders to reopen "The Trail of the Peacemaker," that had been closed for 130 years, he was walking the trail their ancestors had used for centuries.

They were to carry Pounamu of various sizes to the sacred lake and taken far beyond the shores of Aotearoa. It is understood by some that as it sits in the sacred lake waters, peace and love are anchored into the stone. When the stone is given as a gift, it imparts its healing to both the people and the land that receive it.

As Barry noted, "Long ago, when there were different stars in the heavens, the Ancestors sailed the oceans seeking the stone of the Gods. When they came to the shores of Aotearoa, to the Arahura River, they found a stone born of the stars, and held it close to heal the people and the land. They called it Pounamu. Pounamu is of the jade family and is a superb stone for jewelry, one that also served the Ancestors when they needed sharp, fine edged tools."

> **Everything is a Garden**
>
> *Name your stone for it is your companion on the trails of life. In accord with ancient lore it is usually gifted, its enduring power is being given with love.*
> *It's a stone of the wairua, the world of the spirit realm that surrounds all.*
>
> **—Barry Brailsford**

We are in the age of returning to our roots, to the wisdom of our ancestors and, for many of us, this is a time to listen, and correct our course. It is a time to understand and consciously choose to be in sacred relationship with our selves, and with reverence receive the ancestral wisdom being offered to us.

For too long many of us have dismissed our relationship to the land, which holds so much of the knowledge now needed to restore and heal ourselves and the Earth. This is relevant to the dowsing of the land and one's relationship to the Nature Spirits, supporting the rebalancing of the Earth and all her relations.

Barry was told the task at hand was for the Pounamu to help mend the sacred hoop, or circle of life, an ancient symbol used by indigenous tribes. It represents the interconnectivity of all life. As I understood at the time, he was referring to the restoration of the safety, sovereignty, and sacredness of all Native tribes of North America.[120]

I was reminded of this universal quest for peace the day I stood in my copper dowsing tensor ring a few months earlier in Australia with Lynn Pearce, on my first visit to this part of the world.

The message from White Buffalo Calf Woman had found a resonant tone in me in Australia and here now, in New Zealand, I was reminded through Barry's stories of how the Pounamu was carried across the ocean to other lands, to bring peace to them, as well. This also brings me full circle back to the exploration of the Cathars through *The Book of Love* and Sanna's teachings of peace and love. Again, my mind stretched as I considered again the possible connection between the Cathars and the Waitaha nation.

The Waitaha Elders

The warrior tribes began arriving in Aoteara/New Zealand from Polynesia only 800 years ago. They destroyed the peaceful Waitaha Nation that had existed for 77 generations. Some killed tribes related to their own Polynesian lines. Waitaha have a history of occupation of this land that goes back to 2,000 years.

Waitaha: The People of Peace

Since learning about Waitaha, every dowsing presentation and program I offer begins with the Karakia, the ancient ritual Waitaha prayer that I learnt from Barry. I start with this because a Karakia's vibration evokes such a resonance in my clients and students that they are compelled to discover the ancient teachings for themselves.

---

[120] Barry Brailsford, "The Story of Pounamu The Sacred Stone of Aotearoa," *The Stone Studio NZ,* www.stonestudionz.co.nz.

Apparently the Waitaha secretly passed the sacred knowledge of their travels on the old tides, of Creation and of the Cosmos in song; people of each generation were given the responsibility of learning the history and singing it on to the next generation.

Many generations of their genealogy was hidden, even the very fact of their existence was shrouded in secrecy to protect their sacred truths.

The Creative Force of AROHA

On our return from the Temple of the Four Winds, Jo and I stopped off at Makuini Ruth Tai's family marae, where Ruth and her husband had created a center for people to learn about permaculture and how to live sustainably on the land. While we were visiting, she told us, "The old ones didn't just 'talk,' they also intoned or chanted, or sang, and they were very passionate orators." In her personal research over many years, Makuini has focused her time on recovering this wealth of information and sharing it with those wishing to understand the old ways.

But I felt my greatest liberation was when I discovered "AROHA" and AROHA education.

"AROHA" is a word that expresses unconditional love. Makuini Ruth Tai says it defines great leadership, ensures personal success, and inspires us to go the extra mile. Aroha is a compound word, whose parts include Aro, Ro, Hā, Oha.[121]

> ARO is *thought*.
>
> How we breathe or emote that thought will either bring it to life or, if we do not breathe it deeply, and emotionally involve ourselves in it, our lack of action will cause it to lie inertly before us.

---

[121] "Makuini Ruth Tai Decodes REO," GreenplanetFM Podcast.

RO is *introspection*

HA is *life force, or the love force, the breath, energy and love behind the thought*

OHA is *generosity, prosperity, abundance, and wealth*

I reveled in the mystery of how similar the energy and expression of the acronym "AROHA" was to the acronym of "ALOHA" which I had previously taught as an embodied practice for transforming stuck survival patterns and beliefs. My "Aha" moment allowed for a volcanic release of energy that had been long suppressed. For more than a year since I had left San Diego for Australia, I had not been able to speak nor teach the ALOHA practice. The mere thought of saying the word "Aloha" seemed to aggravate a deep wound in my body.

Yet, learning and hearing about AROHA, liberated me! Breaking into a hilariously fulfilling, expanded belly laugh, I was sure these tsunami waves of energy rippled across the entire Southern Ocean. Like the release of steam from the vent on a pressure cooker, I no longer had to hold my love back, and I relished this humorous tide of events, never mind the fascinating connection between ALOHA and AROHA. I was finally free! From the time I had learned of my husband's betrayal and his unwillingness to undertake any counseling, right up until this moment, I had unconsciously vowed to not speak the word "Aloha" aloud, nor use this potent integrative process in working with any new clients.[122]

As Makuini Ruth Tai teaches "When we lead from a place of Aroha our dreams become possible, and we are inspired to achieve beyond what we have previously imagined."

AROHA ignited a crack in my consciousness. I had loved my work as a spiritual mentor, using the acronym "ALOHA" as a pathway to embodied living. This practice

---

[122] Damian Chaparro, "Aro Ha-layers of meaning," *Aro-ha Journal*, https://aro-ha.com.

allowed my clients and students a greater sense of love and joy for themselves, which later translated into a greater sense of peace and aligned purpose. As I deepened my understanding of AROHA, the vibrational transmission of unconditional love, I felt excited, empowered, and open to interweaving this knowledge into my work, and even into my dowsing teaching.

> ### Wairua / Spiritual Dimension
>
> *I am a Spirit having a physical journey. My spirit is made up of "two waters." One "water," Waiora, is directly linked into the Central Sun, the Divine Spark. Waituhi, the other "water," records everything that I do, whether it be good or bad. It is second nature for me to link in with the Divine Source from whence I came, in terms of communication through prayer, to ensure that I vibrate to Aroha the Presence and Breath of the Divine Source which is Unconditional Love. My day begins, flows, and ends with the Aroha I have for our Divine Source.*
>
> **—Dr. Rangimarie Turuki Rose Pere, CBE**

The challenge now lay in connecting the part of me that knew who I was with the part of me that was afraid to be who I was.

Standing in the waka, I'd been navigating many deep emotional tides as I left behind my home, my husband, and my business, and trusted the call to visit Australia and New Zealand. I was at the edge of my own horizon, andI now silently asked to open to the deeper understanding of this odyssey, without expectation or forcefulness. I was shifting from an old survival pattern that compelled me to run, hide, or push away my feelings,

There is a Maori saying, "Ma te wa" push nothing; may things happen in their own time. May we let things unfold, as they will, and may we leave room for Spirit to move."

Within the whispering of my own heart, I heard "Ma te wa...Ma te wa..."

Golden Promise

Still integrating my understanding of the fully balanced Masculine, I realized that when we embraced it, we are able to stand in our loving power. I was thus able to open myself to the return and integration of my true gifts, and so I began the evolution of my life as a Spiritual Navigator.

A powerful reclamation of my personal power took place at that moment in New Zealand. I was humbled and filled with gratitude to know that although this journey had its challenges, it opened the way for a state of profound newness to emerge. My commitment to my own healing, through my journey to both Australia and now New Zealand was opening the way to fulfilling a golden promise of transformation.

Here I was, determined, to navigate my way back to my soul. My journey had begun when the cry *"What about the promise,"* met my vision of a heartbroken little girl sitting with her head bowed on a dank set of dungeon stairs, yearning for the fulfillment of a promise. I was going back to find that sad little girl who was waiting, and who knew I was coming.

The Cathars, the Waitaha, and Dowsing

The Cathars, the Waitaha and Dowsing were the stars in my chart that were now helping me to navigate home.

In the past, I had felt driven to know more, to be more, and to do more. I found that through this journey I was finally settling into myself and, possibly for the first time, I was experiencing a sense of inner contentment and joy.

Everything was now coming into focus, and through the kaleidoscope of my past fears, truth, beauty, and brilliance were now emerging.

Songline of the Heart / Shelley Darling

For me, dowsing was, on the sea of my life experience, a navigational compass that helped me find my way back to the *Songline of my heart*.

I reveled in how subtle and not-so-subtle awakenings occurred personally for me during the course of dowsing my clients' homes or businesses. I witnessed their delight as they consciously partook of this dynamic, transformational experience, which was my greatest joy.

With the energy raised in their home and habitat, I watched as they easily sustained access to a higher octave of consciousness. Dowsing offered them the same gift it had offered me: a portal to the reunion of their light and truth.

Dowsing opened the energetic connection to each person's heart-mind, which acted as a touchstone for inner stability and calm, all within the natural chaos of life. It also supported their awareness of their connection to their divinity, and their sacred relationship to the land.

Contrary to the average person's understanding, dowsing is not just about finding water, dowsing is an alchemical instrument that unlocks the magic within us, allowing the transmutation and elevation of our consciousness.

I returned home again a changed person, ready to resume my life and my path, and eager to see what was to happen next in the ever-changing unfolding of my journey. In considering my lineage as a Spiritual Navigator, I felt a deep commitment and responsibility calling me forward.

My evolutionary purpose was to light the way in circumnavigating the inner realms of the resonant heart. This was not what I had been consciously seeking. And it found me.

I was at a nexus point. Hidden within the bones of this odyssey were the converging messages of the Cathars and the Waitaha. Nature and Spirit were now speaking with one voice.

Songline of the Heart / Shelley Darling

The Cathars on one side, and the Waitaha on the other—like sympathetic strings—harmonized within my being. This passage upon the ocean of my consciousness was clearly about standing up, finding my feet again, and finally standing tall.

My journey was a pilgrimage, a return to wholeness at the behest of my soul, to discover and integrate a golden promise, a promise held within the very depths of my heart, a treasure within that lay in the frames of these experiences.

Magically, the emerging trinity with the Cathars, the Peaceful Nation of Waitaha and my Essential Self allowed for a mystical initiation into the full authorship, authentic power, and manifestation of myself as a Navigator, a humble but shining guiding beacon of light and love, assisting others to find their way home.

Through the alchemical magic of this journey, I was ultimately navigating my way home. Trust in the intuitive nature of my heart's song was the bowline that connected me to my purpose and power. I could feel how this voyage had been steering me towards an intimate and peaceful safe harbor.

I remembered hearing Barry speak about the Waitaha—the navigators of the long tides—as the "One-Hearted" people. They understood their sacred relationship to the stars, Spirit and Nature, and lived in harmony with life on all levels.

They also understood that everything is energy, and as Earth-bound spirits they lived in resonance with their hearts, working with the elements and land, honoring the magic and mystery of all life.

In my search for intimacy, consistently honoring and listening to the direct messages from Spirit, spoken as a love song to my heart. This was my story, this was my truth, and this was my song.

Songline of the Heart / Shelley Darling

> ### Song of Waitaha
>
> *Song of Waitaha, tells how the voyagers to Aotearoa wove together people from three parts of the world: tall, big-boned, dark-skinned people with dark eyes and black hair who were superb gardeners; short, light-skinned people with fair or red hair and blue eyes who were skilled at reading the geometry of the stars; and small, fair-skinned people with long black hair and green eyes who had deep knowledge of stone. They became a peaceful confederation of over two hundred iwi (tribes).*
>
> *Star Walkers joined the stars to the land and were skilled navigators. Water Seekers explored the rivers and tasted the waters until every stream had been sung to and sung about. Stone People carried pounamu (greenstone or jade) across mountain passes and shaped this stone of peace.*
>
> *Sea Gardeners tended sea nurseries and nurtured the many children of Tangaroa, God of the Sea, Rivers, and Lakes. They created trails and trading systems that moved foods, sacred and industrial stone, and other resources the length of the country. All followed Rongo Marae Roa, God of Peace*
>
> **—Linda Jean Shepard**

Songline of the Heart / Shelley Darling

Epilogue: Return to the Birthplace of the Gods

There are moments in a lifetime when you realize something of great importance. There is a tiny gestalt, a momentary suspension of the norm, then everything goes on with everyone knowing that somewhere a profound change has occurred.
—Stephen Harrod Buhner, *Ensouling Language*

By a strange twist of fate, I found myself back in Australia and New Zealand two years later.

I travelled first to New Zealand with Cheryl, my close friend from Montecito, the one who had originally introduced me to Waitaha and inspired my first meeting with Barry.

We had planned to convene with Barry at his home in the South Island of New Zealand. In his kindness he offered to take us to Castle Hill.

Castle Hill is a supernatural place where thousands of years ago, situated in the hills was a school of higher learning, known as a "Wananga." Those chosen by the elders, were the ones to be entrusted to carry the sacred lore of the nation.

In his visit in 2002 the Dalai Lama was awed by this enchanting landscape. And after having a spiritual experience there, he proclaimed Castle Hill, the "Spiritual Center of the Universe."

The morning of our visit Barry, his wife Cushla, Cheryl, Michael—our guide—and I paced ourselves, mesmerized by the magnificent towering stone beings that stood sentinel over our approach.

Barry and Cushla, hand in hand, headed up the trail together ahead of us, and I marveled at the genuine simplicity and splendor of their love for one another. The air was embedded with anticipation and awe. I sensed a miraculous unfurling was taking place.

Barry hailed us to stop before stepping over a small stream to invoke a Karakia, a blessing honoring the Ancestors who long ago had walked this very same trail.

As he spoke, my eyes scaled high above to the right, to the uppermost ridge, where the two ancient limestone tors, Marotini—named after a goddess of the kumara—and Ra Kai Hau Tu—named for a famous Waitaha navigator—were resting at a spot I later learned was sacred to the Star Walkers, the Celestial Navigators.

The Starwalkers had understood the geometry of the stars and as navigators of the long tides, they steered the ancient travelers' wakas to Aotearoa, the Land of the Long White Cloud, what we now know as New Zealand.

I felt overtaken with emotion as I experienced the great masculine energy of Ra Kai Hau Tu and the strong feminine energy of the beloved Marotini. As Barry and Hamish Miller wrote in their book *In Search of the Southern Serpent*:

"Within these high mountain ramparts stood the greatest school of learning in the land and maybe in the world. Here the old lore, the most sacred knowledge of all, was taught and stored. Here Waitaha placed their cosmology, their understanding of creation, for all who visited to see and record."

The energy of this place took hold as I began to weep, barely able to catch my breath. There seemed to be no end in sight to the cascade of tears until Barry came over, and ever so gently looked me in the eyes, as he held up a strand of my hair. *"Don't you know who you are?"* he asked.

My mind swirled as he reminded me of the ones known as the Navigators. He said their physical appearance was similar to mine. He noted my complexion, as well as their hazel eyes and light hair color.

Slowly, I followed him up to a small rock where he revealed the old way of introducing our self to this powerful place; a simple ritual, followed by a few moments of silence

I thought about how my father actualized his dream of sailing with my mother around the world for more than 10 years. Today my father, the great navigator, my childhood hero, is still renowned for his exceptional navigational skill.

We are all learning to be Navigators.

After we all passed by the monolithic stone landscape guardians I sat down in the grass.

In the stillness of what felt like a forever moment, I found myself contemplating the Cathars. I profoundly resonated with the passion of those who had walked into the fires of genocide waged against them, the descendants of Abraham, Moses, Jesus, and Magdalene, those who had known and lived the "Way of Love."

As well, I had come to realize that within my bones was held the ancestry of Waitaha, a nation that had navigated the long tides, honoring the "Way of Peace." These were the Ancestors, my guides, and teachers.

A renewed strength and conviction began to flood through my veins. I was aware this journey was about the reunification of my soul, heart, spirit, mind and body. In fact, through this experience, I had finally walked through the doorway of my own dream, into the Christ light of my being.[123]

---

[123] Barry Brailsford, "Polynesian World Calling," *Barry Brailsford*, http://barry-brailsford-indigenous-knowledge.blogspot.com/2012.

> ### We Can Heal the Past
>
> *With compassion and courage, we have the power to heal the pain of the nations and the planet. While we cannot change the past, we can heal the past, and heal it now. That is the challenge and the way of hope.*
>
> —**Barry Brailsford**

Tracking Ancestral Lines

Is it possible our ancestors have left us a living map?

After the experience at Castle Hill, and prior to leaving New Zealand, on my way back to Australia to lead the two-week Ancestral Wisdom Journey, I received what appeared to be a message in my morning gratitude ritual that seemed to encapsulate my entire journey.

Some people call these experiences "downloads." I didn't feel the need to put a label on this experience, I just listened and received the wisdom it left behind:

> *As author of your own destiny, we ask that you be open to the vibrational thread and divine design of your living energetic blueprint. You, as master of your Soul Destiny, are called to awaken the planetary grid lines of our most beloved mother. You have the "star keys" to open the heart-field of the planet. You are of the purest light essence and have the quality of love to move through any consternation and confusion.*
>
> *You're now attuning to the full mastery of your life's purpose. Your light will pervade any discolorations, and these crystalline activations will support and uplift any*

dormant energy and absolve any renegade frequencies. Yes, you are seeing them as the free radicals that are destructive to our beloved mother.

Presently you are a navigator of the stars, dear darling, darling. Prepare yourself by clearing your etheric body. Be present in a state of illustrious joy, bound for glory. Allow us to do our work, dear one, as we of the higher dimensions are in constant connection with Divine Source.

We love you. Know the power of this unification process. Stay attuned to this station, beloved sister of the stars, and we will adjust and accelerate what is necessary for your individual and collective calibrations.

We are the sum of all that has come before...
We are the Ancestors.

When dowsing came into my life it was a surprise, a magical moment when the course of my life needed to take a drastic turn. May you, too, learn to navigate the invariable wild, gusty winds of life with steadfast knowing.

My gratitude flows to you, dear reader, as you near the end of this book. Thank you for accompanying me on this Sacred Evolutionary Dowsing journey.

We are here to remember what is essential to our heart and bring our attention to the vitality and health of our beloved Earth. Together let's learn to track the *Songline of our Hearts*, so we may know and embrace the beauty of our inherent wholeness.

Thank you for stepping into this Waka of Love...

Songline of the Heart / Shelley Darling

Blessed We Are

*Blessed we are
to dance on this ground,
The rhythm of saints to carry the sound.
We hold a prayer for the earth,
for the ones yet to come,
'May you walk in beauty and remember your song.'*

*Remember why you came here,
Remember your life is sacred."*

Song by **Peia Luzzi**

Acknowledgments

I would like to express my gratitude to my Ancestors, both seen and unseen, for their guidance, unconditional love, support, and evocative presence in my life. And, to everyone who has graced my life and helped to open new doorways of understanding, through being direct messengers or co-creative partners, challenging me to shine brighter and stand in my passion and evolutionary purpose, I thank you, ALL of you.

Specifically, Marie Diamond, who came my home in San Diego one evening with her dowsing rods, and instigated a transformational life change that led me to Mary Magdalene, Jesus, the Cathars, and the *Book of Love*. The sacred journeys to Australia and New Zealand opened my consciousness to hear the voice of the land, and through dowsing connected me to the Aboriginal people. The adventure has never stopped to this day.

To Annette Rugolo, dowsing mentor and once close friend, may collaboration and co-creation be the way of the future, in service to the whole of humanity.

To Sanna Purinton, reverence and humility have been the umbilical cord connecting us to this pathway of Love, to which I owe my heart's healing. Your dedication to truth, honesty and wisdom has been the torch guiding my way home. I thank you, dear sister, for the integrity you Be.

To Cheryl Tomchin, who listened to the whispering winds, and without whom the extended journey to New Zealand to meet Barry Brailsford might not have happened. I am grateful for our growing friendship and "waka" journey, which continues to sail us through the mightiest of ancestral waters. You are truly a beautiful blessing of ever-expansive joy!

To Barry Brailsford and Cushla, with deep respect, love, and honor for your journey, wisdom, and for choosing the "Songline of your heart" to help us broaden our understanding of the Power of Place and the Way of a Peaceful Nation.

To Dr. Julie Krull, my co-creative sister-in-love. Thank you for standing beside me, together building a field, where every individual feels valued, connected, and whole.

To the Resonance Council, I love your joyful presence.

To my first husband, Peter, whose love of the Elementals and the cosmos gave me three most beautiful children, who over the years—and especially most recently—reminded me to have the courage to stand in my truth.

To my beloved children, Isaiah, Heather, and Nina, I thank you for always being there and stretching to understand my nomadic ways. You are my greatest teachers. I love you dearly, and delight in how you love and stand by each other.

To my grandchildren, Obediah, Adrian, Alon, Liam and Celeste, I love and adore you!

To my second (former) husband, who traveled both an ecstatic and bumpy road with me... I own my life 100%.

To Johnny for opening the gateway to a source of untapped creativity, power, and light.

To Gloria Burdett for your deep insight, wisdom, and kindred spirit, which led me to Martha and Mim, without whom this book would never have manifested.

To Mim, thank you for your trust in handing me the key, and offering the summer of quiet stillness and communion with the land and river of my childhood.

To Peter, Bernie, and Cathy Carson, for your dedicated service to all relations. I revel in our connection and am grateful for your healing wisdom that shifted my health and my life.

To Lisa Rawlinson who year after year, provided a haven by the sea to nurture this journey and book.

To Ellen Epstein and Global Joy Team, may waves of light and joy reach the shores of millions of hearts! Thank you!

To Patty Cotton my long-time childhood best friend. Your continuous generosity in sharing your family Chalet as a serene, beautiful writer's retreat has been a haven for the gestation and birth of my greatest expression.

To all my dowsing students, and clients, thank you for listening to the call of your hearts and trusting your guidance in restoring resonance to our beloved Earth and all her inhabitants.

To the Sacred Evolutionary Dowsing Consortium (SED); blessed am I am to stand beside you, weaving our wisdom while evolving our co-creative template for others.

To Charlie Riverman, Earth angel and official sacred water guardian - *how fortunate am I!*

To Tyhson Banighen, extraordinary dowsing detective - *may the hawk continue to inform us!*

To Deborah Harnett for honoring our sacred journey together, and for your meticulous polishing of this book.

To Susan Crossman, my writing coach, and editor, there are no words that can express my gratitude for the fecundity of this journey. This book has birthed itself in full form because of your wisdom and skill, yet it's your heart that empowers those who are lucky enough to work with you.

Special thanks of gratitude go to Michael Davie, for this golden opportunity to work with Manor House Publishing and for having faith in the expression of this book.

Finally, my grateful heart goes out to Ruth Brown, Earth angel, whose expression of unconditional love calmed my heart, even after 30 years had gone by. May I humbly continue this path in service, with the same heartfelt love you always so generously bestowed unceasingly to others.

...And to God, the creative source of all love itself, that energy which birthed the words in this book, I love you...

—Shelley Darling

Appendix A
Evolutionary Dowsing

In the book, *In Search of the Southern Serpent*, Barry Brailsford wrote about the positive signatures that each sacred site generates. Traveling with the Hamish and Ba Miller, two English Dowsers, they would dowse each sacred site and return sometimes weeks or a year later to find, to their wonder, that the site signature would stay the same yet would have expanded in size.

In trying to understand this, Hamish and Barry at one point were astounded at the direct relationship of our attention and its effect on the Earth's Field. I too, was having the same experience. My realization was that Earth indeed was radically changing and as we focus our conscious loving attention on her, we create a "quickening" in the positive frequency of the land.

My findings were absolutely confirmed when I returned to Canberra, Australia to visit with Julie. Excited to take me to a stone circle in the hills above her home, we were dismayed when we arrived to notice someone had painted some abhorrent graffiti on the tallest stone.

Dowsing for the signature, we found that wherever there was graffiti, there were no longer radials defining the signature. Matthew, Julie's husband, began lovingly scrubbing the paint off the stone, while we offered a prayer, and sang to it. Thirty minutes later, when we were complete with our ceremony, we checked again and were elated to find the radials had expanded, revealing the stone's star shaped signature.

It was this "quickening" I had been experiencing with my clients. In the same way that each sacred stone has a signature, every person has an energetic signature.

Through the dowsing process, their signature—also known as an auric field—would energetically brighten and expand. Further, as the dowsing elevates someone's personal resonance, their property and home simultaneously expand their vibration, prompting subtle and not-so-subtle shifts in the neighborhood and community.

As Barry and Hamish found, when we collectively focus our loving attention somewhere in honor of our beloved Earth, at the same time, there is a growing coherence within the collective Field itself. One might even say the Earth herself, as an elemental being, responds in gratitude by expanding her "Heart-Field."

Focused on concentrating on aligning my heart's vocation, my business, once called Golden Light Dowsing/Earth Medicine Alchemy, Evolutionary Dowsing, became the aggregate of all my previous experiences and the fullest expression of my soul.

My world expanded as I delighted in the effects of dowsing as a catalyst for community connection, and I rejoiced in knowing that dowsing a few houses in an area helped people find greater clarity of purpose, and helped their homes become natural gathering spaces within their communities. One might say that as a house is optimized, all the subterranean "infections" rise to the surface to be healed by the sun. The electromagnetic field seems to be naturally activating greater awakening, connection, and co-creation. People evolve into a more powerful version of who they could be, who they were here to be. Evolutionary Dowsing has become a pathway to remembering our original Divine Soul Design.

Evolutionary Dowsing has far-reaching effects on our families, neighbors, and our communities. It is a whole-system approach to balancing energy, and it optimizes our personal field, as it orientates with the Earth's constantly changing Field. This energy clears and uplifts an individual, while healing and balancing the energies that are held in their home and land.

Our homes and land want to support us in ways we cannot imagine. Similar to our brain waves, our homes have waves, too, which are made up of energy, frequency, and vibration. Through science, we now know these waves can be measured.

We know we can raise our own consciousness through meditation, prayer, and positive thinking, so consider that our houses, too, need to hold a higher vibration to support greater health, wellbeing and illuminated access to our soul's purpose.

Dowsing is a tool that allows us to gather information not directly available to the conscious mind and it takes us on a journey beyond our five senses. It bypasses the conscious mind, accessing a deeper state of awareness and allowing us to attune to a much broader range of energetic signals.

Today, we recognize that dowsing includes the mystery of human consciousness as well as that of the Earth. We are always in constant dynamic interaction with the natural world and forces around us, even if we are not consciously aware of these energies.

With the completion of my journeys to Australia and New Zealand, I continue to this day teaching Evolutionary Dowsing,[124] clearing harmful frequencies from homes and the land, and witnessing each person as they reap the benefit of this transmutational journey in their "return to wholeness."

---

[124] Evolutionary Dowsing Specialist www.evolutionarydowsing.com.

Appendix B
Ancestral Bridge Wisdom Journey

Only a few hours' hop from New Zealand, five years later, I again found myself back on the mountain on the South Coast of Australia, where I was called by the vision of the Ancestors standing on top of the ridge.

I had created the "Ancestral Bridge Wisdom Journey," a two-week dowsing journey leaving from Scotland Island on the northern beaches, and finishing up in Uluru, an Aboriginal sacred site and massive sandstone monolith in the heart of the Northern Territory's arid Red Centre. Uluru is considered the solar plexus of the Earth, the power center of the planet.

The trip offered a magnificent experience with the land and the Ancestors similar to what I myself had encountered in Australia.

We began in the Ku-ring-gai preserve where the group immediately connected with the power of place through experiencing the 10,000-year-old rock carvings high above Pittwater. It was an invitation for fellow travelers to explore Australia and discover more about their own essential nature, while opening to the heart of the Aboriginal voice and message.

The brochure spoke from my heart as it described the trip:

> *Envision yourself arriving in Sydney, Australia, embarking on an experiential odyssey which kindles your innermost Soul remembering. An illuminating travel experience, which combines learning and expanding your dowsing skills, with the dreamtime voice of a land infused with generosity, and the communion of Spirit and Matter as a way of life.*

Songline of the Heart / Shelley Darling

Envision awakening each day to the delightful song of the Kookaburra's laughter, while opening to the voice of the Ancestors, being guided by the "Songline of your heart."

The first Ancestral Bridge Wisdom Journey took place in 2017 and it was magnificent, an answer for those looking to be enriched by a culture that dreams with the whales, sings to the land, and respects the nature of all life.

Joining forces with two Evolutionary Dowsing Specialists, Najma Ahern and Julie Armstrong, both from Australia, allowed for a phenomenal Divine synergy and an on-the-ground experience. This pilgrimage is a sacred journey that holds within it the keys for full self-expression, co-creation, and magic.

To discover more about the Ancestral Bridge Wisdom Journey: www.shelleydarling.com.

Join us on an upcoming journey!

Email: connect@evolutionarydowsing.com

Appendix C
SED Consortium

"All of us share a common destiny. Through this revelatory journey, my passion and joy expanded to include working with groups, with our focus on the direct experience of heart resonance, which naturally harmonizes the individual energies into a coherence whole."
—Shelley Darling

Under the influence of a full moon in January 2015, I was guided to initiate a co-creative collective experience with advanced Dowsers, Alchemists, and Planetary Healers.

Those who felt called to participate, met weekly in a sacred circle of 12. The model followed a metaphysical, and evolutionary, "12 around 1" model, an architectural principle which reveals the inseparable relationship of the parts to the whole. As a consortium[125] of planetary healers, we focused on the healing and harmonizing of Earth Energies.[126]

In these times of needed restoration and greater global coherence, the Sacred Evolutionary Dowsing Consortium is a model of collaboration, connection, trust, and co-mentoring, recognizing that the whole is greater than the sum of our parts.

---

[125] A "Consortium" is an association of two or more individuals who pool their resources to achieve a common vision.
[126] "12-Around-1 Whole System Framework," *Cosmometry*, https://cosmometry.net/12-around-1.

> **12 Around One**
>
> *The 12-around-1 framework is fundamental as it is found in the cosmometry of both the Vector Equilibrium and Icosahedron – two of the primary geometric configurations of the cosmos. In essence, the concept of a 12-around-1 whole-system model of the basic areas of human concern has the intention of providing an organizing framework that can assure that, as we apply ourselves to the design and application of solutions to our worldly challenges, we do so with a minimum-sufficient set of considerations at the outset and throughout the whole process. Each sector can be seen as a fractal "whole" unto itself, and yet each one is always in relationship to the others and the dynamics of the whole as it evolves over time.*
>
> **—Martial Lefforts**

When we work together in resonance the shift is monumental. Each week, through quietening our minds and opening our hearts, we tap into the current of our collective flowing genius which informs and enriches us all. Our vision is to steward the Evolution of Consciousness and the healing of our planet, through weaving our knowledge, energy and skills together and focusing on areas that need to be cleared of old non-beneficial energies and which need rebalancing for the planet and for humanity.

  I was given the vision to do this after having dreamt of being in a small wooden boat on a very serene lake with Barry Brailsford. He was teaching me a Karakia. I saw this as a sacred dowsing canoe, like the ones that had been built by the peaceful nation for more than 2500 years. Each person carried their own specific skill and purpose with them, uniting in a shared vision of peace and love. The Dowsers loved the idea that the group was sailing in a "waka." [127] The Sacred Evolutionary Dowsing Consortium was to be convened with the understanding of gaining wisdom from each other, while listening to the fabric of the Field, co-creatively working together, with me acting as the navigator, using dowsing and other modalities to remotely remedy any abhorrent energies still left in a home or land as a result of past massacres, fighting, or other brutal events. Our goal was and is to assist natural areas on the Earth while supporting the planet's waterways.

Our shared intention was to collectively birth a template others could use to expand their knowledge and skill as Evolutionary Dowsers. Through the sharing of this information, we saw the possibility of exponentially raising the vibrational frequency of our collective heartbeat, homes, and habitat, while restoring and healing our Mother Earth.

I was provided with direct guidance and downloads from the ones who call themselves the "Evolutionary Council of Light." On the night of the full moon in January, prior to our first call, I received this transmission:

This is not a quest for grandeur, just a space from which the intrepid voice of the void can speak to our collective hearts and minds. Creating the space for the glow of love's glory will bring joy, harmony, and peace to the planet. The sands will shift as the radiance catapults its rays, penetrating even the finest discordant vibrations. Be not concerned, the gifts of this group will work its magic. Each one will bring their voice to the awareness of the others. Each call will have time for the growing joy that will come from this engagement. The fruits of each sacred action will lead the course to its next step. Trust implicitly.

---

[127] A waka is a Maori word for "boat."

In this course we ask that each one be in their holographic knowing, bestowing the wider whole of your being with your loving intent. The magnitude of this collective will grow as you all come together. You will be purifying, protecting and vitalizing the field with the collective force of your love and knowing.

Gather now the tribe. And tell them it is done it is done it is done.

—*Evolutionary Council of Light*

We embarked upon an initial five-month program, meeting online weekly. We engaged the services of a few SED Field Advisors, originally people I called in who were adepts in their field of energy work.

Later, we relied upon continuing SED mentors, who assisted us to lay the foundational understanding for the evolution of Earth Energy, while substantiating our collective vision. The SED Field Advisors were chosen to help the group achieve a deeper understanding of the Laws of the Universe, Harmony, and Frequency as they relate to Vibration, Sound, and Geomancy in the application of healing a home or landscape.

Each week we would call in the Ancestors, always beginning the evening's journey with a Karakia, offering our gratitude, blessing this "waka of love."

We honored the ones who had come before us and who lived in peace. We honored our circle of 12, empowering each other's strengths, and with respect and love embracing that which we might call our weakness, knowing that what we call weakness is simply the growing edge of our being.

Each week we were like bees returning to the hive, bringing the "nectar of experience" that we gathered in between our calls back to the group. We grounded our vision and collectively attuned our energy to the Unified Field, while focusing on the Earth, her sacred sites, and the places and situations in our personal locales that needed healing.

The group followed each week with a weekly action, as shared by Guidance. For example, we were asked to create a silent five-minute gathering, each in our respective places, at the same time each day connecting with each other as a unified collective.

We paid particular attention to the world news in areas that captured our attention, and we would work together using specific protocols to support the energetic shift needed in those areas.

I also invited the SED Consortium to investigate the history of the area, noticing anything that stood out for them.

Then we applied our group dowsing protocol, which involved bringing the energy of the group together and protecting ourselves from any misguided energies. We used techniques to clear the water and the adjacent land by checking for negative vortices, geopathic stress, imbalanced elemental energy, and entities. For example, in one case we worked with a highway in South Dakota where there had been many accidents.

Three weeks later, after working on this one area, we learned there had been no further accidents, and when we checked in even one year later, that area of the highway was still accident-free.

The success of that initial program led us to continue the connection and the Sacred Evolutionary.

Dowsing Consortium is now in its sixth year; the invitation stands open for those who are ready to work as a co-creative heart-based group to join us.

What I have seen over the years is how each person's toolbox exponentially expands through the sacred communion and sharing of this group. Through the safe space that is created, each person is personally transformed through the collective experience.

Each year we embark on a new cycle of the Sacred Evolutionary Dowsing Consortium, initiated by Spirit, calling for humanity's healing. We continue to meet with new participants and a growing group of SED Field Advisors.

If you feel the calling to expand your horizons in this field of work, whether you're a beginner dowser or advanced at the craft, you are welcome to call or email for a personal invite to join this group of 12 via connect@evolutionarydowsing.com.

For some the urge is simply to learn to dowse. There are various ways to bring this about, either privately, in a group course, or learning while having your house or business dowsed. This transformational modality will always create an opening for your clients, friends, and family. Understanding the nature of spirit communication, land healing and dowsing is vital to living a harmonious and resonant life. What's more, dowsing creates a high vibrational and safe space for our children to play and develop, and we need to understand it is an investment in their long-term happiness and health as well.

Join me as we together shine our light, navigate, serve, and co-create a world that is for the good of the whole...

To explore the Sacred Evolutionary Dowsing Consortium email Shelley: connect@evolutionarydowsing.com.

Comments from SED Consortium Field Advisors:

"There are moments in everyone's life that we will never forget, and meeting Shelley was one of them. Learning from and joining with her as a member of Sacred Evolutionary Dowsing Consortium changed my relationship to everything."

—Charlie Riverman Bergeron

"Belonging to the Sacred Evolutionary Dowsing Consortium has both anchored and expanded my earth healing skills. It has also blown open my knowledge of what is possible while working as a collective. None of this invaluable experience would have happened without Shelley's creation and guidance of the group."

—Deborah Kruse

"The SED Consortium has provided me with the opportunity to work with likeminded eco-spiritual dowsers to deepen our connection to the unseen world and the ancient earth wisdom of our ancestors who communed with Mother Earth, before undertaking any important activity that would affect the whole of life."

—Tyhson Banighen

"I met Shelley Darling while studying and becoming a Conscious Evolutionary through Barbara Marx Hubbard's work. I was easily drawn to Shelley's heart resonant way of being. It was a natural progression to study dowsing with her. Learning dowsing as something both sacred and evolutionary has informed my growth as a healer. Working with the collective consciousness of the Consortium has expanded my knowledge. This profound education has informed my healing work as a Reiki Master teacher and dowser. Thank you, Shelley, for generously sharing your gifts with the world."

—Shanti Heart Janice Hollinger

Songline of the Heart / Shelley Darling

"As an international collective, the SED has been working with sacred sites around the world, educating each other, and doing collective remote dowsing on places that have been crying out for help. (Such as an unsafe corner of a state highway where there had been fatalities, clearing EMF radiation around schools in the US, and performing coordinated simultaneous land ceremonies working with the leylines). Hearts Across the World in 2015 brought people together for a 24-hour online experience. It's been and continues to be amazing."

—*Najma Ahern*

Songline of the Heart / Shelley Darling

Praise for the Author

Dreams Manifested: Anonymous, Engineer, CA

"I am basking in the afterglow! ...I haven't experienced anything like this except after sex!"

Addiction Recovery: JD-Nutritional Counselor, Standard Process Distributor

"When Shelley came to my house, I didn't know what to expect. My husband was having troubles with addiction and I was concerned about his life and our financial situation.

We sat for a few minutes and as I was very emotional, she sat with me and helped me relax, connect with my heart, and open to what the dowsing could shift in our [lives]. Was I surprised when she found a negative vortex exactly where the year before my husband had been found after he had an overdose! The second negative vortex was where I always found myself tripping down the stairs.

News!!! *My Husband got a FULL-TIME job offer at the Rehab for Music Therapy Program, as well as the Record Label for Recovery!"*

Financial Abundance: Katherine Wolf, Financial Planner, San Diego, CA

"Thank you so much for the dowsing of my house. Before the dowsing I had been experiencing stagnation in my relationship and in my finances. After the dowsing I experienced incredible clarity in my thoughts and feelings. Within a week I found I had made decisions that increased my wealth by $24,000/year! I also experienced greater clarity of

my goals and desires of my relationship! Once my decisions were made it was if the Universe already had everything aligned to support me - everything fell right into place, easily and effortlessly! I am a believer! Thank you again Shelley!"

Beachfront Sale: Lisa Rawlinson, Agricultural Scientist, Gerringong, Australia

"When Shelley arrived in town, I discovered she was a Dowser, I had purchased 400 acres and needed to sell my beachfront property to help pay for the property.

After a year and a half, there was still no offer. Shelley offered to Dowse and Feng Shui the home to clear what was needed in order to sell. The biggest surprise was when she found a negative vortex in the exact spot where my husband had died of cancer two years before I hadn't said anything to her about it.

She also helped me to clear any energy that was still stuck around my issues about his death. The house sold in less than two months!"

Feng Shui and Dowsing: Deborah Harnett, Feng Shui Master & Founder Cinnabar Designs

"Shelley has an amazing passion about her work and the desire to heal structures. I am a Feng Shui Master and keep my house's energy as balanced and clear as possible. Shelly's work added a missing piece by dowsing my home.

There were certain places in a few rooms that never felt as comfortable as the rest of the house. She located those spots.

Now I can be in any room and feel completely calm and grounded. Also, I had neighbors that were difficult, and they put their house up for sale a couple of months later and moved. I am very happy with Shelley's gift and can highly recommend her to dowse a residential or commercial building."

Expanding Consciousness: Dr. Julie Krull Ph.D., LMHP, Talk Show Host-All Things Connected, Co-Founder: Good of the Whole

"Shelley is a master dowser in the cosmic sense. Her intuitive gifts complement her well-developed skill and universal understanding of energy, consciousness, and the unified field. What I appreciate most about Shelley is her depth and breadth of understanding when it comes to living in resonance and the co-creative process. Shelley lives and breathes resonance and shares her authentic passion generously from the heart."

"Through her dowsing and resonance coaching, I have witnessed Shelley assisting others to create high levels of coherence, expanded Consciousness, and harmonic resonance in their lives, homes, workplaces and communities. I, personally, have benefited in all those realms. I have been genuinely blessed by Shelley's gifts and have experienced a greater clarity, alignment, and expression of my Soul's purpose. With great gratitude and immense respect, I say "Thank you, Shelley Darling and (Golden Light Dowsing/) Evolutionary Dowsing."

Business and Relations: Elizabeth Cotton, Therapist, SF

"Since the dowsing there have been amazing shifts. While we were dowsing our studio, I could feel the energy lift and lighten and have continued to experience that lightness on subsequent visits.

Our plans to build my office here at home have been smooth and easy, and my mood and excitement continue to lift and brighten daily. My husband is filled with more energy and excitement, but the most remarkable effect is the total 180 in the relationship between our co-tenants, which has gone from stand offish and adversarial to an easy, polite, and friendly collaboration.

We never imagined that this would be the case and were preparing ourselves to be forever at odds and out of synch with them. Halleluiah!! Three cheers for dowsing!"

The Five-Plex Sold: Valerie, Real-estate Investor, Sydney, Australia

"The Five-Plex sold! I wanted to let you know that the Five-Plex closed this morning. It is done and dusted! After two years of ownership, and a very smooth selling process in the end, I wanted to take this opportunity to tell you how grateful I am for your, all your work around me and my property to assist in this great result. Thank you, Shelley!"

Imminent Dowser: Sharon Joy, Connection Partners, Tampa Bay, FL

"I congratulate you and your team for hosting the spirited inquiry and encouraging important ponderings about what Dowsing may mean to our lives. You are primed to be The Imminent Dowser of the region. The field was cultivated...and now it is time to reclaim this important art, science and evolution."

Quantum Leaps: Najma Ahern, Cranial Sacral Practitioner. SED Field Advisor

"I have such a deep and profound reverence for dowsing. Learning dowsing in 2013 made a quantum leap for me in following my intuitive abilities. I am now focused on healing for the planet. I am deeply grateful what each one of us in the Sacred Evolutionary Dowsing Consortium hold, week after week. I am feeling the alignment, connection, and support. I am excited to be joining with the Dowsing Consortium, learning to connect more deeply and bring harmony wherever it is needed."

Songline of the Heart / Shelley Darling

Land Healing Empowerment: Mary Kay Anderson, SD

"Watching Shelley dowse, I began to realize it was so much more then Dowsing just the house. I experienced a huge shift in my awareness and power. The dowsing was actually a journey in opening to a new frequency, not only in the house, but also within me. During the Dowsing a very large snake showed up, I was so afraid, yet Shelley spoke to me about Animal Totems and I began to see the gift in his showing up...I was able to get over my fear and see more clearly the Dowsing Journey and how it not only shifts the frequency of the house, but showed me how to move into my own power in so many ways."

Financial Success: Karen Archipley, Owner, Archi's Acres, Veterans Sustainable Agriculture Training, San Diego, CA

"Thank you so much for the dowsing of our house and farm. Before the dowsing we were in a year-long process of obtaining a farm loan, and with the changing market we were losing ground seemingly by the day.

Once Shelley dowsed our house and farm, it was like a series of miracles started to happen. First our house was appraised for the needed amount and then some. And our loan funded within six weeks. Secondly, it had been our dream to farm on our neighbor's property, and within weeks we had the opportunity to lease our next-door property.

We are now in the process of expanding! Recent News! We have been in a myriad of newspapers, CNN and more!"

Creating Harmony: Julie Armstrong, Act for Bees, AU

"The work with you, Shelley, has helped me be clearer and stronger. Thank you so much for your enthusiasm and positivity. Your light shines brightly and brings harmony into people's lives. Go Dowsers!!!"

Growing Trust: Ange Bambach, Options Process® Mentor, I Am and Essential Business, AU

"One memory of you stands out for me.... that was of you setting up your home base in our living room sleeping on our couch over the course of many days and trusting you will be guided to your next step, as you had no plans other than to listen to your angels and guides and God.

You were my first introduction to such a way to be, and I will always remember that moment. I understood what you were doing. I was intrigued and admiring you as I watched your next move appear miraculously from "co-incidental meetings." You're such an inspiration to me."

Unity Consciousness: Alice Bitetzakis

"Shelley was magnetic as she bestowed her gifts of dowsing to each of us. Her stand for the Earth and Unity Consciousness was so palpable that she drew me into her passion as a moth to the light! She was wonderful and so was all the information she conveyed with clarity and light. Thank you."

Doctors of the Land: Jill Buzan, Sarasota, FL

"What I took away from Shelley's Dowsing weekend is that dowsing is another way to truly assist the earth and all of us who inhabit it in our ascension process, as we heal the land and allow "heaven" back into these places that have been "dark" or deadened by stagnant energies. I love how specific and tangible it is. As I said last weekend, we become doctors of homes and land!!"

Dowsing Detective: Nancy Chaconas, Legal Shield - Ladies of Justice, Somis, Ca.

"This is something very new for me, a bit scary, though mostly exciting. I'm choosing to open to receive this gift that I always had, and yet never opened. I am experiencing a new awareness

coming in, a sense of heightening intuition and practicing trust and faith in my life. I am elated as the Dowsing has helped me to get information about lost objects!

"I have just had my house Dowsed and I am amazed at how it shifted the energy. It's not just dowsing it's so much more than that! Clutter is flying out the door easily, and remodeling projects on hold are falling into place. Things are organized in a new way. My husband's home office became a delightful place to work. Clients are calling me out of nowhere. I feel a renewed sense of joy being here, working here and gathering people together."

Spiritual Ease Darin Coats, President, Coats and Coats LLC, South Dakota

"The frequency in the house was so changed that I have no words to express my experience of the Dowsing. Just simply this: 2 +2=5! The Dowsing... says that you can expand in space and be more of that. I was able to access more of myself. The Dowsing energy gives permission for miracles to happen. I saw the pathway to choosing more ease in my life."

Manifesting More Joy: Margi Flint - Earth Song Herbals, International Herbalist, Marblehead, MA

"Ah, to be humbled. I thought I was doing you a favor! Standing in the middle of the street with Shell felt perfectly normal. As we entered into the seeing, expressing the "dreaming of" how I envision my space I knew we were going into rapid-growth time.

Diving into the realm of remembering the previous owners – their thought patterns and how they lived in the house, yikes, I was doing the same thing! The simple statement 'Okay, we can begin there,' set into motion radical change. Since dowsing the house and following through with simple suggestions I have felt lighter, and am perceived as lighter. Lighter, in the sense of joy manifest.

The rods are placed, the rings—oh baby! The ring under my bed has allowed perfect sleep, and little pains are gone from the body. Bonus!

Shell has a way of sharing advice that is gentle and kind, sipping tea or standing in the street gazing at the home. Do those little things and you are set free!"

Transformation: Judy Gabriel, Energy Landscaper, Ojai, CA

"I watched someone transform today. I watched my dear friend take in the full spectrum of her true being. I watched her accept the bliss and the release of her fears. It was not a logical nor linear process and was guided by the intuition and insight of Shelley Darling.

We dowsed the house and the house was now vibrating at a level high enough to allow my friend to step into her full vibration. I watched Shelley quietly, with patience, listening and in tune with each step [of] my friend's consciousness, lead[ing] the gentle unfolding and blooming.

"I can't explain the process. I just know that Shelley saw the opening and created a safe space for my friend to choose it for herself. I am honored that I was able to witness and participate in this beautiful transformation.

I would highly recommend Shelley Darling as your partner in bringing your home and your life into its fullest potential."

Land Healing: Kara Breese, Expand Community, Kittery, ME

"Thank you for an amazing whirlwind of love and teachings. The gift of your stories and energy inspires me to take this beautiful modality across the world. Many blessings to you."

Live Your Potential: Kyla Mawson, Starlight Clearing. AU

"I felt the pull so strongly that I flew to Florida to study with Shelley. Over the last three years my connection to the earth and to (Golden Light Dowsing/) Evolutionary Dowsing has led me on a journey of self-discovery and truth.

I am now able to enter a home or business, knowing how to check the energies and share how they affect the occupants, owners or tenants.

I am able to transform the space into a higher frequency so people can reach their highest potential and *live knowing they are supported by their home, free of interference from geopathic stress and other negative energies that may be impacting their home."*

Effectiveness of Dowsing: Jenny Procter, Kittery, ME

"Many of us associate the word dowsing with the old timers who used a forked branch to find water underground.

Dowsing is so much more. It is a practical, ancient and evolutionary tool that raises the frequency of your home and/or business and creates coherence in all areas of life.

Dowsing creates far-reaching effects in your family, your business, and your community."

Emotional Opening: Janet Smith Warfield, Word Sculptures, Sarasota, FL

"All my senses were wide open as I watched Shelley and her dowsing rods in action. Shelley asked questions. The rods, with no obvious manipulation on Shelley's part, gave unbelievably accurate answers that brought me to tears.

The experience Shelley helped facilitate was one of those amazing aha experiences that cannot be understood but will always be remembered."

Investment Property: Elaine Silver and James Alexander, Sarasota, FL

"My husband and I put an investment property on the market in January 2018 and purchased an exchange property investment property.

In late February 2018 We had six months to sell the property number one to benefit from the tax laws. And unfortunately, that house wasn't selling. We had a wonderful responsible and creative realtor but no luck.

It was stressful to be paying two mortgages and in May we asked Shelley darling to dowse the house.

Within two months, the house was sold. We are grateful to show his input and support in time to receive the benefit!"

About the Author

Traveling internationally for the past 12 years as a professional Dowsing master and speaker, Shelley synthesizes her knowledge of Emotional Integration, Heart Resonance and Feng Shui with Dowsing, which evokes an energetic "quickening" in the field, uplifting the home, land, and business environment.

Shelley's dedication to Love as a practical pathway, combined with her understanding of Ancient Wisdom and Conscious Evolution, delivers a dynamic whole-systems model which speaks to Evolutionary Dowsing as a transformational journey whose vision is to restore personal power, prosperity aligned with purpose and planetary peace.

Shelley currently lives where the eagles soar at the delta of Merrymeeting Bay in Maine, USA.

Evolutionary Dowsing References and Resources:

The information contained below is a compilation of articles and resources Shelley Darling deems particularly valuable.

Shelley Darling's Personal References:

Sanna Purinton: Spirit Consciousness Facilitator
Exploration of Spirit Consciousness / www.SannaPurinton.com.

Kat Adami: Human Design Facilitator
Empowering People with Purpose
http://www.humandesignresources.com.au/

Angela Bambach: Option Process® Mentor, I'm an Essential Business Supporting Parents of Children with Autism
http://angelabambach.com/

Dave Bambach: Bio-Optic Holography
Living Your Fullest Potential / www.uniquelyyou-boh.com

Thyson Banighen: The Wellness Academy
Exceptional Courses on Health, Wealth and Enlightenment
https://thewellnessacademy.ca

Brian Besco: Twisted Sage
Tensor Field Technology / https://twistedsage.com/

Kara Breese: Land Healer
Intuitive Healing
https://www.karabreese.com.

Ellen Epstein LICSW: EFT, Channeled Guidance
Living Supernaturally / https://www.livingsupernaturally55.com.

Kyla Mawson: Environmental Alchemist AU
Environmental Alignment / Starlight Space Clearing

Nina Patrick: Milagro World Center
Transformational Community Events and Retreats for the Evolving Human / www.milagroworldcenter.com.

Songline of the Heart / Shelley Darling

Websites of Interest:
American Society of Dowsers: http://www.dowsers.org.
Evolutionary Dowsing: www.EvolutionaryDowsing.com.
Barry Brailsford: http://www.stoneprint.co.nz.
HeartMath Institute: www.heartmath.org.
Questers: https://questers.ca.
Brian Besco:Twisted Sage: www.TwistedSage.com.
Slim Spurling Products: http://www.ix-el.com.
Anne Baring: https://www.annebaring.com.
Tom Kenyon: https://tomkenyon.com.
Good of the Whole: https://www.goodofthewhole.org.
Loving Waters: https://www.lovingwaters.life.

Books:

In Search of the Southern Serpent by Barry Brailsford and Hamish Miller

Beyond the Boundaries of Time by Barry Brailsford

The Book of Love by Kathleen McGowan

In the Mind of a Master by Slim Spurling

Resonance Alchemy: Awakening the Tree of Life by Katherine Parker

Our Moment of Choice: Evolutionary Visions and Hope for the Future by Robert Atkinson

St. Germain on Alchemy by Elizabeth Prophet

WEE Book of Dowsing by Hamish Miller

Gene Keys: Embracing Your Higher Purpose by Richard Rudd

The Songlines by Bruce Chatwin

Emergence: The Shift from Ego to Essence by Barbara Marx Hubbard

Earth Calling by Ellen Gunter & Ted Carter

Black Elk Speaks by John C. Neihardt

Songline of the Heart / Shelley Darling

Manor House Publishing Inc.
www.manor-house-publishing.com
905-648-4797

www.ingramcontent.com/pod-product-compliance
Lightning Source LLC
Chambersburg PA
CBHW071428070526
44578CB00001B/30